The nature of fiction

D1351392

The nature of fiction

GREGORY CURRIE

UNIVERSITY OF OTAGO

CAMBRIDGE
UNIVERSITY PRESS

CAMBRIDGE UNIVERSITY PRESS
Cambridge, New York, Melbourne, Madrid, Cape Town, Singapore, São Paulo, Delhi

Cambridge University Press
The Edinburgh Building, Cambridge CB2 8RU, UK

Published in the United States of America by Cambridge University Press, New York

www.cambridge.org
Information on this title: www.cambridge.org/9780521381277

First published 1990
Reprinted 1993
This digitally printed version 2008

A catalogue record for this publication is available from the British Library

ISBN 978-0-521-38127-7 hardback
ISBN 978-0-521-09098-8 paperback

"And the poets – the perverse follow them; hast
thou not seen how they wander in every valley and
how they say that which they do not."

The Qu'ran

"The good ended happily, and the bad unhappily.
That is what Fiction means."

The Importance of Being Ernest

Contents

Contents

Preface

There are fictions that contribute to the enterprise of philosophy. And there are intellectual traditions for which fiction is a natural means to the expression of philosophical ideas. But the tradition in which I feel most at home is not one of them, and I leave it to others to explore the ways in which fiction does or could contribute to a philosophical explanation of the world. Instead I shall treat fiction itself as something that needs explaining. This is a book written in the belief that there are certain very general questions about the nature of fiction, the answers to which can be discovered more or less a priori by appeal to the methods of philosophy rather than to those of the critic or literary historian. How we come to have the kind of fiction we do have is one question; how it is possible for us to have any fiction at all is another, and that is the question I want to ask. It is a question that resolves into several others: What, if any, are the characteristics that distinguish a work of fiction from a work of nonfiction? What sorts of entities must the world contain in order for there to be fiction? What psychological and linguistic resources must we bring to the world in order to be producers and consumers of fiction?

I said that the method I favor is more or less a priori. But it is tempered by the knowledge that we must not abandon our common, everyday perception of what sort of thing fiction is, or we shall be in danger of constructing an elaborate theory that relates only marginally to the phenomenon it seeks to explain. Throughout the book examples of fictional works of various kinds will appear, sometimes as test cases against which we can judge the explanatory power of a hypothesis, sometimes merely to relieve the sense of abstractness generated by extended philosophical arguments. But there is something that we must bear in mind in choosing our examples and our arguments: Fiction is a category that includes the bad and the mediocre as well as the good. If literature rather than fiction were our subject things would be different, for we cannot separate the enterprise of explaining literature from an understanding of good literature. To say of something that it is literature is, except in certain special circumstances, to ascribe to it a certain kind of value. Not so with fiction; I learn nothing about the merit of what I'm reading when I learn that it is fiction. Good fiction is no better a guide to the nature of fiction than the characters of saints are a guide to human nature.

Distinctions of form will be no more relevant here than distinctions of quality. *The Canterbury Tales, Purple for a Shroud, The Man from Ironbark, The Turn of the Screw, The Garden of Forking Paths* are all fictional works in my sense. The theory embodies no preference for the printed or even the written word; an impromptu story for the children, told and forgotten, will count as fiction in my sense. It applies also to those kinds of fiction that appear in media of visual presentation, plays and movies being the obvious examples. I shall argue that paintings, sculptures, and even photographs can be works of fiction. Any medium that enables us to represent, enables us to make fiction.

I have not in general tried to give self-contained explanations of philosophical ideas that I borrow from other areas and other writers: possible worlds, counterfactuals, proper names and definite descriptions, conventions. A comprehensive account of these things would have doubled the length of the book and been a poor substitute for the exemplary clarity of Kripke, Lewis, Stalnaker, and others. So I've made do with brief explanations and references to the relevant literature. The exception is Grice's theory of meaning, dealt with in Chapter 1. Because it is central to my account of fiction and because I need to emphasize certain features of the theory at the expense of others, I have chosen to give it a fuller exposition. Partly for this reason, and partly because I have tried to be explicit about the fundamental assumptions I make, Chapter 1 moves rather more slowly than the rest of the book. Readers familiar with the sort of material that would be contained in an elementary course in the philosophy of language will be able to move very quickly up to Section 1.8. Thereafter the exposition gets a little denser, but anyone at or above the level of advanced undergraduate work in philosophy should be able to follow the arguments. Agreeing with them might be more difficult.

The philosophy of fiction lies at the intersection of aesthetics, the philosophy of language, and the philosophy of mind. The problems I have chosen to deal with, and the manner in which I deal with them, make this book rather heavily weighted in the direction of the last two of these disciplines. Some of the issues that arise when we think of fictional works as works of art – issues concerning, for example, the nature of appreciation, the differences between literary, visual, and musical works – I have explored in *An Ontology of Art* (London: Macmillan; New York: St. Martin's Press, 1989).

I have a number of people to thank for their criticisms and suggestions concerning various parts of this book. Among them are Ismay Barwell, Frank Jackson, Don Mannison, Alan Musgrave, Graham Oddie, Roy Perrett, Graham Priest, Barry Taylor, Pavel Tichý, and Aubrey Townsend. Special thanks are due to David Lewis. The comments of two readers for the Press were most helpful. Penelope Griffin's careful reading has helped to improve the clarity of this book. The errors and unclarities that remain are my own responsibility.

While this book was being written I knew of Kendall Walton's work on fiction and make-believe only through his articles, published mostly in the 1970s. Later, with the book already at the Press, I was fortunate enough to obtain a copy, in typescript, of his *Mimesis as Make-Believe: On the Foundations of the Representational Arts*, to be published by Harvard

University Press. I was then able to make some emendations
to those parts of the text where I discuss his views. I thank
Kendall Walton for allowing me to see his book, and I heart-
ily recommend it to the reader.

It will be apparent that I have been greatly influenced,
through his writings, by the late Paul Grice.

Some material published elsewhere and now much revised
is included in this book. That material appeared originally in
the following places: *Journal of Aesthetics and Art Criticism* 43
(1985); *Philosophy and Literature* 10 (1986); *Philosophical Studies*
50 (1986); *Australasian Journal of Philosophy* 66 (1988). I thank
the editors of these journals for permission to reprint this
material.

Chapter 1

The concept of fiction

There can hardly be a more important question about a piece of writing or speech than this: Is it fiction or nonfiction? If the question seems not especially important, that's because we rarely need to ask it. Most often we know, in advance of reading or hearing, that the discourse before us is one or the other. But imagine we did not know whether *The Origin of Species* is sober science or Borgesian fantasy on a grand scale. We would not know whether, or in what proportions, to be instructed or delighted by it. No coherent reading of it would be possible.

What makes a piece of writing or speech fictional? Despite the apparent ease with which we judge that this is fictional and that is not, and despite the significance that judgments of this kind have for our subsequent experience of the work, most of us are in no good position to answer the question. Fiction is one of those concepts like goodness, color, number, and cause that we have little difficulty in applying but great difficulty in explaining. Conceivably, no general account of what fiction is can be given. Fiction might be so basic a concept that any attempt to explain it will be circular, or the concept might dissolve on closer inspection into a variety of subcases with no more in common than the name. Neither possibility can be ruled out a priori. But the best answer to those who think either one a plausible option is simply to *give* a general account of what fiction is in terms that do not presuppose an understanding of fiction itself. That is what I shall do in this chapter.

What can we expect from a general theory of fiction? Such

1

1. The concept of fiction

a theory ought to tell us what it is about a work (written, spoken, or in some other medium) that makes it fiction rather than nonfiction. If the theory is adequate it will sort items of the relevant kinds into the fictional and the nonfictional in a way that seems intuitively correct, perhaps after the theory itself has had a chance to shift and to sharpen our intuitions a bit. If it is a really good explanation it will help us to answer other questions about fiction as well; it will help us, for example, to understand the kinds of effects fiction typically has on those who read it. The theory I shall offer is, I believe, a theory of this kind.

1.1. FICTION AND LANGUAGE

Let us begin with the drastically simplifying assumption that all fiction employs the medium of language. It's natural to think that we can discover whether the work before us is fiction simply by reading it. In that case, we might say, its being fiction (or not, as the case may be) is determined by the work's verbal structure; reading a work is, after all, a matter of reading the words and sentences that go to make it up. If we find out whether the work is fictional by reading it, that must be because there is some quality of its words and sentences – perhaps a quality of its sentences taken as a whole – that makes it fiction. But here we confuse constitutive and evidential issues. It is true that facts about style, narrative form, and plot structure may count as evidence that the work is fiction, but these are not the things that make it so. It is possible for two works to be alike in verbal structures – right down to the details of spelling and word order – yet for one to be fiction and the other not. A diarist and a novelist might produce texts identical in their words and sentences.

Characteristic of literary theory in this century has been the view that the text is, in Northrop Frye's words, "an autonomous verbal structure."[1] Older schools of criticism, with their emphasis on affect, history, and biography, have been castigated as impressionistic and unsystematic. There's truth

1 *Anatomy of Criticism* (Princeton, N.J.: Princeton University Press, 1957), p. 122.

1.1. *Fiction and language*

in the accusation, and the benefits of close reading can hardly
be denied. But a purely textual inquiry, whether it employs
the methods of Formalism, the New Criticism, Structuralism,
or Frye's own archetypal analysis, must leave important
questions unanswered, and one of them is the question that
interests us here.[2] There simply is no linguistic feature necessarily shared by all fictional works and necessarily absent
from all nonfictional works.[3]

It has been claimed that all fictional works belong to one or
another of a limited number of narrative kinds or genres. Perhaps an exhaustive enumeration of these kinds will amount to a
definition of fiction.[4] But the question is not whether fictions
are all of these kinds and no others, it is whether they *must* be. A
definition by cases must always be accompanied by a proof that
the enumeration of cases is complete. To my knowledge, no
such proof has ever been attempted for the case of fiction, and
on the rare occasions when something like one can be recon-
structed the premises look suspiciously parochial; they can't
sustain the generality necessary to cover not merely the fiction
we actually have but the fiction we or any rational beings might
have. Frye's postulation of mental archetypes based on the distinctions between seasons would be an implausible framework
for fiction-producing inhabitants of Mercury – or for us if we all
lived in equatorial regions.[5] In the absence of a convincing argu-

2 For a useful introduction to these and other modern schools of criticism, see Terry
   Eagleton, *Literary Theory* (Oxford: Basil Blackwell, 1983). For the work of the Rus-
   sian Formalists, see L. T. Lemon and M. J. Reis (eds.), *Russian Formalist Criticism:
   Four Essays* (Lincoln: University of Nebraska Press, 1965). On Structuralism, see
   Jonathan Culler, *Structuralist Poetics* (Ithaca, N.Y.: Cornell University Press, 1975).
   For an influential employment of the methods of New Criticism, see Cleanth
   Brooks, *The Well-Wrought Urn* (London: Dennis Dobson, 1949). Frye's most important theoretical work is *Anatomy of Criticism*.
3 Significantly, all these schools have taken literature as their subject; they say little
   about the concept of fiction itself.
4 Here I simply grant that genre membership can be regarded as a feature determined by the linguistic structure of a work. My own view is that it cannot; genre
   membership depends upon a variety of extrinsic features including the historical
   relation of the work to other works and the intentions of its author. For further
   remarks on genre, see Section 3.4.
5 See Frye, *Anatomy of Criticism*, Third Essay. For a critical view of genre based
   methodology, see John Reichert, "More Than Kin and Less Than Kind," in Joseph

1. The concept of fiction

ment to the contrary we ought to say that membership in one or another of a given range of genres is neither a necessary and a sufficient, nor even a necessary, condition for being fictional. And the presence of a preferred set of structural-generic features in a work cannot be a sufficient condition for its being fictional. A historical narrative does not become fictional by being given the structure of a tragedy.

1.2. SEMANTIC PROPERTIES

If fictionality does not reside in the text itself, it must be a relational property: something possessed in virtue of the text's relations to other things. Among a text's relational properties will be its semantic properties, such as reference and truth. A text will be true or false (or partly true and partly false) insofar as the sentences that compose it are true or false (have truth values). It will make reference to real people and places insofar as it contains terms like "London" and "Napoleon" that so refer. Truth value and reference are characteristics determined by the text's relations to the world. Sentences are true and words refer because there are things they are true of and refer to. Perhaps fictionality, while not a purely linguistic matter, is a semantic matter.

Philosophers and critics have sometimes argued that fictional works do not possess semantic features, that they are neither true nor false, and make no reference to anything outside the text. These claims are sometimes the product of a general skepticism about semantics according to which no text ever succeeds in making extralinguistic reference. This strikes me as one of the great absurdities of the contemporary cultural scene, but we need not make this the occasion for an assault upon it.[6] After all, even if the theory were correct, it

Strelka (ed.), *Theories of Literary Genre, Yearbook of Comparative Criticism*, vol. 8 (University Park: Pennsylvania State University Press, 1978).

6 This doctrine derives ultimately from Saussure's doctrine of the arbitrariness of the sign (*Course in General Linguistics*, ed. Charles Bally and Albert Sechehaye, [New York: McGraw-Hill, 1966; first published in French in 1916]). It is prominent in, for example, Terence Hawkes, *Structuralism and Semiotics* (London: Methuen,

would leave us where we began: without a means of distinguishing between fiction and nonfiction.

Somewhat less extreme, and certainly more relevant to our present concern, is the view that it is only fictional works which are characterized by their lack of semantic connections with the world. But this position, while not manifestly absurd, is hardly plausible. Surely the reader of the Sherlock Holmes stories is supposed to understand that "London," as it occurs in the stories, refers to London. Someone who did not have the slightest idea what city London was, or who thought that the location of the story was as fictional as any of the characters in it, would not properly understand the story. The Holmes stories are about (among other things) London, not "the London of the Holmes stories," if that's supposed to be something other than London itself. Certainly, Doyle says things about London that are not true of London; he says, for instance, that a detective called "Sherlock Holmes" once lived there. But this shows merely that what Doyle said was false.

In speaking falsely, Doyle was not lying, because he was not making an assertion; a lie is an assertion made in the knowledge that what is asserted is untrue. It is sometimes said that where no assertion is made, as the author of fiction makes no assertion, there is nothing said that could be either true or false.[7] But in one perfectly good sense, the author of

---

1977). For critical comments on the treatment of language as "a self defining system," see John Holloway, "Language, Realism, Subjectivity, Objectivity," in L. Lerner (ed.), *Reconstructing Literature* (Oxford: Basil Blackwell, 1983), as well as the essays by Cedric Watts and Roger Scruton in the same volume. See also the defense of fiction's mimetic function in Robert Alter, "Mimesis and the Motive for Fiction," in *Motives for Fiction* (Cambridge, Mass.: Harvard University Press, 1984). Michael Devitt and Kim Sterelny's *Language and Reality* (Cambridge, Mass.: MIT Press, 1987) contains a useful chapter on Structuralism that highlights, and criticizes, the Structuralist's rejection of reference.

7 See, for example, Margaret Macdonald, "The Language of Fiction," in C. Barrett (ed.), *Collected Papers on Aesthetics* (Oxford: Basil Blackwell, 1965); J. O. Urmson, "Fiction," *American Philosophical Quarterly* 13 (1976), pp. 153–7; and David Novitz, "Fiction, Imagination, and Emotion," *Journal of Aesthetics and Art Criticism* 38 (1979–80); 279–88, 284. (Of course, assertions do often occur *in* fictional works. See Section 1.10.)

fiction does say something: he utters a meaningful sentence, a sentence with a certain *content*. Imagine that Doyle had written "It rained in London on the night of January 1, 1895." In that case Doyle would have written a sentence the content of which is that it rained in London on the night of January 1, 1895. And this content is straightforwardly either true or false, depending on the historical facts about the weather. For Doyle not to have said anything in this sense he would have to have written something with no content – something that isn't meaningful – and that is not what writers of fiction usually do. Competent language users have, after all, no trouble in understanding what is written in fiction: no more, at least, than they do when they read history.

Here it's useful to distinguish between meaning and force. We can identify what is said in terms of meaning alone (as I did while discussing Doyle's utterance), or in terms of force together with meaning. When we identify what is said in terms of meaning alone we identify the content, or the proposition expressed. When we add considerations of force we identify what is said as a certain act of saying, as with the act of asserting or requesting. But identification at the level of force is not relevant to the question of whether the utterance has a truth value. The truth value of a sentence is determined by its referential relations to the world: "Fred is tall" is true just in case the reference of "Fred" is in the extension of the predicate "is tall." And referential relations are, in their turn, determined by the meanings of expressions and facts about the world: the extension of "is tall" depends upon what "is tall" means and upon who happens to be tall. There is no room here for considerations about force to intrude in the determination of truth value. The claim that sentences in fiction have no truth value is based on a confusion of meaning with force.

Another way to put the distinction between meaning and force is this. Force can vary where meaning does not. If Doyle had been writing history instead of fiction when he wrote "It rained in London on January 1, 1895," he would have been making an assertion. The transition from history to fiction is

6

marked, at least, by the loss of one kind of force: assertative force. (Whether it is also marked by the gaining of another kind of force is a question we shall consider presently.) But the transition is not marked by any change of meaning. In the sense relevant to the determination of truth value, Doyle would have said something in writing that sentence, regardless of whether he was asserting it or not. And what he said would be the same in either case.

I rely here on the assumption that words as they occur in fiction may have the same meanings they have in non-fiction.[8] For sentence-meaning is a function of word-meaning; if words mean different things in fiction and in nonfiction, then a given sentence could mean one thing in fiction and another thing in nonfiction. But it is very implausible to suppose that words mean different things in fiction and in nonfiction. In reading a fictional story we bring to the work our ordinary understanding of language. We don't learn special meanings for words as they occur in fiction.

Notice that in the examples of sentences that might occur in fictions I have avoided using what we might call "fictional names": expressions like "Othello" and "Sherlock Holmes" – though in the sentence "Someone called 'Sherlock Holmes' lived in London" one of these expressions is mentioned. The use of fictional names in works of fiction raises problems I don't want to consider here. In Chapter 4, where I discuss the semantics of fictional names, I argue that sentences containing fictional names do have truth values. Just at present I'm concerned to deny the claim that it is because sentences in fictions are not asserted that they have no truth values. The sentences I have considered are counterexamples to that claim; they are sentences, true or false, that the author of fiction may produce without asserting them.

I said just now that the claim that sentences in fiction have no truth value is based on a confusion of meaning with force. The notion of force will turn out to be of the utmost impor-

---

8 "May" rather than "must" because, as we shall see, there are problems about the nonliteral usage of words. But this does not affect the present issue.

tance for us in distinguishing fiction from nonfiction, and I shall soon return to it.

Sometimes it is not sufficient merely to argue that a view is incorrect. Sometimes one needs, in addition, to undermine the motivation that makes the view attractive. The view that statements in fiction have no truth value might be grounded in the thought that if they did, many of them would have to be counted as false. And to admit that the story according to which ghosts exist says something false seems to clash with our perception that it is true *in the story* that there are ghosts. But as I shall argue in Chapter 2, sentences can be "true in the story" and false *simpliciter*. Even with this granted, the worry is not at an end: If fictional statements are false, we ought to disbelieve them – and this would interfere with our appreciation of the story. But this objection seems plausible only so long as we fail to distinguish two different ways in which we may disbelieve a proposition. We may actively, occurrently, disbelieve a proposition; we may have the falsity of that proposition vividly before our minds. Usually we do not disbelieve the propositions of a fiction in this sense, at least while we are attending to the story. But there are many things we disbelieve at a given time without occurrently disbelieving them. I disbelieve that the moon is made of cheese; I am permanently disposed to deny it if the question comes up. In this sense we disbelieve in ghosts in general, in the ghost of Hamlet's father, in Hamlet himself. If someone somehow took *Hamlet* for a reliable historical narrative, we would tell him straight off that the play's eponymous hero does not and never did exist. We dispositionally, rather than occurrently, disbelieve the propositions of a fiction. As readers and theatergoers we do not have the falsity of the story vividly before our minds. If we did we should probably not be able to engage with the story as we desire to do.[9]

I conclude, then, that fictional texts, like texts of other

9 A point I shall make more of in Section 4.3. "The willing suspension of disbelief" is best understood as an operation of the mind whereby we suppress our *occurrent* disbelief in the story.

kinds, can have the semantic properties of truth value and reference. This result will be extremely important to us, but it can't help to *distinguish* fiction from nonfiction. A historical novel might refer to exactly the same people and places that a work of history refers to. Fictional works are typically false, but so are many scientific treatises, and they are not to be classed as fiction on that account. Fictional works often contain true sentences, and a fictional work might even be entirely true. Suppose an author writes a historical novel in which only real people and places are referred to, and in which he sticks rigidly to known fact; the author's inventive powers are exercised only when filling in the gaps between our bits of historical knowledge. It might just happen that his imaginative filling in coincides exactly with what actually occurred. In that case the story is entirely true, but surely it is fiction still. Truth value offers no theoretically decisive test for fiction.

Suppose, contrary to what I have claimed, that we had good reason to say that fictional works essentially lack semantic relations. I don't think we could base the distinction between fiction and nonfiction on this alone. A lack of semantic relations to the world could hardly be a basic feature of fictional works. If semantic relations are suspended in fiction, we require an explanation of this in terms of how these sentences are being used. And this explanation in terms of use would be the more likely explanation of what makes the work a fictional one. Although considerations of use will not, I believe, tell in favor of the idea that semantic relations are suspended in fiction, they will play a crucial role in distinguishing fiction from nonfiction.

1.3. READERS AND AUTHORS

Texts have other kinds of relational properties: among them are properties we specify when we describe people's attitudes toward the texts. A work's being popular, or successful, or influential, are properties of this kind. That a work is popular just means that a large number of people enjoy it.

1. The concept of fiction

Properties like those just listed we might call *community based;* they depend upon the prevailing attitudes of the community, or of a subgroup of the community, rather than on the attitudes of a single individual. One way to suppose that the fictionality of a work is community based would be to endorse an "institutional theory of fiction," parallel to the familiar institutional theory of art. According to the institutional theory, something is a work of art if a member or members of a certain institution, sometimes called "the art world," have conferred upon it a certain kind of status, sometimes called the status of "candidate for appreciation."[10] It has proved immensely difficult to give a plausible and relatively precise formulation of this view; it will be at least equally difficult, I think, to formulate an institutional theory of fiction. But a community-based theory of fiction might not appeal to a "fiction world" or to any kind of conferred status; it might claim simply that a work's fictional status depends in some broad sense upon attitudes within the community. Such a theory might deliver the result that a work is fiction if it is generally acknowledged within the community to be fiction: a result that, while patently circular, might be thought to tell us something important about the concept of fiction in the same way it is said to be an insight into the nature of colors to point out that a thing is red just in case it looks red to normal observers in normal conditions.[11] But whatever the truth about colors, the fictionality of works cannot be community based in this way. It is surely possible for the community to be mistaken about the fictional status of a work. We might think a work is fictional and learn subsequently that it isn't. And although it is arguably the case that the colors of things would change if, because of some change in our sensory apparatus, they came systematically to look different colors to us, there is no comparable sense in which a work could go

10 See, for example, George Dickie, "Defining Art," *American Philosophical Quarterly* 6 (1969): 253–6. Later, and progressively less "institutional," versions of the theory are to be found in Dickie's *Art and the Aesthetic* (Ithaca, N.Y.: Cornell University Press, 1974) and *The Art Circle* (New York: Haven, 1984).
11 See Colin McGinn, *The Subjective View* (Oxford: Clarendon Press, 1983).

from being fiction to nonfiction or vice versa. It makes good sense to ask when a work was popular, but it would be bizarre to ask when it was fiction.

Readers, collectively and individually, do not make and unmake fiction.[12] Fictional status is acquired by a work, not in the process of its reception but in the process of its making. I am going to argue that there is a kind of act engaged in by an author of fiction and in virtue of which his text is fictional; we may call it an act of *fiction-making*.[13] Fiction-making involves overt behavior. That is, it involves the production of some publicly accessible object that, again on the assumption that we are dealing with linguistically encoded fictions, we may call a text. The behavior may involve speech or writing, or some less conventional performance like tapping out morse code. But fiction-making is not just the utterance (in a generalized sense) of words and sentences, for that would not distinguish it from the production of history, journalism, or scientific theory. Fiction-making is distinguished by the performance of a *fictive* utterance, an utterance produced in order to fulfill certain specific intentions; we may call them *fictive intentions*. My aim in the next five sections is to develop a precise account of the nature of these intentions. I shall begin this task by distinguishing my proposal from another with which it may easily be confused.

First, though, a brief remark about multiple authorship. In what follows I shall speak of authors and their actions as if a work is always the product of a single author, and this, of course, is not strictly true. Although it is not true, no great harm will be done by assuming that it is. For I take it that an act of joint authorship is exactly that: an act engaged in by more than one person rather than several distinct acts undertaken individually and patched together. This does not mean that every word must be the joint product of all the authors, merely that it should be understood between them that they

---

12 See also Section 1.9.

13 I borrow the term "fiction-making" from Kendall Walton. See his "Fiction, Fiction-Making, and Styles of Fictionality," *Philosophy and Literature* 7 (1983): 78–88.

are engaged in a common project and that each has, in engaging in it, the kind of intention I have called a fictive intention. Cases – however unlikely they are to occur – where there is misunderstanding between the participants, one thinking that the other is providing a sort of nonfictional commentary on the other's story, will result in something that can hardly be called a single work. No doubt there are variations on the theme of cooperation that will produce some puzzling cases that are hard to classify. But for the sake of simplicity and in the belief that such cases will not provide serious problems for the theory I shall propose, I choose to ignore them.

1.4. THE PRETENSE THEORY

I have said it is not any linguistic or semantic feature of the text that determines its fictionality, nor is it anything to do with the reader's response. Rather, it has to do with the kind of action the author performs in producing the text. In one form or another, this view is quite widely held. Unfortunately, the most popular version of it is wrong. According to the popular and incorrect version, the difference between fiction and nonfiction is this: When I utter a sentence as part of a nonfictional discourse I am asserting it, and when I utter it as a part of a fictional discourse I am merely pretending to assert it. On this view fiction is to be explained not at the level of meaning, but at the level of *force*. A sentence uttered in a normal, nonfictional context will be uttered with a certain kind of force; if it is an indicative sentence, it will be uttered with an assertative force – the speaker will be making an assertion. The same sentence uttered as part of the production of a fictional work will not have that force; its utterer will be merely pretending to utter it with an assertative force. Let us call this the "pretense theory."

The pretense theory seems to have a good deal of intuitive appeal, and many writers on fiction have adopted it, often without offering much in the way of explicit arguments for

1.4. The pretense theory

it.[14] It is not without truth: authors of fiction do not assert when they make fictive utterances, and it is questions about force rather than questions about meaning that need to be settled if we are to understand what fiction is. But the theory goes wrong in saying that the author of fiction is *pretending* to assert something. On the contrary, the author is performing a genuine communicative act that is not merely the pretense of some other act, assertative or otherwise.

John Searle is one writer who defends the pretense theory in some detail.[15] On Searle's view the author of fiction engages "in a nondeceptive pseudoperformance which constitutes pretending to recount to us a series of events" (p. 65). In doing so, "an author of fiction pretends to perform illocutionary acts which he is not in fact performing" (p. 66). Writing an indicative sentence, the author of fiction pretends to engage in the illocutionary act of asserting.

As will be clear from the last statement, talk of illocutionary acts is connected with what I have been calling "force." When we know that an utterance was an assertion, or a question, or a request, we know what illocutionary force the sentence was uttered with. To assert is to perform one kind of illocutionary act, to request is to perform another.[16]

Searle offers two arguments in support of the pretense

---

14 See, for example, D. M. Armstrong, "Meaning and Communication," *Philosophical Review* 80 (1971): 427–47; Barbara Herrnstein Smith, "Poetry as Fiction," *New Literary History* 2 (1971): 259–81; Richard Ohmann, "Speech Acts and the Definition of Literature," *Philosophy and Rhetoric* 4 (1971): 1–19; M. C. Beardsley, "Aesthetic Intentions and Fictive Illocutions," in P. Hernadi (ed.), *What Is Literature?* (Bloomington: Indiana University Press, 1978), D. K. Lewis, "Truth in Fiction," *American Philosophical Quarterly* 15 (1978): 37–46, reprinted in his *Philosophical Papers*, vol. 1, (New York: Oxford University Press, 1983), see esp. p. 40 of the reprint; and, to be examined in detail below, J. R. Searle, "The Logical Status of Fictional Discourse," *New Literary History* 6 (1974–5): 319–32, reprinted in Searle's *Expression and Meaning* (New York: Cambridge University Press, 1979). Searle's theory is conditionally endorsed in John Reichert, *Making Sense of Literature* (Chicago: University of Chicago Press, 1977), pp. 53–4.
15 See Searle, "The Logical Status of Fictional Discourse." Parenthetical references in the text of this section are to the reprint of this paper in *Expression and Meaning*.
16 On illocutionary acts, see Searle, *Speech Acts* (New York: Cambridge University Press, 1969), and J. L. Austin, *How to Do Things with Words*, 2nd ed. (New York: Oxford University Press, 1975), chap. 8.

theory: one to the effect that the theory is preferable to another theory, the other to the effect that the theory has important explanatory power. Both arguments fail.

Searle's first argument is particularly important because the theory he contrasts with his own is, roughly speaking, the theory I want to defend in this chapter. This alternative theory says that the difference between fiction and nonfiction is a difference between *kinds* of illocutionary acts performed; whereas the writer of nonfiction performs the illocutionary act of asserting, the writer of fiction performs a different, characteristically fictional, illocutionary act: Searle calls it "telling a story" (p. 63).[17] On this view the author isn't pretending to perform an act of one particular kind; he *is* performing an act of some (other) kind. Now, Searle argues that his own theory is preferable to this one because his satisfies a principle that the other theory fails to satisfy. Searle formulates the principle in this way: "The illocutionary act (or acts) performed in the utterance of a sentence is a function of the meaning of the sentence" (p. 64). In other words, once we fix the meaning of a sentence we thereby fix the illocutionary act it is to be used to perform. In yet other words, (token) sentences with the same meaning must be used to perform the same illocutionary acts. Let us call this the "functionality principle" (hereafter *FP*). Searle notes that it is inconsistent with *FP* to claim that fiction-making involves the performance of a distinctive illocutionary act. For it is agreed that the same sentence, with the same meaning, may occur in fiction and in nonfiction. According to the theory which says that fiction-making involves the performance of a peculiarly fictional illocutionary act, we would then have the possibility that distinct illocutionary acts could be performed on two occasions of utterance of one and the same sentence. We could try to deny that sentences in fiction can mean the same

---

17 "Telling a story" is not an especially appropriate description of the act, since one can tell a story that one didn't have any hand in writing. "Fiction-making" is a better description, and I shall revert to it further on.

as sentences in nonfiction.[18] But I have already said that this is quite implausible.

So everything depends upon whether we accept *FP*. As stated, *FP* seems to be straightforwardly wrong. I may utter the sentence "You will leave now" in the act of asserting that you will leave now, or in the act of issuing a request (or more likely an order) for you to leave now. The same sentence *can* be used to perform distinct illocutionary acts. Of course, to have a counterexample to Searle here it must be the case that the sentence "You will leave now" has the same meaning on both occasions of use, which it does: that this sentence can be used to perform different illocutionary acts is not a result of any ambiguity in the sentence itself. Rather, it is the result of the fact that *what the speaker means by the sentence* varies from one occasion of use to the other. But perhaps Searle's statement of *FP* was incautious. Perhaps Searle should have said that the illocutionary act performed in the *literal* utterance of a sentence is a function of the meaning of the sentence. The addition of the word "literal" would rule out such counterexamples. Saying "You will leave now" and meaning it as a request would not be a case of literally meaning what you say.

But now consider again the case of Doyle, who writes, "It rained in London on January 1, 1895." Here Doyle's utterance is literal in the sense that the proposition he intends to convey to his audience is exactly the proposition expressed by the sentence he utters; he intends his words to be taken literally.[19] On nobody's account – and certainly not on Searle's – is Doyle here asserting anything. But a historian might make an assertion by engaging in a literal utterance of exactly that sentence. In that case the revised *FP* is wrong; for here we have a case of two literal utterances of one and the same sentence, the one resulting in an assertion, the other not. To protect the revised *FP* Searle will have to claim that

18 Once again, "can" and not "must." See Section 1.8 for a discussion of nonliteral usage in fiction.
19 Searle himself says that the author of fiction speaks literally. See "The Logical Structure of Fictional Discourse," p. 60.

one of these two utterances – presumably Doyle's – is not, in fact, a literal utterance. But if Searle does claim this, he will have saved the *FP* at the cost of making it irrelevant to the present debate. The revised *FP* may be stated like this: "If someone engages in a literal utterance of a sentence, then the illocutionary act he performs is a function of the meaning of the sentence." If the maker of fiction is not engaged in a literal utterance, then his utterance fails to satisfy the antecedent of the revised *FP* and so that principle says nothing whatever about the kind of act (illocutionary or otherwise) in which he is engaged. The conclusion is, then, that the *FP* is either false or irrelevant to the debate between Searle's theory and my own.[20]

Searle's second argument for his theory is that "it should help us to solve some of the traditional puzzles about the ontology of a work of fiction" (p. 70). In fact there is just one puzzle Searle attempts to solve: How can I say something true when I say, "Holmes never married," given that Holmes does not exist? A theory that could answer this question would indeed have something to recommend it.

According to Searle, I, as a reader of the Sherlock Holmes stories, may truly say that Holmes never married, this being an assertative utterance *about* the fiction. In saying it "I did not *pretend* to refer to a real Sherlock Holmes; I *really referred* to the fictional Sherlock Holmes" (p. 72; italics in the original). This, of course, presupposes the existence of a fictional Sherlock Holmes, and can hardly be said to solve the problem of fictional existence. The matter becomes more puzzling

---

20 In "Austin on Locutionary and Illocutionary Acts" (*Philosophical Review* 77 [1968]: 405–24) Searle states the following principle that is very similar to *FP*: ". . . for every illocutionary act one intends to perform, it is possible to utter a sentence, the literal meaning of which is such as to determine that its *serious* literal utterance in an appropriate context will be a performance of that act"(p. 418, my italics). And Searle meakes it clear that fiction-making does not count as "serious" utterance (see "The Logical Structure of Fictional Discourse," p. 60). For an excellent critical discussion of Searle's views on the relation between meaning and illocutionary force, see Dennis Stampe, "Meaning and Truth in the Theory of Speech Acts," in P. Cole and J. L. Morgan (eds.), *Syntax and Semantics*, vol. 3: *Speech Acts* (New York: Academic Press, 1975).

still when we note that Searle says, "Holmes and Watson never existed at all, which is not of course to deny that they exist in fiction" (p. 71). Now, existing in fiction is presumably not a way or manner of existing, otherwise Searle would be contradicting himself, saying both that Holmes never existed at all and that he existed in some way. So existing in fiction must be different from existing, in which case the problem about how we can refer to Holmes remains unsolved – at least it remains unsolved for anyone who, like Searle or myself, thinks we can refer only to things that exist.[21] But at the same time Searle seems to be arguing that Holmes does exist, that he is created by an act of pretended reference that is part of the author's act of pretended assertion: "It is the pretended reference which creates the fictional character" (p. 71). What Searle does not tell us is how the author acquires or exercises these mysterious powers of creation. These are certainly difficult problems, and I take them up in Chapter 4. But we need a clearer statement of Searle's solution and its relation to his theory before we regard that theory as having much explanatory power in this area.

We have seen that Searle has done nothing to establish his thesis, but we have yet to find a reason for thinking it false. One such reason is this: There are cases of pretended assertion that do not produce fiction. I don't have in mind here cases of *deceptive* pretense at assertion (however such cases might be constructed) for Searle claims only that fiction is nondeceptive pretense. But suppose I put on a verbal performance to illustrate an idiotic line of reasoning, or to imitate the conversational manner of an acquaintance. Such an act could fairly be described as an act of nondeceptive pretense; I pretend (nondeceptively) to be someone who habitually thinks or speaks that way. But the words I utter don't count thereby as a work of fiction, however truncated or impoverished.

---

21 I consider this problem in more detail in Sections 4.2 to 4.4. Joseph Margolis makes essentially the same point in criticism of Searle in "The Logic and Structures of Fictional Narrative," *Philosophy and Literature* 7 (1983): 162–81.

1. The concept of fiction

At best the pretense theory is incomplete. The author of fiction must be doing something more than merely pretending to assert. What I shall do now is suggest what it is that the pretense theory needs by way of supplement. We shall then see that the supplement does very well on its own; we don't need the pretense theory at all.

1.5. MAKE-BELIEVE

What distinguishes fictive utterance from the cases of imitation and parody I have just considered? I think it is that the speaker intends the audience to respond in different ways in these different cases. In cases of imitation and parody the speaker wants, presumably, the audience to see, and perhaps to be entertained by, the bad logic or the odd manner, perhaps to attribute the logic or the manner to a person or type of person, and perhaps to appreciate the speaker's witty performance. An author of fiction might also have such intentions as these concerning his own verbal (or written) performance. But he certainly need not have any such intentions as these. What the author of fiction does intend is that the reader take a certain attitude toward the propositions uttered in the course of his performance. This is the attitude we often describe, rather vaguely, in terms of "imaginative involvement" or (better) "make-believe." We are intended by the author to *make believe* that the story as uttered is true.

It was the work of Kendall Walton that first suggested to me an explanatory connection between fiction and make-believe.[22] But there are differences between us concerning the nature of this connection. Most importantly, Walton denies the central thesis of this chapter – that we can define fiction itself in terms of the author's intention concerning our make-believe. I consider his argument in Section 1.9. And

22 See his "Pictures and Make-Believe," *Philosophical Review* 82 (1973): 283–319; "Fearing Fictions," *Journal of Philosophy* 75 (1978): 5–27; "How Remote Are Fictional Worlds from the Real World?" *Journal of Aesthetics and Art Criticism* 37 (1978): 11–24; and *Mimesis as Make-Believe: On the Foundations of the Representational Arts* (Cambridge, Mass.: Harvard University Press, in press).

1.5. Make-believe

Walton claims that we can explain pictorial depiction in terms of make-believe, which I deny (see Section 2.9). A further difference between us will emerge in Section 5.6. Putting these disputes aside for the moment, I want now to clarify a little the concept of make-believe as it will be used in this and later chapters.

"Make-believe" is not a term of art as I use it, any more than "belief" and "desire" are terms of art for the philosophical psychologist. These latter terms may take on an unfamiliar aspect as they occur in the context of propositional attitude psychology, where they keep company with alarmingly theoretical notions drawn from decision theory and possible worlds semantics. All the same, the aim is to make precise a piece of intuitive theory about ourselves as rationally motived actors – folk psychology. Because the study of propositional attitudes has largely been driven by an interest in explaining action, the role of make-believe has tended to be pushed to one side, although some interesting work has been done on it by psychologists.[23] I suggest that we shall not get a comprehensive picture of the mind's workings until we acknowledge the place of make-believe in the folk theory we are trying to capture. Some of the distinctions and terminology I use when I speak of make-believe will be somewhat unfamiliar. But in using them I am attempting to clarify a notion I take to be well known. Even discounting its role in fiction, make-believe plays a quite pervasive role in our lives. Our daydreams and fantasies, as well as our encounters with fiction, involve us in "making-believe" that such and such is the case. Indeed, folk psychology affirms the reality of make-believe just as it does the reality of belief and desire. Talk about make-believe tends to be loose and unsystematic, but some commonly acknowledged generalizations are discernible: that make-believe allows us to achieve in imagination what we are denied in reality, that we gain vicarious experience through make-believe, that disaster can follow if we

23 See the fascinating account in Jerome Singer, *Daydreaming and Fantasies*, (London: Allen & Unwin, 1976).

confuse what we make believe with what we believe. We acknowledge, in other words, a body of complex connections between belief, desire, experience, sensation, and make-believe.

Imagine how the activity of fiction-making might come about. People enjoy daydreaming, and construct various scenarios that they run through when they desire to turn aside from the outer world. As in other things, some are more skillful at this than others. The less talented among us naturally turn to those with greater talents to construct the material for these fantasies. Fiction is born. And fictions do not differ essentially from daydreams in their capacity for realism, complexity, formal structure, and cognitive significance. As modern research has made clear, daydreams and fantasies are often related to real-life concerns, have a high degree of structural complexity, and are significant instruments for cognitive development. That fiction reading is a phenomenon continuous with our fantasies has even been exploited by recent authors whose works allow the reader to become one of the characters of the fiction, choosing, according to taste, between alternative paths of development for the story.[24]

Modern philosophy has managed to correct at least one traditional error: the identification of thought with the having of "ideas" or mental images. We now think of beliefs and desires as characterized by their abstract propositional content rather than by the introspectible processes that accompany them. I think of make-believe as itself an attitude we take to propositions. We can believe that P, desire that P, and make believe that P. I shall make occasional use of expressions like "make-belief," "made believe," and "making believe." These are not particularly attractive terms, but if we think of make-believe as a propositional attitude, they will seem quite natural. Like belief and desire, make-believe earns its place in our commonsense psychology by its ability to explain, and a good deal of this book is devoted to showing how much we can explain in terms of

24 See, for instance, Anthony J. Niesz and Norman N. Holland, "Interactive Fiction," *Critical Inquiry* 11 (1984): 110–29.

make-believe. Skepticism about propositional attitudes is possible, and it's a position currently adopted by certain writers, but I see no reason to be more skeptical about make-believe than about the other attitudes.[25]

So I do not think of make-believe as a "qualitative" or "phenomenological" state, introspectible in the way pains and bodily sensations are – although, like belief and desire, it is a kind of state that can be accompanied by or give rise to introspectible feelings and images.[26] It is, perhaps, as unfamiliar to think of make-believe as propositional as it once was to think of belief and desire in this way. We still think of make-believe as closely connected to imagination, and one quite ordinary sense of "imagination" is "that which creates mental images."[27] Certainly our fantasies are strongly marked by the presence of visual and bodily sensation. But a fantasy or daydream, however vivid, is primarily to be characterized in terms of the events, happenings, states of affairs, or whatever, that the images make vivid to us. When we read and become absorbed by a work of fiction we may find compelling images before our minds, but a work of history or a newspaper article can stimulate the imagination in the same way. What distinguishes the reading of fiction from the reading of nonfiction is not the activity of the imagination but the attitude we adopt toward the content of what we read: make-belief in the one case, belief in the other.

1.6. THE AUTHOR'S INTENTIONS

Having introduced the idea of make-believe, we can better understand those cases of parody and imitation which are problematic for the pretense theory. In the parody–imitation

---

25 For skepticism about propositional attitudes, see, for example, Stephen Stitch, *From Folk Psychology to Cognitive Science: The Case Against Belief* (Cambridge, Mass.: MIT Press, 1983).

26 I say more about this in Section 5.4.

27 According to Mary Warnock, this is "perhaps the most ordinary sense of the word 'imagination' that there is" (*Imagination* [London, Faber & Faber, 1976], p. 10).

cases the speaker does not intend that we should engage with the *content* of the performance as we would with a piece of fiction; he does not intend that we should make believe that what is said is *true*. If we did, we would misunderstand the point of his performance. Possibly in the parody–imitation cases there is make-believe of some kind intended. The speaker may intend the audience to make believe that he, the speaker, is someone who believes the bad argument to be a sound one, or that he is the person whose conversational manner is being imitated. But he does not intend the audience to take the attitude of make-believe to the propositions he utters in performing the parody–imitation.

The idea of an author intending that the audience make believe his story is central to the explanation of what fiction is. The author's intention that we take the attitude of make-believe to his story is part of what I have called the author's fictive intention. As we shall see, there is more to fictive intention than this; I shall explore the structure of this intention in the next section. In Section 1.10, I shall argue that having a fictive intention is necessary but not sufficient for the production of fiction. The extra condition required has nothing to do with the author's intentions but concerns the relation of his narrative to actual events. This account, as it is elaborated, will make no reference to the notion of pretense. So if the account is satisfactory, it will have been shown that authorial pretense contributes nothing to the explanation of fiction. Showing that the account is satisfactory will occupy the rest of this chapter and a great deal of the rest of this book. But I can offer here an admittedly rather sketchy argument suggesting that authorial pretense plays no useful role in explaining fiction.

Note that we have already one important result. It is possible to engage in an act of pretended assertion without having a fictive intention; the cases of parody and imitation show us that. So the class – call it *PA* – of acts of pretended assertion is not a subclass of the class – call it *FI* – of acts performed with a fictive intention. Pretense, we might say, does not entail fictive intention. Does fictive intention entail pretense?

1.6. The author's intentions

(Is *FI* a subset of *PA*?) Either it does or it doesn't. If it does, we don't have to talk about pretended assertion any longer; talk of fictive intentions gives us everything we want by entailing the relevant facts about pretense. If it doesn't, then it must be possible to utter something with a fictive intention and *not* be pretending to assert anything. Suppose this is possible. Would someone who uttered words and sentences with a fictive intent, but *without* pretending to assert anything thereby, count as someone who was producing fiction? I think the answer is yes. To have that fictive intent the speaker must think it reasonable to believe that his intention can be fulfilled. Barring massive error based on some skeptical scenario, it would then *be* reasonable in at least some circumstances (though not necessarily in all) to speak with a fictive intent and to suppose the intention will be fulfilled. In that case it is possible to tell a story and to have someone make believe it, without pretending to assert anything. But if I can do *that*, then surely what I have done is produce a piece of fiction. My utterance achieved, and was intended to achieve, the primary (but not, of course, the only) purpose of fiction: the reader's involvement with the story. The same could be said if I wrote down my story and sent it off to the printer. Fictive intent is sufficient to produce fiction, and, by the argument of Section 1.4, which resulted from the need to distinguish fiction-making from parody, it is necessary. So it is necessary and sufficient.

There is a dilemma for an advocate of the pretense theory. Either pretended assertion is consequent upon having a fictive intent, in which case we get it as a free bonus from our account of fictive intent, or it isn't, in which case it turns out not to be a necessary condition for fiction-making at all. So any account of fiction-making in terms of pretended assertion must be either redundant or wrong.

In fact, I suspect the pretense theory is more likely to be wrong than redundant. A writer who types out his work and sends it to the publisher is surely not *pretending* to do anything (in which case *FI* is not a subset of *PA*). In certain cases an author may be engaged in an act of pretense (and so *FI*

1. The concept of fiction

and *PA* have a nonempty intersection). Perhaps the campfire storyteller who makes up his tale is pretending to tell us of things he knows to be true. But this is at most an incidental fact about certain acts of authorship. It tells us nothing about the nature of fiction.

1.7. COMMUNICATIVE ACTS

F iction is essentially connected with the idea of communication. Perhaps there could be creatures who made up imaginative stories for their own personal enjoyment, and who never (out of either choice or necessity) communicated these stories to each other. Such beings produce fantasies rather than fiction. Fiction emerges, as I have said, with the practice of telling stories. The author who produces a work of fiction is engaged in a communicative act, an act that involves having a certain kind of intention: the intention that the audience shall make believe the content of the story that is told. My next aim is to embed the theory of fiction in a general theory of communicative acts. So I shall explain the theory of communication I favor. It is based on ideas of Paul Grice.[28]

I say, in your presence, "It's raining." What makes this an act of communication on my part? Not the verbal behavior alone. If a parrot had uttered the sentence, no act of commu-

28 See these papers by Grice: "Meaning," *Philosophical Review* 66 (1957): 377–88, reprinted in P. F. Strawson (ed.), *Philosophical Logic* (New York: Oxford University Press, 1967); "Utterer's Meaning, Sentence Meaning and Word Meaning," *Foundations of Language* 4 (1968): 225–42; reprinted in J. Searle (ed.), *Philosophy of Language* (New York: Oxford University Press, 1971); "Utterer's Meaning and Intentions," *Philosophical Review* 78 (1969): 147–77; "Meaning Revisited," in N. V. Smith (ed.), *Mutual Knowledge*, (New York: Academic Press, 1982). See also P. F. Strawson, "Intention and Convention in Speech Acts," *Philosophical Review* 73 (1964): 439–60, reprinted in J. Searle (ed.), *Philosophy of Language*. Grice's theory has undergone various changes, and there are alternative elaborations; see, for example, K. Bach and R. M. Harnish, *Linguistic Communication and Speech Acts* (Cambridge, Mass.: MIT Press, 1979). In what follows I choose one path of development, but it is possible to present a Gricean account of fictive intention along different lines. The reader who prefers some other version of Grice's theory is invited to substitute the details of that version in the definitions I give in Section 1.8.

nication would have taken place. And there would be no act of communication even if the parrot's behavior was a reliable guide to the weather, as it might be if the parrot was trained to utter the sentence when and only when it saw signs of rain. If my ears turn red when it rains, and you see my ears turn red and infer that it's raining, I have not communicated anything to you, in the sense of "communication" I'm trying to explicate here. Parrot talk and involuntary ear-reddening are not instances of communication, because they are not intentional acts. When I *say* to you that it's raining I do so *intending that you shall believe that it's raining*. But this intention is still not enough for communication in the full and proper sense to take place. If I point to the window, intending you to see the rain, I have not yet communicated to you that it's raining. We are here interested in communication in the sense of "openly telling someone something," and that is more than directing someone's attention to a state of affairs. When I tell you that it's raining I expect you to form the belief that it is raining (at least in part) *because you recognize my intention*. When I merely direct your gaze to the rain-streaked windows I expect you to form that belief simply because you see that it's raining.

For communicative purposes it is important, therefore, not only that I intend you to believe what I say; it is also important that you recognize this intention. And usually it will be easy for you to infer that this is my intention because that is the only reasonable hypothesis that makes sense of my behavior. ("Why on earth would he say 'It's raining' in this situation if not to get me to believe that it's raining?") Understanding people's speech behavior is just like understanding the rest of their behavior; it is a matter of making assumptions about their intentions that will make their behavior seem rational and appropriate.

Now for a slight complication. How is it that when I say "It's raining" I can expect you to grasp my intention to get you to believe that it's raining? One initially attractive answer is that I can rely on our sharing a common language; I know you will understand the meaning of what I say, and infer

25

from what it means to what I intend. But the inference from the one to the other is not immediate. You must assume not merely that my utterance has this feature – a certain meaning – but that it was intended by me to have that feature. Suppose you hear me utter the sentence "It's raining," but that, for whatever reason, you think I don't know what the sentence means. Or suppose you think I just like the sound of the sentence. In that case you will not think that I uttered the sentence *because* it has the meaning it has; you will think I uttered it because of the way it sounds. In either case you will have no tendency to believe the sentence I uttered, even though you understand it.[29] And the reason is that you won't infer that I intend you to believe that it's raining. So it is your knowledge of the meaning of what I say, together with your belief that I intended to produce a sentence meaning exactly *that*, which enables you to make a specific hypothesis about what I was doing.[30] The point is that I cannot hope to get you to recognize my intention that you should believe that it's raining just by relying on your knowledge of meaning; I have to rely on your making the inference from the fact that my utterance has a certain meaning to the conclusion that I intended my utterance to have that meaning.

Your reasoning, made tediously explicit, goes something like this: "He has uttered a sentence that means *it's raining*. He must have had a reason for doing this. It is likely (at least in this situation) that he knows what the sentence means, and intended to utter a sentence that means exactly that – that it's raining. Therefore he probably intends me to believe that it's raining. It is unlikely that he wants to deceive me (at least in this situation). It is unlikely that he is wrong (again, in this situation). So probably it's raining." You add this to your belief system and my purpose is achieved.

In order for communication to take place it's not essential that you do come to believe what I want you to believe. We

---

29 At least, your hearing and understanding my utterance would not make you any more prone to believe it than you otherwise would have been.

30 The inference here becomes more complicated when we deal with cases of nonliteral meaning, as we shall in Section 1.8.

frequently end up not believing what people tell us. What is essential is that you should perceive my intention in saying it. When you perceive that I intend you to believe that it's raining you know what I *meant* by uttering the sentence "It's raining." (Notice that "knowing what I meant by uttering the sentence" and "knowing what the sentence means" are different things.)

I have been talking here as if communicative acts always involve using language. But it is an important aspect of Grice's theory that they need not. The structure of communicative intentions I have ascribed to the speaker here could be ascribed to someone whose performance was nonlinguistic. To use a familiar example, I hold my hands a certain distance apart intending to get you to realize you are at a certain distance from the car behind; I intend to get you to infer from the nature of my performance that that is my intention, and to pass from recognizing the intention to believing you are at that distance. If everything goes smoothly, as well it might in such a situation, I have communicated with you without the use of language. It isn't just that my performance is *nonverbal*, since there can be nonverbal language. It is that my performance is, or may be, "one-off." There may be no established practice of using that gesture to signify that state of affairs. But still, I can expect you to see what I'm getting at. So although it is important there be some feature of the performance that I count on you to recognize as a sign of my intentions, that feature need not be the accepted or "conventional" meaning of what is said, because the performance may not consist of saying ,anything (or doing anything) with a recognized meaning. In the case of signaling to the driver that feature will be the disposition of my hands; it is from this that I intend you to infer my intention. Someone can mean something by a performance even when performances of that kind don't have any conventionally recognized meaning.[31]

---

31 On conventions of meaning, see Section 3.3.

1. The concept of fiction

Before I extend this account of communication to cover fiction-making, it will be useful to note a complication in the account that will also apply to fictional cases. In fiction-making, as in other forms of writing and speech, we don't always take, and are not always intended to take, the utterance literally. The words a person utters don't always express the thought he intends to communicate. Here again we need the distinction between meaning and force. If Doyle writes "Holmes was a smoker," we don't take this as an assertion, but we take it literally in the sense that we realize that the literal content of what is said is what we are intended to make believe.[32] But there are times when things are said in the narrative that we realize do not literally express the content of what we are to make believe. If a character is described as having fallen off the wagon, we have little trouble in realizing that our make-believe should be that the character has failed in an attempt to stop drinking. Clearly an author may use the full range of nonliteral devices: metaphor, metonymy, irony, understatement, and the like. We do not, for instance, take Chaucer's almost uniformly approving remarks about his characters at face value. We realize that we are intended to make believe that some of the characters are deplorable.

So the decisions we make about what to make believe when reading a story are partly dependent upon the literal meanings of what is said, but they depend also on our perception that the narrative is the product of an intentional agent, whose meaning in making a certain utterance may be different from the literal meaning of the utterance. Earlier I distinguished between knowing what a sentence means and knowing what the speaker means by uttering it. Anyone who thought that this is a distinction without a difference will now see, I hope, that there is a real difference here.

Grice, extending his investigations into the nature of communication, has suggested a general framework within which we can distinguish between what is said and what is

---

32 See this chapter, text to note 19.

meant, when these are different.[33] He distinguishes quite generally between what is said, and what is *implicated* by an act of saying, and he identifies an important class of what he calls *conversational* implicatures. Grice's framework is easily applicable to fictional contexts and I will briefly indicate how conversational implicatures work in fiction.

Grice's idea is that a conversational exchange is governed by a principle of cooperation tacitly agreed to by the conversational partners. In a conversation one normally intends to make one's contribution appropriate to the purposes and direction of the talk exchange, and one expects that one's partner will intend likewise. Grice has listed a number of specific maxims we follow in order to be cooperative in this sense. Among them are (*a*) be truthful, and (*b*) be relevant. Now suppose we are discussing Harry and his drinking. Your comment "Harry has fallen off the wagon," if taken literally, seems to violate (*b*) because any encounter of Harry's with a wagon has nothing obviously to do with his drinking. And it may seem to violate (*a*) if I have good reason to believe that Harry has not been near any wagons lately. In order to preserve the supposition that you are obeying conversational rules, I shall suppose that what you are trying to get across to me is something else. I then make an inference, involving, no doubt, premises concerning the topic of our exchange so far, to the conclusion that what you are trying to tell me is that once again Harry has taken to drink. In this situation you may be said to have *conversationally implicated* that Harry has gone back to drink, because you know that in order to see your conversational contribution as conforming to the conversational maxims, I will assume this is likely to be what you are trying to communicate to me.

I suggest we think of reading as a limiting case of a conversation: a conversation in which one party does all the talking. And it's not hard to see how the conversational maxims will apply in such a situation. At any stage in my reading I have

33 See his "Logic and Conversation," in P. Cole and J. L. Morgan (eds.), *Syntax and Semantics*, vol. 3: *Speech Acts* (New York: Academic Press, 1975).

certain expectations about relevance, and certain presuppositions about truth, and these will entrench or shift as my reading proceeds. If I'm reading about the struggle of someone called "Harry" with a drinking problem, and I read that Harry has fallen off the wagon, I can use the maxims of truth and relevance (as well, perhaps, as others) to infer what the author intends to communicate to me.

This can operate equally well with a fictional narrative as with a nonfictional one. The difference between them is, of course, that if the narrative is a fictional one, it will be my presuppositions about what is "true in the story" that guide me, rather than my presuppositions about what is true. We require, therefore, an account of what it is for something to be true in a fiction. This question, which has its own intrinsic interest for us, is addressed in Chapter 2.

1.8. FICTIVE COMMUNICATION

Now we have an account of communication, we can describe the author's act of fiction-making. The author intends that we make-believe the text (or rather its constituent propositions) and he intends to get us to do this by means of our recognition of that very intention. The author may expect his intention to be recognized in a number of ways: by the manner of his writing, the nature of his story, or simply because he knows his work will be advertised and sold as fiction. He may on occasion explicitly signal his fictive intention by using a prefatory formula like "The characters in this story bear no relation to persons either living or dead." Of course, the signaling of their intentions is something authors rarely give any thought to. They don't normally worry that their work will be taken in the wrong way, that their fictive intent will not be recognized. In fiction as in conversation, it's only when things go wrong that we give thought to these matters.

It is as true of fictive communication as of other kinds of communication that it can be achieved without language. One can tell a story in mime or shadow play as well as in words, although in doing so one puts serious restrictions on

30

what can be expressed. Proust could hardly have conveyed the full subtlety of *A la Recherche du Temps Perdu* without using words. But fiction is not always so marvelously complex, and while fiction is essentially connected with communication, it is not essentially connected with language. This will be important when we come to consider works in visual media.[34]

I must now specify what it takes for an utterance to be fictive. First of all, informally: I want you to make believe some proposition P; I utter a sentence that means P, intending that you shall recognize this is what the sentence means, and to recognize that I intend to produce a sentence that means P; and I intend you to infer from this that I intend you to make believe that P; and, finally, I intend that you shall, partly as a result of this recognition, come to make believe that P. Complex as it is, this account is only a start. There are further complications to consider, although I shall go on to examine only two kinds. Now a bit more formally:

(D_0) U's utterance of S is fictive if and only if (iff) U utters S intending that the audience will

(1) recognize that S means P;
(2) recognize that S is intended by U to mean P;
(3) recognize that U intends them (the audience) to make believe that P;
(4) make believe that P.

And further intending that

(5) (2) will be a reason for (3);
(6) (3) will be a reason for (4).

One important simplification in this is that it applies only to utterances with a certain conventionally recognized meaning, and where what the sentence means – the proposition it expresses – is exactly what the speaker intends the audience to make believe. This is a simplification for two reasons. First, we have seen that a speaker may utter the sentence meaning it nonliterally, intending that the proposition the audience will make believe be different from the proposition

---

34 See Sections 1.9 and 2.9.

expressed. In the preceding section we discussed the mechanism that underlies this. Second, we have seen that it is not essential to the making of a fictive utterance that the speaker use language at all. What the speaker "utters" might not be a sentence – something with a conventionally recognized meaning – but a piece of dumb show, shadow play, or whatever. In cases of these kinds the speaker makes movements or creates an object where the movements or the object have some feature that he, the speaker, counts on as providing a clue as to what he intends. When the speaker utters a sentence, but means it nonliterally, he still intends his utterance to have the meaning that sentences of that kind conventionally have. One important clue to the intended meaning of nonliteral speech is the conventional meaning of what is said; I cannot hope to understand that you are speaking ironically or metaphorically unless I understand the sentence you utter. And when the speaker engages in shadow play or dumb show he intends his movements to be movements of a certain kind – to be, for example, reminiscent of the movements of a bird – and to be recognized as movements of that kind in order that the audience should grasp the meaning he intends. In either kind of case the speaker intends his utterance to have some publicly available feature (e.g., a certain meaning, or a certain visible shape). So let Φ be a variable ranging over such features of utterances. Then we have:

(D_1) U's utterance of S is fictive iff there is a Φ such that U utters S intending that the audience will

(1) recognize that S has Φ;
(2) recognize that S is intended by U to have Φ;
(3) recognize that U intends them (the audience) to make believe that P, for some proposition P;

with further clauses as for (D_0).[35]

A definition like this, while it covers both literal and nonliteral utterances, will still apply in only a restricted range

---

35 This formulation is derived, with some simplification, from that of Schiffer; see his *Meaning* (Oxford: Clarendon Press, 1972), chap. 3. (Schiffer's formulation is not intended to apply to fictive contexts.)

of circumstances. It presupposes that there is an audience the author has in mind. But the author may not have any particular audience in mind. Unless he is in the position of a campfire storyteller he probably won't. And if being a member of his audience involves buying his book, he may not think of himself as guaranteed an audience of any kind. In such cases the author's intention is not of the form "that the audience shall make believe that *P*." Rather, it is of the form "if anyone were *C*, they would make believe that *P*." The author's intention is conditional rather than categorical.[36] *C*, the condition the author thinks of as sufficient to evoke the desired response, might be simply *reading this book*. There are, however, imaginable circumstances in which the author assumes further, more recondite constraints on the audience. I might tell a story that I know most people will take as fact but that will, I believe, be recognized as fiction by the few who recognize the clues I put into the text and with which I signal my fictive intention. It could reasonably be said that in uttering such a work I was performing more than one kind of communicative act: I would be asserting and fiction-making in one breath. Having communicative intentions of one kind does not always exclude the possibility that one has communicative intentions of another kind as well.

We can revise the definition in order to take these considerations into account. Let χ be a variable ranging over characteristics of persons:

(D_2) *U*'s utterance of *S* is fictive iff there is a Φ and there is a χ such that *U* utters *S* intending that anyone who has χ would

(1) recognize that *S* has Φ;
(2) recognize that *S* is intended by *U* to have Φ;
(3) recognize that *U* intends them (the possessors of χ) to make believe that *P*, for some proposition *P*;

with further clauses as for (D_0).[37]

---

36 The conditional is subjunctive rather than material. The author's intention will not be satisfied merely by the failure of the antecedent.
37 This formulation owes something to Grice, "Utterer's Meaning and Intentions."

1. The concept of fiction

Suppose the author writes a story he intends no one to read. He does not even intend it for the consumption of his own future self. Wishing only to refine his literary skills, he writes the story and burns it immediately it's done. It seems he has engaged in an act of fiction-making. But what sort of communicative act has he performed? After all, he intends that no one shall read his story; he intends, consequentially, that no one shall make believe it. But this does not preclude him from intending that if someone were to read it, he would make believe it. This kind of hypothetical intention is covered in (D_2).

Suppose the author is in a position to *know* that no one will read his story. Can I know that A will not happen, and yet intend that if A were to happen, then B would happen? Suppose a boxer is practicing with a punching bag. He knows that no one is in a position to receive his blow, so he knows his blow won't floor anybody. But he can surely intend his blow to be such that if someone were in the way, he would be floored by it. Just so with our crypto-author: he intends his writing to be such that if someone were to read it, he would make believe its content. The boxing analogy is apt. The boxer may never intend to fight anybody, but it pleases him to exercise the skills appropriate in a boxing match. His activity is made understandable in terms of its relation to a game that involves an opponent. So it is with the crypto-novelist who intends his work never to reach the public. He takes his place among the makers of fiction by virtue of the relation of his activity to the activity of those with a more publicly oriented intention. And just as not all boxers can be punching bag hitters (for then there would be no boxing), not all fiction makers can be crypto-authors.[38]

I have explained what it is for an utterance to be fictive. I assume there is a relation of *production* that may hold

I am grateful to Graham Priest, who suggested a revision, along the lines here presented, of an earlier definition.

38 See Patrick Suppes, "The Primacy of Utterer's Meaning," in R. Grandy and R. Warner (eds.), *Philosophical Grounds of Rationality* (Oxford: Clarendon Press, 1986).

between an utterance and a work. An author produces a work by performing a verbal or written utterance; his utterance is productive of the work. This relation is not, of course, peculiar to fiction. A historian's utterance is productive of his historical work. What kind of work is produced depends upon the intention of the utterer. Let us provisionally say that a work is fictional if and only if it is the product of a fictive utterance. We must now see whether this provisional analysis is correct.

1.9. OBJECTIONS TO THE NECESSITY OF THE ANALYSIS

Fiction requires a fictive utterance, which requires in turn a fictive intent. So I claim. But is a fictive intent really necessary for the production of fiction? Kendall Walton has argued that it is not: there can be fiction that consists entirely of statements asserted by the author, and there can be fiction that is not the product of any intention whatsoever.[39]

Walton says little about the supposed possibility of entirely asserted fiction. But such a possibility is consistent with my view. In Section 1.8, I said that an author might have multiple communicative intentions, intending his utterance to be taken in more than one way at the same time. The author of a fictional work may intend his audience to believe what he says and also intend that the audience (perhaps a different audience) will take the attitude of make-believe toward what he says. He engages simultaneously in acts of fiction-making and assertion. Such a thing would not be possible according to the pretense theory, which has it that fiction-making consists in pretending to assert, and one cannot assert something and pretend to assert it at the same time. If Walton has an objection to anybody's theory here, it is to Searle's, not to mine.

Walton's second argument would, if it were correct, be an

---

39 See his "Fiction, Fiction-Making, and Styles of Fictionality," *Philosophy and Literature* 7 (1983): 78–88. See also his *Mimesis as Make-Believe*, sections 2.4 to 2.6.

objection to my theory. He claims that our interest in a piece of fiction is an interest in the story that is told, not in the act of telling it. If the structure of naturally occurring cracks in a rock spells out a story, we may read it and respond to it as fiction, much as we would if it was told to us by someone. But we ought not to take the pattern as an assertion, or as the product of any communicative act at all, since it is not intentionally produced by anyone.

The most this argument could establish is that we may treat the shapes on the face of the rock *as if they were fiction;* we can respond to them as we would to a fictional work. But this is not enough to make something fiction. If it were, the Bible would undoubtedly be a work of fiction, since many people read and enjoy Bible stories *as* fiction. What makes the Bible nonfiction (if that's what it is) is exactly the absence of the right kind of intention on the part of its authors.[40] Just about anything can be read as fiction, but not everything is fiction.

It is conceivable that there are works we commonly regard as fiction that are not the product of fictive intentions. It has been suggested to me that Defoe's intention in writing *Robinson Crusoe* was to get the audience to believe the story.[41] I don't know whether this is the case, but it certainly might have been. If we discovered that it was, would we have to say that *Robinson Crusoe* is not fiction after all? Many would resist such a revision of the canon. This seems to be a difficulty for my theory and, of course, for Searle's also. For the case would be describable in his terms as one where the author performed a genuine rather than a pretended illocutionary act, and therefore as a case of nonfiction.

But the difficulty is, I believe, only apparent. There is an appearance of difficulty because we do not readily distinguish between the question of whether something is fiction

---

40 Of course, the Bible, or parts of it, may be fiction. For it may be that the biblical authors, or some of them, had the kinds of intentions that would make it fiction. See the work of Robert Alter (especially *The Art of Biblical Narrative* [New York: Basic Books, 1981], chap. 2), who probes the intentions of the biblical writers. (I owe this reference to a reader for the Press.)

41 By Roy Perrett.

and whether it is (or should be) *treated as* fiction by the reading public. If Defoe had had an assertive intention in uttering
Robinson Crusoe – intending the reading public to believe his
story – then his was a lying utterance. And there is no firmer
doctrine in the poetic tradition than the doctrine that fiction
makers do not lie in the act of making fiction. If we discovered that Defoe's intention had been assertive rather than fictive, we would conclude that *Robinson Crusoe* was not, after
all, fiction. But such a discovery would be unlikely to affect
the attitude of the present reading public toward the work. It
would continue to be read as fiction; readers would continue
to take the attitude of make-believe toward the story. To say
that *Robinson Crusoe* is not fiction is not to say that readers
ought to change their attitudes toward it. Since the story isn't
true (or even close to the truth) there is no point in readers
treating it as assertion; there is nothing factual to be learned
from it. No doubt the most profitable way to read the work
is *as if it were* fiction. So there is a category of works rather like
fictional works – let us call them "pseudofictions" – and
membership in that category is determined by there being a
widespread practice of reading the work as if it were fiction.
The category of fictions and the category of pseudofictions
overlap; for all I know, they are coincident. But at most they
are actually, rather than necessarily, coincident. Making a
discovery about the intentions with which Defoe wrote *Robinson Crusoe* wouldn't cause us to revise our attitude to the
pseudofictional status of that work, but it might alter our attitude to its fictional status.

   Perhaps it will be argued that this just begs the question,
because the possibility remains that what I call pseudofiction
is what most people call fiction. In that case my definition of
"fiction" would not be an explication of the intuitive concept
fiction, but a theory-driven attempt to put something else in
its place. But the distinction between being fiction and being
regarded as fiction is surely one that would be widely
(though perhaps not universally) acknowledged, and it
would be acknowledged by many who do not accept the
theory I'm proposing (e.g., Searle and other advocates of the

pretense theory). If we don't make the distinction, we have to say that *The Origin of Species* would be fiction if some or most people adopted the attitude toward it appropriate to a reading of fiction: surely an unacceptable result. Recall the example of the Bible from our discussion just now. If atheism becomes more widespread than it is, I can imagine Christians (the few who remain) admitting that the Bible is pseudofiction (in my sense) and denying that it is fiction. To call the Bible fiction is much more inflammatory to a believer than to say it is often read as fiction. There is another work by Defoe, *A True Relation of the Apparition of one Mrs. Veal*, which used to cause some confusion. Until sometime in the last century it was thought to be fiction.[42] Anyone who says, reasonably enough, "It was widely and mistakenly thought to be fiction," must be making a distinction between being fiction and being regarded as fiction. So my answer to Crusoe-type counterexamples is this: Don't confuse the (historically revisable) claim that these works are fiction with the (less revisable) claim that they are pseudofictions.

Walton raises an important question about the fictional status of works of visual art – paintings and sculptures. He makes the point that the painter or sculptor is not pretending to do anything. If there are fictional paintings and sculptures, this seems to be an excellent objection to the pretense theory. But how on my own theory can we account for the fictionality of works of visual art?

I have not so far discussed works in visual media, and this is a convenient point at which to integrate them into the theory so far developed. Discussions of fiction do not usually seek to include paintings and sculptures, although, of course, plays and films naturally come to mind as candidates for fictional status. Perhaps the basis for this discrimination is the thought that pictures and sculptures have no narrative structure. Rather, they capture an instant. But to give meaning to a representational picture we often have to set it in a context of temporally flowing events, and usually we have

---

42 I owe the example to Lawrence Jones.

1.9. Objections to necessity of analysis

sufficient collateral information to do this successfully.[43]
Even a painting without any obvious narrative structure can
be fictional. In a unicorn painting with no background or suggested mythological setting it may be fictionally true that
there is a unicorn. We recognize that we are intended to
make believe there is a unicorn that this picture depicts.

But if we agree that paintings and sculptures may be fictions, we should not say they always are. Goya's portrait of
the Duke of Wellington, for instance, does not strike me as
any more fictional than a photograph of the Duke would be.
Of course, a painted portrait is less directly related to the
Duke than a photograph would be; it is more dependent
upon the artist's decisions than a photograph would be.[44]
But then a writer's description of the Duke is as indirect, as
intentionally mediated as the painting, and such a description need not be fictional. There are fictional paintings and
nonfictional ones. Incidentally, photographs can be fictional
too. A photograph of people dressed up to look like fairies
would be fictional, unless it were intended to deceive us into
thinking it was a photograph of real fairies. The fiction–
nonfiction distinction cuts across all the representational
media I know of.[45]

What is it that makes a painting, sculpture, or photograph
fictional? I say it is this: that the artist intended the audience
to make believe the content of what is represented. I don't
perceive in Goya's picture any intention on Goya's part that
we make believe there is a man with the depicted character-

---

43 See E. H. Gombrich, "Moment and Movement in Art," in Gombrich, *The Image and the Eye* (Oxford: Phaidon, 1982).
44 See Kendall Walton, "Transparent Pictures," *Critical Inquiry* 11 (1984): 246–77. Walton offers an interesting argument to the effect that photographs, but not paintings, are "natural signs" in something like the sense of "natural" that Grice uses in distinguishing between natural and non-natural meaning. But I don't think Walton manages to establish that when I see a photograph of my grandfather I see my grandfather in the full and literal sense of "see." Thus, I'm prepared to speak, as I do speak in the paragraph above, of photography as a representa-tional medium (see my "Photography and the Nature of Perception," forthcom-ing). For more on the nature of fictional works in visual media, see Section 2.9.
45 Music is a problem here, because of the problematic status of the claim that music can represent.

istics. I do perceive – at least I believe I perceive - an intention on his part that we should believe that this is how the Duke looks, or at least that this is how the Duke looks to Goya. Of course, this wasn't Goya's only, or even his primary, intention in producing the work. Goya intended to produce a work with certain aesthetic qualities. But I do perceive an assertative intention among the rest: Goya is saying, this is how the Duke is.

This might sound an implausible account when applied to less realistic pictures, for instance, Picasso's portrait of Kahnweiler, a portrait that displays strongly cubist conventions. Surely Picasso is not telling us that Kahnweiler has the fractured appearance of this picture. But we need to bear in mind two things here. First, a portrait, like a verbal description, can contain metaphorical (or otherwise nonliteral) elements. We would go wrong if we took a description of Churchill as a "giant" literally, but the description might still be part of a purely factual account of Churchill. There are pictorial metaphors as well as verbal ones and it might be argued that the portrait of Kahnweiler is a nonfictional, but also a nonliteral, presentation of Kahnweiler's appearance.[46] Second, the information we take from a portrait about the appearance of the sitter is relative to assumptions we make about the medium. The image in Picasso's painting is flat, but we don't conclude from this that Kahnweiler is flat. We ignore flatness in judging representation because flatness is a feature of the medium of painting, not a piece of information conveyed by the medium. It is what is done within the constraints set by the medium that we take as relevant information about the appearance of the sitter. Cubism itself is in this sense a medium. Rearranging the geometry of surfaces is what you

46 Kinds of nonliteral meaning other than metaphors can occur in pictures. A picture of the crown can represent the king (metonymy). A picture of a very prominent nose can represent de Gaulle (synecdoche). Exactly how one should describe the nonliteral devices that Picasso uses to depict Kahnweiler is a difficult question that I shall not try to answer here. Probably, pictorial representation makes available nonliteral devices that have no clear counterparts in verbal description.

have to do to produce a cubist painting, just as coloring a flat canvas is what you have to do to produce a painting. So it might be argued that the fracturing of the image is to be interpreted in the same way we interpret the flatness of the image – as part of the medium and not as a piece of information about the sitter.[47] I shall not try here to decide which of these two hypotheses best accounts for the present case. Plausibly, they will both play a role in explaining our response to many kinds of pictures and to fictional works of visual art generally.

So the sense in which paintings and sculptures are fictional works is accommodated by my theory. They are fictional works because the artist performed a fictive act in producing them.

David Lewis (in conversation) noted an interesting case that appears to be fiction without fictive intent. Kingsley Amis tells a story called "Who or What Was It?" in which he begins by saying that the events described actually happened to him. At first one is inclined to believe that this is a piece of autobiography. But events soon take a wildly supernatural turn. At some stage we are supposed to realize that this is fiction.[48] Amis does not intend that we make believe the whole thing – that would spoil the effect – but the whole thing is surely fiction.

I think Amis intends us *retroactively* to make believe the whole thing. His effect is achieved by getting us to start off by believing, to realize at some stage that this is inappropriate (the tale is too implausible to be true), to realize the whole thing is just a story, and to revise our attitude toward the bits of text that took us in. He intends us to make believe the

---

47 Perhaps the conventions of cubism are best described as *ways* in which information is conveyed. See Kendall Walton, "Categories of Art," *Philosophical Review* 79 (1970): 334–67, for an interesting discussion of the distinction between what he calls "standard" and "variable" features of works.

48 Amis reports that a number of people stubbornly went on taking his word for it to the end. See the Introduction to his *Collected Short Stories* (New York: Penguin Books, 1983). (The story was told by Amis in a radio broadcast before it was published.)

whole story, but he doesn't make that intention clear until late in the piece.

1.10. OBJECTIONS TO THE SUFFICIENCY OF THE ANALYSIS

Fictive utterances produce fictional works. But not all fictive utterances do. If I read a fairy story to the children, I may do so intending them to make-believe the story, but I produce no fiction thereby. The fiction has already been produced. Here we have fictive intent without fictive utterance, because a fictive utterance is one *productive* of fiction, and not merely an utterance in which a fiction is told. Pierre Menard, the quixotic hero of Borges's tale, performed a fictive utterance, even though the fiction he produced was verbally indistinguishable from Cervantes's.[49] But if Menard had simply copied out Cervantes's text, he would not have produced any work.

The same holds if I take a newspaper item and repeat it word for word, hoping that my audience will see it as a story of my own invention that they are intended to make believe. My fictive utterance does not produce fiction because it does not produce a work. No counterexamples to my theory here. The theory says that a work is fictional if it is the product of a fictive intention. To have a counterexample we need a case where a fictive intention is productive of a work, but not of a fictional one.

Suppose I'm a bit more imaginative: I don't just copy out the newspaper article, I retell it in my own words, but without materially affecting the story. This might count as an act productive of a work – retelling an old story in a new way often does. I tell the reworked tale to an audience intending them to make believe it. (I know they will assume, unless I

---

49 See Jorge Luis Borges, "Pierre Menard, Author of the Quixote," in *Ficciones* (New York: New Directions, 1964). I follow the philosophical tradition of making some simplification to Borges's story. I assume that Menard's act is entirely independent of Cervantes's, and that Menard's story matches, in verbal structure, the whole of Cervantes's story. Neither of these things are true in Borges's tale.

tell them otherwise, that the story is one I made up.) Intuitively, I am not the author of a work of fiction. According to the definition (D_2) I am, since I have the right kind of intention and my intention is productive of a work. Here is another problematic case. I have led an amazing life, full of improbable incident. I faithfully report these events in a work I intend people to make believe, intending also that they recognize my intention. (The events are so unlikely, I can count on the audience's assuming the story is made up.) Once again, this ought not to be regarded as fiction, but (D_2) makes it so.

Such cases as these involve deception, and we might suspect that they are cases of a kind that have troubled Grice and his followers: cases that satisfy the Gricean conditions stated in the definition but involve a "higher order" intention to deceive. The speaker intends that the audience's response will depend upon their recognition of an intention that they believe (falsely) they are not intended to recognize.[50] But the cases just described are not of this kind. In presenting the newspaper article and the autobiography as fiction I have no hidden higher-order intention that the audience shall recognize a lower-order intention of mine. My deception is of a different kind. I am recounting events I know or at least believe have occurred. But I don't tell my audience this, hoping, reasonably enough in the circumstances, they will not be able to work it out for themselves.

We could avoid this problem by stipulating in our definition of fictive utterance that the author's utterance be not deceptive in this sense. But this will not rule out all counterexamples. Here is one based on another kind of deception. Suppose that Jones, an impecunious and failing author, discovers a text, T, which he takes to be a hitherto unknown work of fiction. He determines to plagiarize the story and offers it to the public as a fiction of his own devising. He does

---

50 For cases of this kind, see Strawson, "Intention and Convention in Speech Acts," and the generalization discussed in Schiffer, *Meaning*, sec. II.I. Grice discusses these cases in "Utterer's Meaning and Intentions" and again in "Meaning Revisited."

not simply reproduce the text (some shreds of artistic integrity are left to him) but presents the material in his own style. He does not, however, materially alter the events described. But as it happens Jones was wrong in his original assumption that T is fiction. T is a reliable account of known fact.[51] Again, (D_2) has it that Jones is the author of a fictional work. This can hardly be right.

Here Jones can fairly be described as the author of the work, but the work isn't fiction even though Jones has a fictive intent. And Jones does not intend to hide from his audience the fact that these are events he knows to be true. He does not know them to be true.

Notice there might be complications about reference here. If Jones changed the proper names in T, then presumably his version of the story would not refer to the same people the original text refers to (it would not, presumably, refer to any people), and so it is no longer an account of known fact. We can assume that Jones changes none of the names in T, but that won't solve the problem. Even if Jones uses the same names, he does not use them with the intention of referring by means of them to whoever was referred to by them in T. After all, he thinks T is fiction, so why should he think that the names in T refer to anybody? The names in Jones's story can be paired homophonically with the names in T, but they are not co-referential with the names in T. So the sentences in Jones's story will not express the same propositions as the sentences of T, and the stories will be different. Their being different might then be enough for us to say that Jones's version is fiction after all. To get around this difficulty we must assume one of two things. Either T contains no names but only descriptions, or, if T contains names, it contains only names that Jones *knows* to be referring and the referents of which he intends to preserve. T might be a piece of history, naming only historical characters with whom Jones is familiar, and which he takes for an historical novel.

This time Jones's deception involves him in getting the

---

51 I owe this example and the next to Don Mannison.

reader to think that he, Jones, is more original than he is. But we cannot protect the definition against cases like this by adding to it the stipulation that fictive utterances must not be intended to be deceptive in this way. Suppose that *T* really had been fiction. In that case Jones's own work would surely be fiction, too, despite the presence of such a deceptive intent.

Here is a counterexample involving no deception of any kind. Smith has certain real-life experiences of so horrible a kind that he represses them. He then invents, so he supposes, a story, and this story exactly retells these events. This is no coincidence; Smith's subconscious somehow provides him with the information for his story. Here again, Smith has fictive intent, but his work isn't fiction. And Smith is not being deceptive about anything.

It is time to take a step back and assess the damage done by this confusing array of counterexamples. They suggest, most obviously, that there can be works produced with a fictive intent that are not fictional works. Also, all the examples of this kind that we have constructed have been cases where the narrative is *true*. But we have already seen that this cannot be the feature that prevents them from being fiction: recall the case of the accidentally true novel. Notice, however, that all the cases explored in this section have been cases of narratives that are true *but not just true by accident*. They are in different ways *based on* the truth. The purportedly fictional autobiography is based on the facts of my life known to me; Jones's plagiarized novel is based (although he does not know it) on facts known to the original author; Smith's novel is based (although he does not know it) on his own repressed experiences. On the other hand, our true historical novel is not based on the truth – at least parts of it are not. Recall that the author of that novel followed known historical events, and filled in the gaps in our knowledge with incidents of his own invention. That his descriptions of these incidents are true is just an accident.

We can now say that being the product of a fictional intent

is necessary but not sufficient for a work to be fiction. There is another condition required: a "background condition," activated in certain unusual circumstances. Because the circumstances are so unusual one can scarcely imagine them arising in real life, the original proposal – that fiction is the product of a fictive intent – is an extremely good approximation to the truth. In just about any real case it will give the right answer to the question Is this fiction or not? But to turn the approximating formula into a precise one we need to add an extra condition. We need to say that a work is fiction iff (*a*) it is the product of a fictive intent and (*b*) if the work is true, then it is at most accidentally true.

I shall try to clarify a little the contrast between accidental and nonaccidental truth. The sort of account I'm going to give will probably need a lot of refinement, but that can wait until another occasion. To think of a particular newspaper as reliable is more than just to think of it as printing the truth. An unreliable newspaper might print the truth just by accident. To be reliable a newspaper must be such that, had things been different in various ways, it would still have printed the truth. We say, of a reliable newspaper, "If the story hadn't been true they wouldn't have reported it," or "If the story had been different in some important respect the paper would have reported it differently." Of course, when we say these things we don't assert the indefensible thesis that this newspaper is incapable of being wrong. We can all imagine circumstances in which even the most reliable newspaper is wrong. When we say that the paper wouldn't have reported the story if it hadn't been true, we mean that in the most likely scenarios where the story isn't true, the paper doesn't report it. Our reasoning here seems to involve judgments about what happens in various *possible worlds* where the facts of the story are different, but which do not deviate more than minimally from the actual world in other ways. In these worlds, so we believe, the paper's report is correspondingly different. Our reasoning also, if less obviously, involves judgments about what happens in other worlds where the facts of the story are not assumed to vary, but certain other things are. If we think the paper reliable, we think that in a world of minimal deviation the story is still correctly reported by the paper – the paper's getting it right doesn't depend just on who they happened to send along.

We can sum all this up by saying that the reports in a reliable newspaper *display counterfactual dependence on the facts.*[52] What the paper says is true not merely in the actual world but in other worlds too. Not, of course, true in every world, but true in those worlds which would make the following counterfactuals true:

(1) If different events had occurred, the paper's report would have been correspondingly different.

(2) Were those events, in otherwise changed circumstances, to have occurred as they did, the paper would still have reported them.[53]

So it is with our problematic narratives. Being true, they describe the facts correctly; being nonaccidentally true, they display counterfactual dependence on the facts. In each case we think that if the events had been different in various ways, the narratives would have been correspondingly different. (If the horrible events Smith witnessed had been different in some way, his story would have been correspondingly different). In each case we think that if these events had been the same, and certain other features different, the narratives would have been the same also. (If Smith had witnessed the same horrible scene but had witnessed it on a different day, his story would have been the same.) Not so with our accidentally true novel. Its being accidentally true just amounts to this: The author's imaginative filling in of the plot

---

52 The use made here of the idea of counterfactual dependence is derived from ideas of David Lewis. See, for instance, his "Veridical Hallucination and Prosthetic Vision," *Australasian Journal of Philosophy* 58 (1980): 239–49, reprinted in his *Philosophical Papers*, vol. 2, (New York: Oxford University Press, 1986). It is also related to Robert Nozick's idea of "tracking." (See his *Philosophical Explanations*, [Oxford: Clarendon Press, 1981], chap. 3.) For more on possible worlds and their role in explaining counterfactual discourse, see Section 2.3.

53 This formulation was suggested by the one in Crispin Wright, "Keeping Track of Nozick," *Analysis* 43 (1983): 134–40.

does not depend on what actually happened. And so we cannot say, "If the events in which the historical characters were caught up had been different, the novelist's account would be correspondingly different."

My account of fiction now turns out to be *intensional* as well as intentional. It is intentional in that it makes reference to the author's intentions; it is intensional, as opposed to extensional, in that it makes use of the notion of nonaccidental truth. Being true is extensional; it is just a matter of what is actually the case, what is the case in the actual world. Being nonaccidentally true also involves consideration of what would have been true in other circumstances – what is true in various nonactual worlds.

I have claimed that a fiction can be true – wholly true, that is. No doubt this sounds like an odd, even paradoxical, claim. We can now see why. A fiction can be at most accidentally true. If its relation to the facts is anything closer than actual world truth, it is not fiction. Most usually what we say is true, when it is true, because our methods for determining truth are to some degree reliable and so the true things we say usually display the kinds of counterfactual dependencies exhibited in conditions (1) and (2). It is only in odd cases or by an effort of reflection that we clearly distinguish between true narratives and reliable ones. If "true fiction" sounds oxymoronic, that's because we haven't distinguished between truth *simpliciter* and reliable (i.e., counterfactually dependent) truth.

Clearly, there will be statements in a fictional work that are nonaccidentally true. The Travis McGee novels of John D. MacDonald are (I take it) a reliable guide to certain aspects of sailing technique. Homer turned out to be sufficiently reliable to lead Schliemann to the site of Troy.[54] Most works of fiction are to some extent based on fact. We encounter the same kind of mixture when we consider how we are to take the author's utterances, for they will tend to be a mixture of fiction-making and assertion. Walter Scott breaks off the nar-

54 As a reader for the Press reminded me.

1.11. Make-believe and pretense

rative of *Guy Mannering* in order to tell us something about the condition of Scottish gypsies, and it is pretty clear that what he says is asserted. A work of fiction is a patchwork of truth and falsity, reliability and unreliability, fiction-making and assertion. We can say that a work as a whole is fiction if it contains statements that satisfy the conditions of fictionality I have presented, conditions we can sum up briefly by saying that a statement is fiction if and only if it is the product of an act of fiction-making (as defined in Section 1.8) and is no more than accidentally true.

Is a work fictional if even one of its statements is fictional in this sense? Must the greater proportion of the whole be fiction? These are bad questions. One might as well ask how many grains of sand make a heap. If we wanted to, we could define a numerical degree of fictionality, but it would be artificial and unilluminating. What is illuminating is a precise account of the fictionality of statements. For in some perhaps irremediably vague way, the fictionality of works is going to depend upon the fictionality of the statements they contain. As long as we are clear about what water molecules are, it hardly matters for purposes of definition that most things we call "water" actually contain much else besides.

1.11. MAKE-BELIEVE AND PRETENSE

To be fictional, a statement must meet our two conditions: It must be the product of a fictive intent, and it must be at most accidentally true. We have seen that there might be statements that meet the first condition but not the second, as in the case of the author who wants to pass off a reliably true narrative as fiction of his own making. But there are also cases of statements that satisfy the first condition and where it is *common knowledge* between author and reader that they fail to meet the second.[55] I have already noted that there is

---

55 *P* is common knowledge between *A* and *B* iff *A* knows that *P* and *B* knows that *P* and *A* knows that *B* knows that *P* and *B* knows that *A* knows that *P*, and so on. See the discussion in Section 2.3 of the related concept of overt belief.

49

1. The concept of fiction

often a great deal in a fictional story that is true and that would not be said in the narrative if it were not. You can pick up bits of reliable information about London geography from almost any novel set in that city. Where these pieces of information are an integral part of the narrative ("Lightning illuminated the hideous outlines of the Barbican") we are not intended to bracket them out from the rest of the story. We are intended to adopt the make-believe attitude toward them as much as toward the description of fictive characters and their doings. So it may be that we are asked to make believe things that are nonaccidentally true, even though they are not, strictly speaking, fictional statements.

Sometimes make-believe is identified with pretense. We have seen writers like Searle say that the author pretends to make assertions. David Lewis extends the pretense to include the reader: "The storytellers pretend to pass on historical information to their audience; the audience pretends to learn from their words, and to respond accordingly."[56] If "pretense" here just means the same as "make-believe" as I use that term, I shall not quarrel with the claim that readers pretend the stories they read are reliable narratives. (As we have seen, I do quarrel with the idea that authors pretend that their stories are reliable narratives.) But nothing much is gained by this unless we have a well-developed theory of pretense that will cover the cases of make-believe that interest us here.

There is one fairly clear sense of pretense: giving (and intending to give) the appearance of doing something but not actually doing it. Children pretend to be pirates, actors pretend to fight. But this account of pretense, with its reference to deliberate behavior, will not tell us anything about what the reader of fiction does. And the actor who pretends to do something does not, unless perhaps he belongs to the school of Stanislavsky, make believe that he is doing it. It seems best to say that the reader is engaging in a make-believe but not in a pretense. There is support for this from the conclusion of

56 Lewis, "Postscript to 'Truth in Fiction,' " *Philosophical Papers*, vol. 1, p. 276.

1.11. Make-believe and pretense

two paragraphs back – that when reading fiction we regularly make believe things we know or believe to be true: the architecture of a building, the climate of a country, the date of a battle. In such cases as these make-believe cannot be pretense. You cannot pretend to believe what you do believe, since you cannot do something and pretend to do it at the same time.[57] If someone wants to use "pretense" in so wide a sense as to encompass make-believe, I have no particular objection. But we shall not achieve a better understanding of make-believe in this way.

We may conclude that pretense has little or nothing to do with fiction. In this chapter I have argued that fiction is the product of a certain kind of communicative act, an act of fiction-making, on the part of the author. This is an act with a Gricean structure formally similar to the structure of assertion, but differing from assertion in its intended result. In performing that act the author is not pretending to perform any other act. Nor is he intending that there be any pretense on the part of the audience. Nor need there be any such pretense. At no stage in our explanation of the communicative process do we need to refer to pretense.

57 J. L. Austin once argued that a burglar intent on seeing the contents of a room might be *pretending* to clean the windows, even while he actually removes dirt from them with the appropriate materials in the appropriate way. This seems implausible. See Austin, "Pretending," *Philosophical Papers* (New York: Oxford University Press, 1961).

Chapter 2

The structure of stories

When *Bleak House* appeared as a book Dickens added an indignant preface defending the reality of two things depicted in the novel: the ruinous inefficiency of the Court of Chancery, and the phenomenon of spontaneous combustion. He did not, of course, claim the same for the case Jarndyce and Jarndyce, nor for the death by combustion of Krook. He was content that these things should belong to the story only. That Krook spontaneously combusted is something true in the story but for which no claim of truth is made. That such things happen from time to time is true in the story and, so Dickens assures us, true.

As it happened, Dickens was right, more or less, about the Chancery Court; wrong about spontaneous combustion. The latter phenomenon, like the Jarndyce case and Krook himself, exists in Dickens's story but not in reality. Propositions, both particular and general, can be true in a story and not true. They can be true in the story and true, as with the ruinous nature of Chancery litigation. They can be untrue in the story and true: it is untrue in the story that Charles Dickens falsely believed in spontaneous combustion, but this is, in fact, true. Being true in fiction is thus not a matter of being true in a certain place, or of a certain subject matter. Things that are true in London or true of Londoners are thereby true, but things true in fiction are not. Truth in fiction is one thing, truth another.

Sometimes when we talk about truth in fiction we do mean a kind of truth. Fictions do sometimes express or suggest, and may be valued because they express or suggest, truths of one kind or another. Perhaps *A la Recherche du Temps Perdu* expresses important truths about love, time, and memory. In that case there is much truth in Proust's novels, and in this sense the truth in Proust's fiction is genuine truth. This sense of "truth in fiction," which appears prominently in literary evaluations, is not the subject of this chapter. That it is true in *Bleak House* that spontaneous combustion occurs and that Krook is a victim of it; that it is true in *Othello* that Desdemona is murdered; that it is true in *The Turn of the Screw* that there are ghosts: these claims exemplify the kind of truth in fiction that will concern us here.

2.1. TRUTH IN FICTION AND FICTIONAL WORLDS

Truth and truth in fiction are distinct, but perhaps there is a way to connect them. We call something true when it is true in the actual world. But if there are worlds other than the actual world, presumably there are things true in those worlds but not true in the actual world. These nonactual possible worlds are not distant bits of our universe; if they were, then what is true in them would be true in the actual world, just as what is true on Alpha Centauri is true in the actual world (or, simply, true). Possible worlds are alternative possibilities, "ways things might have been," and for something to be true in a nonactual world is for it to be possibly, rather than actually true. You may treat possible worlds as elements of a useful but theoretically dispensable framework for thinking about such things as necessity and possibility, the semantics of proper names and the nature of attributes. You may treat them as irreducible but abstract representations, not of the same order of being as the real (actual) world. You may treat them as real in the way the real world is real; that is, you may suppose they are made up of planets, people, and atoms, or the strange but equally real kinds of things the

2. The structure of stories

actual world might have been made up of.[1] Adopting any of these three positions (rather than declaring the whole idea incomprehensible rubbish), you may be tempted to think that truth in fiction is truth in a possible world. In the world of Doyle's fiction it is true that Holmes is a smoker; it is just not true in the actual world.

The idea of "fictional worlds" or "worlds of the story" has the appeal of certain vague and comforting metaphors that disguise the gaps in our theorizing. Most of us think we understand phrases like "the world of Dickens" or "the world of Barchester," but could give no satisfactory account of them if pressed to do so. Concerning possible worlds we have at least a few clear principles. If fictional truth is truth in a possible world, fictional worlds will have acquired some respectability. But fictional worlds, if there are any, cannot be assimilated to possible worlds. The few clear principles we have to regulate our thinking about possible worlds could not apply to fictional worlds. Possible worlds are *determinate* with respect to truth; every proposition is either true or false in a possible world. They are *consistent*; nothing logically impossible is true in a possible world. But fictional worlds are always indeterminate and sometimes inconsistent. Fictional worlds are indeterminate because there are questions about fictions that have no determinate answer. Does Holmes, at the moment of his struggle with Moriarty, have an even number of hairs on his head? The text does not tell us, and no answer can be reasonably inferred from background knowledge (about which more in this chapter). But if the answer cannot even in principle be decided, there is no answer. In other words, the following rule applies to fiction: If it's not possible for a reader with all the relevant information to decide whether P is true in the fiction or whether not-P is true in the fiction, then neither P nor

---

1 For a review of the alternatives and a defense of extreme realism about possible worlds, see David Lewis, *On the Plurality of Worlds* (Oxford: Basil Blackwell, 1986).

not-P is true in the fiction. And so it is with countless propositions about fictional characters. Is Lestrade married? Does Mrs. Hudson wear false teeth? There are no answers to these questions.[2] Some fictions also have it that the impossible occurs. The hero shows that Gödel was wrong and arithmetic is complete after all, or turns out, as a result of time travel, to be his own mother and father.[3] Such things are logically impossible. Any "world" in which these things are true is not a possible world.

There is another reason we cannot identify fictional worlds with possible worlds. Suppose there are two possible worlds in both of which things happen exactly as they do in the Holmes story. (I shall treat the stories as one big story.) These worlds differ in other ways, not connected with the contents of the story. Which one is *the* world of the story?[4] Both are equally good candidates and there is nothing to choose between them, so neither is. But no other possible world is a better candidate than either of these for being the world of Holmes. So no possible world is.

The failure to assimilate fictional worlds to possible worlds shows why we cannot explain truth in fiction as truth in a possible world. Later we shall review the prospects for a more complex version of the same idea, a version according to which truth in fiction is a function of what is true in various possible worlds.[5]

If we are going to persist with our talk of fictional worlds, we shall have to add them to our ontology. But such an extension seems undesirable, for several reasons. Realists about possible worlds will object in this way: possible worlds do not increase the kind of things that exist, for a possible world is just another thing of the same kind as the actual

2 At least, my not very diligent examination of Doyle's texts has revealed no answers. If I'm wrong about these examples, make up your own. Later I abandon this "either there is an answer or there is not" approach for something more sophisticated. See Section 2.8.

3 As in Robert Heinlein's "All You Zombies."

4 We may also ask, In which world is it that *Holmes himself* does these things? On this see Section 4.3.

5 See Section 2.3.

2. The structure of stories

world.[6] But fictional worlds are a new kind of thing; they are not things we have reason to believe in before we start our investigations into fiction. They should be resisted on grounds of ontological economy. Of course, additions to our ontology, even such radical ones as fictional worlds, can be justified if they turn out to have high explanatory value. But such a virtue cannot be claimed for fictional worlds. Fictional worlds are supposed to explain fictional truth, and we are invited to say that P is true in the Holmes story if and only if P is true in the world of Sherlock Holmes. But what use is such an explanation to us? Since stories are paired one-to-one with fictional worlds, we would not be explaining more in terms of less. Because we have to infer the characteristics of fictional worlds from the characteristics of fictional stories there is no sense in which we are explaining the unfamiliar in terms of the familiar. And because we work out what is true in a fictional world by working out what is true in the corresponding story, rather than vice versa, there is no light shed on the epistemology of fictional truth by this account. The appeal to fictional worlds seems merely to inflate our ontology without producing growth in understanding.[7]

2.2. BEING FICTIONAL

I shall abandon the attempt to explain truth in fiction as a kind of truth, along with the unilluminating metaphor of fictional worlds. To say that P is true in fiction or fictionally true is not to ascribe to that proposition some peculiar kind of truth, but rather to say that it is *fictional* that P, or that it is fictional that P is true. What is true in fiction is what is fictional, what is *part of the story*. "It is true in the fiction that P," "it is

---

6 The argument is Lewis's. See his *Counterfactuals* (Cambridge, Mass.: Harvard University Press, 1973), chap. 4, sec. 1.
7 There have been various attempts to make sense of fictional worlds. Thomas Pavel's *Fictional Worlds* (Cambridge, Mass.: Harvard University Press, 1986), is a recent one. But Pavel's fictional worlds remain shadowy entities, described in largely metaphorical terms. See my review in *Philosophy and Literature* 11 (1987): 351-2.

56

2.2. Being fictional

part of the fiction that P," "it is fictional that P" I take to be alike in meaning. It is true in the fiction that Holmes smokes; it is part of the fiction that he is not a native speaker of Hindi; it is neither fictional that he has an even number of hairs on his head at the moment of his struggle with Moriarty, nor fictional that he has not.

Being fictional is not the same as being true, but like truth, it is a property of propositions. At least for certain purposes it's useful to think of properties as functions from objects to truth values. *Redness* is the function that takes all red things to the value true, and all non-red things to the value false. Likewise, *being fictional* can be thought of as a function (a "propositional operator") from propositions to truth values. "Holmes smokes" does not express a true proposition, but "It is fictional that Holmes smokes" does, since the operator *being fictional* takes the proposition *Holmes smokes* to the value true.[8] Let us abbreviate "It is fictional that P" to "$F(P)$." Of course, being fictional is always relative to a given fictional work. Strictly, then, we should write "$F_w(P)$," meaning: It is fictional in work W that P. When I am speaking generally, I shall suppress this subscript. Much of the time I shall simply use our original, familiar terminology and speak of P being fictionally true, or true in the story. By this I shall mean just that $F(P)$.

None of this amounts to a theory of fictional truth; it is merely a proposal about how such a theory might be developed. To get to the point where we have a concrete proposal before us we must examine the truth conditions of claims of the form "$F(P)$" – assuming, for the moment, that such statements are capable of being true or false in just the same way a statement like "Tigers are carnivores" is either true or false. Section 3.1 will qualify this assumption.

The operator F is often suppressed in our ordinary talk if it's common knowledge between the conversation partners

8 Here I follow David Lewis, "Truth in Fiction," *Philosophical Papers*, vol. 1 (New York: Oxford University Press, 1983). For disagreement with Lewis about how this proposal is to be implemented, see Section 2.3.

that their topic is *what happened in the story*. The operator makes an appearance when we need to clarify which fiction we are talking about; "Hamlet dies in *Hamlet*" sounds pedantic, but "Flamineo dies in *The White Devil*" does not, for most audiences. It also makes an appearance when the conversation turns to the comparison of fiction with the real world, as in "The Romans really had no clocks, but in *Julius Caesar*, one is heard to strike." There is no doubt, then, that the operator **F** corresponds to something in our linguistic repertoire. But I take a point of Kendall Walton's: Not all of our talk about fictional characters and events can be construed as prefixed by the operator **F**.[9] Consider, for example, the descriptions we give of our responses to fictional characters and events. When I say that I fear Othello will kill Desdemona, this cannot comfortably be construed as an ellipsis for "I fear that F(Othello will kill Desdemona)," and "F(I fear that Othello will kill Desdemona)" is also inadequate. We will examine statements of this kind in Chapter 5.

Nor can we employ the operator **F** to interpret the author's own fiction-making utterances. It should be clear from the results of Chapter 1 that when the author writes "Holmes is a smoker" he is not to be understood as saying that it's true in the story that Holmes is a smoker.[10] The author is not asserting that F(*P*), he is fiction-making that *P*.

---

9 See his "Fearing Fictions," *Journal of Philosophy* 75 (1978); 5–27, and *Mimesis as Make-Believe*, sec. 5.3. Walton somewhat overstates his case. He argues that an utterance of "Tom and Becky were lost in the cave" is not likely to involve a suppressed use of the operator **F**, for we rarely suppress other intentional operators such as "believes that." But we omit such operators more readily than Walton allows. It is common for discussion of a philosophical system to involve statements like "all action is by contact" or "secondary properties are in the mind" rather than "According to Descartes all action is by contact" or "According to Locke secondary qualities are in the mind." At least, it is common to abbreviate in this way when it's clear to the participants whose system is under discussion and that the point of the discussion is to get clear about what the system is rather than to decide whether it is true. In discussing fiction, only rarely are we interested in whether what is said is true, so we have little reason to make the operator explicit.

10 *Pace* Nicholas Wolterstorff. See his "Characters and Their Names," *Poetics* 8 (1979): 101–27.

2.2. Being fictional

The role of the operator **F** in a theory of fiction is a limited one. It isn't going to help us explain everything everybody says about fictional characters. But it is a vital role. The operator is implicitly employed by us whenever we read a fictional work and try to unpack a story from its text. Deciding whether P belongs to the story is deciding whether $F(P)$ is true. As our reading progresses we constantly have to make decisions about what is true in the story. Sometimes the decision is easy: the author writes that P, and we decide that P is part of the story. But as we saw in Chapter 1, we have to be alert to the possibility that a sentence in the text may not be meant literally; in such a case we have to decide what is meant and add that to the story. We also have to decide at what point fictional truth shades off into indeterminacy, where our own imaginative powers may take over. What, exactly, does Dr. Watson look like? Presumably it is true in the stories by Doyle that Watson has some definite look, but there is no definite look that it is true in the stories he has. When it comes to the details of Watson's appearance, it is up to each reader to construct, if he is so inclined, a particular appearance for him, as long as the construction stays within the boundaries set by the work. The reader must also decide on an appropriate background that may not be explicit in the story. It is surely true in the Holmes story that Victoria reigns, that Britain is a great industrial and mercantile power, that people, including Holmes, eat, sleep, and breathe, that Watson is less than seven feet tall. But it is likely that one could not find all these things explicitly stated anywhere in the relevant works.

The idea that a reading of a fictional work can legitimately be informed by an appropriate background has sometimes been denied by critics. John Dover Wilson argued, famously, that there is "a fundamental misconception" in treating a fictional character "as if he were a living man or a historical character, instead of being a single figure . . . in a dramatic composition . . . . Apart from the play, apart from his actions, from what he tells us about himself and what other characters tell us about him, there

59

is no Hamlet . . . . Critics who speculate upon what Hamlet was like before the play opens . . . are merely cutting the figure out of the canvas and sticking it into a doll's-house of their own invention."[11]

If Wilson had been less provoked by the excesses of Ernest Jones's psychoanalytic study of Hamlet, he might not have gone so far. There is much about Hamlet's life before the curtain rises that we cannot know, because there is simply nothing to be known. Perhaps there is nothing to be known about Hamlet's psychological condition in childhood, and perhaps that is what is wrong with Jones's method.[12] But there can be little doubt that what is true in the play extends beyond the boundaries, both temporal and textual, of the play's explicit content. Who doubts that it is true in the play that Hamlet was a living, breathing human being ten minutes before the opening scene? Nor can we avoid applying psychological generalities, for which we will not find explicit support in the text, to Hamlet and the other characters. Otherwise we shall not be able to make sense of the play. The great problems of *Hamlet* criticism – why the apparently excessive reaction? why the delay? – simply cannot be posed, let alone solved, unless we are prepared to treat Hamlet as a human being with a range of motives and responses not radically different from our own. Hamlet's behavior is odd exactly because it is to be judged, more or less, by the standards of behavior that we apply to human beings in general.

How we are to decide upon an appropriate background for *Hamlet* or any other work is a question I try to answer in this chapter. *Hamlet* is an illuminating case that I shall refer to again.

A final preliminary remark. In this chapter I'm going to ignore problems about the existence of fictional characters, and I shall assume that it makes perfect sense to say things

---

11 Introduction to *Hamlet*, 2nd ed. (Cambridge: Cambridge University Press, 1936), pp. xlv–xlvi.
12 For more on this, see Section 2.3.

2.2. Being fictional

like "Holmes takes cocaine," "Holmes is smarter than Watson," and even "Holmes does not exist." In fact, this assumption is highly problematic. One reason it's problematic is that expressions like "Holmes" and "Watson" seem to function in the story as proper names. On one view, proper names are semantically distinctive in that their contribution to the truth values of the sentences in which they occur is simply to pick out some individual of which something is predicated. Their semantic role is, we may say, exhausted by their referential role. A nonreferring proper name would then seem to have no semantic role. But meaning is semantic role, and so a nonreferring proper name has no meaning.[13] Since "Holmes" picks out no individual it has no referential role, and so no meaning can be attached to it. A sentence that contains a meaningless expression must be meaningless, and so no sentence containing "Holmes" can have a meaning. And if "P" has no meaning, then "$F(P)$" can have no meaning either.[14]

No doubt at least some of the steps in this argument are questionable, but it should dispel the complacent assumption that we can insulate ourselves from worries about reference by introducing the operator **F,** or some comparable device. It won't do simply to say: "'Sherlock Holmes' doesn't really refer, but it's true in the story that it does, because it's true in the story that Holmes exists." For the reply will be: "Unless 'Sherlock Holmes' really refers, no sentence in which that name occurs *can* be true in the story, for no such sentence can be meaningful." If the semantics of fiction is not to collapse into incoherence, we are going to have to tell a convincing story about the semantics of fictional names. In Chapter 4 we confront the problem head on. But for now I shall simply assume that sentences containing fictional names are meaningful. I choose the present order because what we decide here about fictional truth will enable us to see

13 I discuss this argument in more detail in Section 4.3.
14 A point made in this context by Gareth Evans, *The Varieties of Reference* (New York: Oxford University Press, 1982), chap. 10. See also Section 4.10.

more clearly what we want from a theory of reference for fictional names.

2.3. LEWIS'S THEORY

David Lewis has given an account of the truth conditions for statements of the form F(P).[15] Lewis's account is a paradigm of the clarity that analytic philosophy can bring to a topic that might otherwise seem amenable only to vague and impressionistic discussion. However, there are what strike me as deficiencies in his theory. Locating some of them will motivate my own proposal. Lewis offers us two distinct analyses to choose from. To be understood they require some scene-setting.

We want first the idea of *a world of the story* (an "S-world," as I shall say, supposing we have in mind some particular fictional story S). This is not a return to the despised fictional worlds. A world of the story will be a possible world in the sense of modal semantics, and there will be *many* worlds for any given story. When is a world an S-world? We cannot simply say: When everything true in S is true in that world. For such an answer appeals to the very notion we are trying to explicate: the notion of truth in fiction. Lewis suggests that we think of an S-world instead as a world where the text of the story is uttered as known fact.[16] The worlds of the Holmes story are worlds where someone knows of the activities of a detective called Holmes and where this knowledge is imparted to others via a text lexically identical to the text produced by Doyle. There will, of course, be many worlds in which the same story is told as known fact, and these worlds may differ quite radically one from another over matters that concern the story, but about which the text is silent or inconclusive. In some of these worlds what we intuitively take to

15 Lewis, "Truth in Fiction." Parenthetical references in the text of this section are to the reprint of this paper in his *Philosophical Papers*, vol. 1.
16 See Lewis, ibid., p. 265. See also David Kaplan, "Bob and Carol and Ted and Alice," in J. Hintikka (ed.), *Approaches to Natural Language* (Dordrecht: D. Reidel, 1973), esp. p. 507.

2.3. Lewis's theory

be the background of the story will be violated. Suppose it is never made explicit in the Holmes story that Holmes is a human being rather than a disguised robot or a Martian changeling. Then in some S-worlds Holmes is a robot, in others he is a Martian. All these worlds have in common is that what is explicit in the stories is told, in those worlds, as known fact. For that reason, it won't do to say that what is true in fiction S is what is true in all the S-worlds, for that would reduce truth in fiction to what is explicit in the text.

To solve the problem Lewis suggests we give differential weight to the S-worlds, according to how similar they are to the real (actual) world. (Think of possible worlds, the actual world among them, as distributed in logical space, their distances from each other being a measure of their overall similarity one to another.) Now we take a proposition P and ask whether it is true in the story. P might be true in *all* S-worlds; in that case we judge it to be true in the story. P might be true in *no* S-worlds; in that case we judge it not to be true in the story. The difficult cases arise when P is true in some S-worlds and not true in others. Lewis's idea is that we should in that case count P true in the story if and only if there is an S-world in which P is true that is *closer* to the actual world (@) than any S-world in which P is false. Let us formulate this a little more concisely. S-worlds where a proposition P is true I shall call S_P-worlds, and S-worlds where P is not true I shall call $S_{\sim P}$-worlds. Let "$F_s(P)$" abbreviate "P is true in fiction S." Then

(1) "$F_s(P)$" is true iff there is an S_P-world closer to @ than any $S_{\sim P}$-world. (p. 270)

Lewis did not invent this technique in order to deal with fictional truth. It was developed in order to explain the truth conditions of counterfactuals.[17] Lewis assimilates, in (1), reasoning about what is true in fiction to reasoning about what is counterfactually true. On the assumption that Lewis's

17 See Lewis, *Counterfactuals*, and Robert Stalnaker, "A Theory of Conditionals," in N. Rescher (ed.), *Studies in Logical Theory* (Oxford: Basil Blackwell, 1968).

analysis of counterfactuals in terms of worlds and their similarity relations is correct, (1) can be restated idiomatically:

(1′) "$F_s(P)$" is true iff P would have been true if S had been told as known fact.

Consider the proposition that Holmes is a Martian in disguise – something we intuitively regard as false in the story, but which, we shall suppose, the explicit content of the text leaves undecided. A world where things that seem to be people are, on occasion, Martians, would be very different from @; there would be many worlds closer to @ than it. Suppose, to simplify the argument, that w_1 is the S-world in which Holmes is a Martian which is closest to @.[18] Let w_2 be an S-world just like w_1 except insofar as there are no humanlike Martians in w_2.[19] Surely w_2 is closer (i.e., more similar) to @ than w_1 is. w_2 is thus closer to @ than *any* S-world where there are humanlike Martians (since w_1 is the closest). In w_2 Holmes is not a Martian, so it is true in the story that Holmes is not a Martian.

Now take a contrasting case. Consider the proposition that Holmes has, at the moment of his struggle with Moriarty at the Reichenbach Falls, an even number of hairs on his head – again, a proposition about which the text itself tells us nothing. As before, let w_1 be the S-world in which he does which is closest to @. Is a world that differs from w_1 just in that the number of hairs is odd, closer to @ than w_1 is? It is not. Having an even number of hairs on your head isn't a deviation from the norm of having an odd number. In that case the proposition that the number is odd fails to be true in the story. The same argument, with "even" and "odd" swapped over, establishes that the proposition that the number is even also fails to be true in the story. This is one of the things left indeterminate by the story.

18 There need not be a unique closest such world, nor even a world such that no other such world is closer to @ than it is. I neglect these complicating factors here.

19 Strictly speaking, w_2 is that world where there are no humanlike Martians which is closest, overall, to w_1; w_2 will differ from w_1 in other ways as well.

2.3. Lewis's theory

Analysis (1) makes fictional truth jointly the product of the story's explicit content, and what is true of the actual world. As Lewis notes, analysis (1) will not suit everybody, since it will license psychoanalytic explanations of a character's behavior, if psychoanalysis is true (p. 271). If psychoanalysis is true, it may be that a world in which *Hamlet* is told as known fact and in which Hamlet's delay is the result of his psychoneurosis (as Ernest Jones argued) would be closer to the actual world than any world in which *Hamlet* is told as known fact and in which Hamlet's delay is caused by something else.[20] Of course, people who endorse such interpretative practices will see this as an advantage of the theory. But the theory legitimates interpretative maneuvers no one would take seriously. Let *n* be the number of hairs on the head of Julius Caesar at the time he died. Nothing in the Holmes story is inconsistent with this fact, or makes it less probable than it otherwise would be. If the Holmes story had been told as known fact, it would still be true that there were *n* hairs on Caesar's head when he died. Employing (1), we must conclude that it's true in the story of Sherlock Holmes that Julius Caesar had *n* hairs on his head at the time of his death. This seems to be an intuitively undesirable consequence. This fact, like countless similar facts that will be true in the Holmes story on Lewis's view as expressed in (1), is quite extraneous to the story.

Perhaps all this shows is that Lewis's definition (1) introduces irrelevant information into the story, and irrelevant information that does not clash with the structure of the story as intuitively understood may not be harmful. But consider

---

20 See Ernest Jones, *Hamlet and Oedipus* (New York: Norton, 1949). I say "it may be that"; whether it is will depend on complex facts about the plot of *Hamlet* and about the availability of alternative explanations of Hamlet's behavior. Conceivably, Hamlet's behavior does not conform to an identifiable pattern of Freudian neurosis, or does not conform to it sufficiently well to make this the most likely explanation of Hamlet's behavior, even for a committed believer in the truth of Freudian theory. For the sake of the argument I assume here that the best explanation of the behavior of someone who behaved as Hamlet does would be that he is suffering from some neurosis describable and explainable in Freudian terms.

the following more worrying case. Suppose there is a Victorian novel in which Mr. Gladstone features as a minor character, although little is said there about his personality or doings. No person's character was more widely regarded as exemplary in Victorian society than Gladstone's.[21] However, post-Victorian historical research has suggested that Gladstone's "rescue work" among London prostitutes was less nobly motivated than most Victorians were willing to believe. Suppose that, in fact, Gladstone was in the relevant respects a morally monstrous person. What the story explicitly says about Gladstone is certainly consistent with this possibility. So the story being told as known fact requires no revision of actual world history with respect to Gladstone's character. So (1) has it that it is true in the story that Gladstone is immoral – assuming he in fact was. But this is not intuitively true in our Victorian novel, which, we will assume, adopts a complacent attitude toward the morals of the day. Its general tone is quite out of keeping with a cynical view of Gladstone.

Here is another difficult case for (1) – a real one this time. It has been argued that Henry James's story *The Turn of the Screw* is ambiguous between two very different interpretations.[22] Is the governess right in thinking that the ghosts of Quint and Miss Jessel threaten the children, or are the ghosts merely figments of her own deranged imagination? Let's assume the actual world contains no ghosts but contains plenty of disturbed people. If the text is ambiguous between the two interpretations, it can be uttered as known fact without requiring any alterations to the actual world concerning the nonexistence of ghosts and the prevalence of mental disorder. So we are obliged to conclude that the governess is

21 There were those, apparently, who gave credence to the view that there was a darker side to Gladstone's activities, but they were distinctly in the minority. Assume, for the sake of the argument, that everyone at the time thought of Gladstone as a paragon of virtue.

22 The argument was developed independently by Harold Goddard and Edmund Wilson. See G. Willens (ed.), *A Casebook on Henry James' The Turn of the Screw* (New York: Crowell, 1960).

mad and that there are no ghosts in the story. But it seems wrong to make our interpretation of James's story depend so decisively on what we believe about the existence or nonexistence of ghosts. Someone skeptical of ghosts is not thereby excluded from believing that *The Turn of the Screw* is a ghost story.

So we have reason to reject (1). For those who dislike psychoanalytic criticism, Lewis offers another definition: one that will also avoid the other difficulties just mentioned. The idea is to make truth in fiction the joint product of what is explicit in the story, and what is *overtly believed* in the author's society. P is overtly believed if almost everyone believes P, almost everyone believes that almost everyone else believes P, and so on (p. 272).[23] Let us call the class of worlds where what is overtly believed in the author's community is true the class of *belief worlds*. Then we have:

(2) "$F_S(P)$" is true iff for every belief world w there is an S_P-world closer to w than any $S_{\sim P}$-world. (p. 273)

Again, we may understand the right-hand side of (2) as expressing a certain counterfactual: that P would be true if some belief world were actual and S were told as known fact. So we may interpret Lewis's second proposal like this: Something is true in fiction iff it would have been true were overt belief correct and the fiction told as known fact.

Analysis (2) fares better than (1). It gets rid of all those extraneous facts (like the number of hairs on Caesar's head) that are not part of overt belief. It preserves Gladstone's integrity in the case just described, since most Victorians believed Gladstone to be morally upright. It preserves the ambiguity of *The Turn of the Screw*, since the Victorian system of overt belief was reasonably tolerant of ghosts.[24] It rules out

---

23 This is what Lewis elsewhere calls "common knowledge." (See his *Convention*, chap. 2, sec. 1.) As he later remarked, this term is somewhat inappropriate because what is common knowledge in his sense need not be true (see "Truth in Fiction," p. 272, note). See also the account of "mutual knowledge" in Stephen Schiffer, *Meaning* (Oxford: Clarendon Press, 1972), sec. II.2.

24 This may be overly generous to Lewis. For the story to be ambiguous on Lewis's criteria it might have to be overtly believed in Victorian society that ghosts are

2. *The structure of stories*

Freudian explanations of Hamlet's behavior, since Freudian theory was not part of the overt belief system of Elizabethan society.

But what happens to fictional truth when the fiction is inconsistent and there are, consequently, no S-worlds for the story (since there are no worlds at which an inconsistent story can be told as known fact)? How are we to calculate truth in an inconsistent fiction? Lewis's original suggestion was this: If the inconsistency is a minor oversight – for instance, as to the position of Watson's war wound – we are then to consider the various possible stories which would eliminate the inconsistency while staying close to the original in other respects. We then say that what is true in the original is not everything but rather what is true in all these revisions (p. 275). What about stories where the contradiction is not eliminable without wholesale destruction of the story? Lewis said that for stories about circle squarers and "the worst sort of incoherent time-travel story" we should just accept that the notion of fictional truth has no interesting application (pp. 274–5). But it isn't easy to accept this. In order to work out whether a fiction is incoherent we sometimes have to work out what the story of the fiction *is*. Even if the story is wildly and manifestly incoherent – the main character turns out to be his own father and mother – there is still a story there. Incoherence of this kind may be a literary vice, but it does not prevent us from making the usual sorts of judgments about what is true in the fiction. And two incoherent stories may be quite different with respect to what is true in them. Lewis's original analysis is not faithful to these intuitive judgments.

More recently Lewis has suggested we adopt the following general strategy for inconsistent fiction: Decompose the original story into consistent segments and then say that what is true in the story is what is true in any such segment. Thus we

as likely to exist as not. That is probably not the case, even if overt belief is construed generously (as it is in the text to note 23) so that something can be overt belief even when not absolutely everybody believes it. See the discussion farther on in Section 2.6.

68

may get the result that P is true in S, $\sim P$ is true in S, but that $P \& \sim P$ is not true in S (since $P \& \sim P$ is true in no consistent segment), and neither is everything that follows from $P \& \sim P$, namely everything.[25] I can see three objections to this proposal. First, it is not clear that every inconsistent story will have consistent segments from which we could obtain a recognizable narrative. What are the consistent segments of a story about the fortunes of a Gödel refuter? In no consistent segment does the hero actually refute Gödel, since Gödel's theorem is necessarily true. If the story has the refutation as its central and unifying idea, we shall not be able to piece together anything that corresponds even roughly to the original story after we have jettisoned the refutation. Second, the shift from Lewis's original proposal to the new one (consider unions of consistent segments) is ad hoc. It is designed to solve the problem posed by inconsistent stories but sheds no light on any other aspect of fictional truth. It therefore represents a "degenerating problem shift" in Lewis's program. Third, the proposal does not cope well with fiction where the inconsistency is an obvious slip on the author's part. If Doyle says that Watson's wound is in the leg on all but one occasion when he locates it in the shoulder, we surely want to say that the wound is in the leg and forget the reference to the shoulder. Lewis could get around this third objection by saying that for such nonseriously inconsistent fictions we are to go back to part of his original view: Take the revision closest to the original story and work with what is true in that.[26] But then my second objection applies with renewed force: we have a further ad hoc move to distinguish fictions that are inconsistent in a superficial way from fictions where the inconsistency is deep. A theory that dealt with all these cases without having to make special provision for them would have much to recommend it. In the next two sections, I shall offer a theory of this kind. We shall also see that it has further advantages over Lewis's theory.

25 See Lewis, "Postscript to 'Truth in Fiction,' " *Philosophical Papers*, vol. 1.
26 See Lewis, ibid., p. 277.

There is one other problem for Lewis's account that's worth mentioning. According to Lewis the worlds of the story are worlds where the story is told as known fact. But suppose (and this is, of course, quite out of keeping with how the story is actually written) there is a general tone of understatement and irony in Doyle's writing, Holmes being described as only marginally successful with his cases. Would the worlds of the story then be worlds in which Holmes was only marginally successful? We would not want to count such worlds as worlds of the story, because we would realize that these statements are understatements; they do not describe what is true in the story – that Holmes is spectacularly successful. But how could Lewis avoid these worlds? They are the worlds where what is said in the text is true. To avoid them we would have to make prior decisions about what is true in the story in order to see where the text is unreliable. But in that case what is true in the story is already playing a role in determining what worlds are worlds of the story. We cannot now explain what is true in the story in terms of these worlds.

2.4. MORE ON MAKE-BELIEVE

In looking for a way to improve on Lewis's analysis, the first thing I want to focus on is the idea of make-believe introduced in the preceding chapter. I begin with some further theses about make-believe and its relation to fiction reading.

Fiction, I have argued in Chapter 1, is the product of a communicative act; an act that shares with other communicative acts like asserting or requesting a Gricean intentional structure. In performing such a communicative act the author attempts to elicit a certain response from his audience; the desired response is that the audience make believe the story told by the author. The reader of fiction is invited by the author to engage in a game of make-believe, the structure of the game being in part dictated by the text of the author's work. What is said in the text, together with certain background assumptions, generates a set of fictional truths: those things that are true in the fiction. Anything that is true in the

2.4. More on make-believe

fiction is available for the reader to make believe. A large part of playing a game of fictional make-believe is to work out what is true in the fiction, and hence what it is appropriate to make believe.[27]

On this view, works of fiction *generate* games of make-believe. Each work of fiction generates its own game, for different works of fiction differ as to what is fictionally true, and hence as to what is to be made believe. Fictional games of make-believe are a subclass of a wider class of games of make-believe that include games played most often by children, for instance, mud pies, pirates, and the like. Games of make-believe differ from games like chess that don't involve any playacting or attitudes of make-believe on the part of the participants. And games like chess have rather precise rules about, for example, the number of players and how the game may be continued at any point. Such games also typically employ principles that specify a winning position. Games like mud pies and cowboys and Indians have a very loose formal structure, depend heavily for their continuation on the creative imaginations of the players, and can be played without an intention on anybody's part of winning. Fictional games are of this latter kind. Consider how one might play the *Anna Karenina* game. The game might be played by a single player, reading the work or merely recalling its narrative. It may be played by several people, one reading or telling the story to the others. As a further extension of the game, the players may chose to discuss the story, hoping for some agreement among them about how the characters and events are to be interpreted. In such an extension, the players make believe they are debating about events that have occurred and about people who really exist.

In order to play a game of fiction, players do not have to work out in every detail what is true in the story. Typically they select for attention those things that are most obviously or saliently true in the story. Some people are better at this than others, and have a quicker and more comprehensive

27 On make-believe, see Kendall Walton, *Mimesis as Make-Believe*.

71

grasp of what is true in the story. Like other games, games of fiction can be played well or badly, better or worse.

We must now distinguish two senses of "make-believe" that are relevant here. Until now I have spoken of make-believe as something we do. "Make-belief" denotes a propositional *attitude:* an attitude we take toward the propositions of a story. But we also speak of something *being* make-believe. It can be make-believe in a children's game that Emily is a pirate captain, that the surface of the carpet is the surface of the sea, that James is about to walk the plank. Similarly, it can be make-believe in a game of fiction reading that there is a heroic detective and a criminal mastermind, and that the reader is getting information about all this from the text. In this sense, make-believe is a propositional *operator* (M). I shall write "M(P)" for "it is make-believe that P," or as I shall sometimes say, "P is true in the game of make-believe." (Strictly speaking, we should write "$M_{GW}(P)$," indicating that P is make-believe in game G generated by work W.)

We must also distinguish between what is *fictional* in a work of fiction and what is make-believe in the corresponding game. The class of M-truths and the class of F-truths (the classes of truths of the form M(P) and F(P) respectively) normally overlap a good deal; something that is true in the fiction may become make-believe by being made believe by the player or players. The reader perceives that P is true in the fiction (that F(P)), and he comes to make-believe that P. As a result it is then make-believe in his game that P (M(P)).[28] But there are things that are make-believe in games of fiction that are not true in the corresponding fictions. It can be make-believe in a game of fiction that I am reading an account of events that have occurred, but that is not part of the fiction itself, since the story says nothing about me.

In this way each reader's reading generates a fiction larger

---

28 As Walton points out, it is possible for P to be make-believe in a game without anybody making believe that P. One can simply be mistaken about what is make-believe. See ibid., sec. 1.5.

than the fiction being read: a fiction in which the reader plays the role of one in touch with the events of the story and whose business it is to determine, in a rough-and-ready way, what those events are and against what background they take place. When we make believe the story we make believe that the text is an account of events that have actually occurred. But for this to be our make-believe we have to see the text as related in a certain way to those events; we have to see it as the product of someone who has knowledge of those events. Our make-believe is not merely that the events described in the text occured, but that we are being told about those events by someone with knowledge of them. Thus it is part of the make-believe that the reader is in contact, through channels of reliable information, with the characters and their actions, that the reader learns about their activities from a reliable source. To make-believe a fictional story is not merely to make-believe that the story is true, but *that it is told as known fact.*[29]

2.5. TRUTH IN FICTION AND BELIEF

This account of games of make-believe bears importantly on the concept of fictional truth. I am going to argue that our strategies for working out what is true in the story are closely connected with the idea that there is a reliable teller who is our access to these events. I shall argue that our strategies for working out what is true in the story are exactly our strategies for working out what the teller believes. Of course, all this takes place within the scope, so to speak, of our make-believe. The author of the story does not really have knowledge of these events, and we know this if we know we are reading fiction. We know the author does not really believe the things he says, at least we know he does not believe all of them. In our game we make believe there is a teller who does believe these things and whose beliefs are reliable.

29 This converges with the idea of Lewis and Kaplan that the worlds of the story are the worlds where it is told as known fact. See text to note 16 in this chapter.

2. The structure of stories

(Later I shall argue that the teller is not the real author but a character, a fictional construct within the work itself.) From now on, when it's clear that we are talking about moves in a game of make-believe, I shall say that the reader infers what the teller believes, taking it as understood that the inference is part of the reader's make-believe.

The idea that there is a connection between the beliefs of the teller and what is true in the story gains support from certain structural similarities between a person's system of beliefs and what is true in a story. The logical structure of fictional truth is very like the logical structure of belief. Let us consider some of the similarities.

(A) Beliefs are "negation incomplete." There are propositions that a person neither believes nor disbelieves. Similarly, we have seen that some propositions are neither true nor false in a given fiction.

(B) Beliefs are not closed under deduction. People do not believe all the consequences of their beliefs. In particular, people do not usually believe the contradictions, if there are any, that follow from their beliefs. We have already seen that fictional truth in the intuitive sense is not closed under deduction either. If what is true in the story has contradictory consequences, it may still be the case that nothing contradictory is true in the story.

(C) A person may have contradictory beliefs, believing P and believing not-P. (We shall see an example of this in Section 2.7.) And in certain stories both P and not-P are to be treated as part of the story. By feature (B), this may not lead to disaster. From a contradiction everything follows, but from a belief in contradictory propositions we cannot infer that everything is believed.

(D) If A believes P or Q, it does not follow that A believes P or that A believes Q. Just so with fiction. It might be true in the story that the murder weapon was either a gun or a knife, but neither true in the story that it was a gun, nor true in the story that it was a knife. The story is indeterminate on this point.

(E) Someone may have a belief that we would express as an existential quantification, without his believing any sub-

74

stitution instance of the quantification. Someone may believe there is a perfect number without believing that 6 (or any other number) is perfect. Similarly, it may be fictional that Holmes has some number of teeth, but not fictional that he has *n* teeth, for some particular *n*. To adopt the terminology of the logicians again, belief and fictional truth are "ω-incomplete."

(F) On at least some theories of belief there is a distinction to be made between explicit and implicit beliefs. Some beliefs may be stored in the brain, encoded in sentences of Mentalese, while others are purely dispositional. Similarly, some things are explicitly true in a fiction – because the text says they are – while others have to be arrived at by subtle methods of interpretation.

Now it may be that Lewis's truth-in-a-set-of-worlds approach to fictional truth can mirror at least some of these features. Perhaps it can mirror all of them (although I think it will do so only by a series of ad hoc approximations).[30] But the truth-in-a-set-of-worlds approach gives us the right results about fictional truth only to the extent that it succeeds in mirroring the familiar features of belief just described. How much better, then, to derive fictional truth from belief itself. That's the strategy I shall adopt.

2.6. FICTIONAL AUTHOR AND INFORMED READER

The suggestion is, then, that what is true in the fiction is what the teller believes. But it is important to realize that the teller is himself a fictional construct, not the real live author of the work, whose beliefs presumably bear little relation to what is true in the work. A number of literary theorists have sug-

---

30 Lewis and others attempt to explain belief itself in terms of possible worlds. The central problem for this approach is essentially the same as that which Lewis faces in accounting for truth in fiction: the problem of making room for inconsistency and deductive error or incompleteness on the part of the believer. Recently Stalnaker has tried to accommodate the possible-worlds approach to this difficulty. But problems remain. (See Stalnaker, *Inquiry* [Cambridge, Massachusetts, MIT Press, 1984] and my review in *Philosophical Quarterly* 37 (1987): 588–90.)

gested that the idea of an "implied," "apparent," "postulated," or "ideal" author is important for understanding the mechanisms by which fiction works, and that the character of this figure, delineated by us as we read, enables us to make sense of the text. Jonathan Culler puts it like this: "As a linguistic object the text is strange and ambiguous. We reduce its strangeness by reading it as the utterances of a particular narrator so that models of plausible human attitudes and of coherent personalities can be made operative."[31] The fictional author (as I shall call him) is that fictional character constructed within our make-believe whom we take to be telling us the story as known fact. Our reading is thus an exploration of the fictional author's belief structure. As we read we learn more about his beliefs, and we may come to change earlier hypotheses about what his beliefs are. Understanding the fictional author is thus like understanding a real person; it's a matter of making the best overall sense we can of his behavior (and here we are limited to speech behavior alone). The *belief set* of the fictional author – the set of propositions he believes – is the set of propositions that go to make up the story. This set of propositions is not literally true, although it is, as we say, true in the fiction. Interpreting real people is a matter of building up a picture of their belief set. So, too, with the fictional author.

To make this proposal plausible we must do two things. First, we must show how it is possible to build up a belief set for the fictional author in a nonarbitrary way. Second, we

31 Jonathan Culler, *Structuralist Poetics* (Ithaca, N.Y.: Cornell University Press, 1975), p. 146. Alexander Nehamas makes a similar point: "The author is postulated as the agent whose actions account for the text's features; he is a character, a hypothesis, which is accepted provisionally, guides interpretation, and is in turn modified in its light . . . . The regulative end is to construct, for each text, a complete, historically plausible author – a character who may not coincide with the actual writer's self-understanding, fragmentary and incomplete as it probably is" ("The Postulated Author: Critical Monism as a Regulative Ideal," *Critical Inquiry* 8 (1981): 145 and 147). The classic account of the implied author is Wayne Booth, *The Rhetoric of Fiction*, 2nd ed. (Chicago: University of Chicago Press, 1983). The concept of a fictional author that I shall employ differs in various ways from that of an implied or postulated author as used by Booth, Culler, and Nehamas.

must show that the belief set so constructed conforms to what we intuitively regard as true in the fiction.

The primary tool for constructing this belief set is the text of the work. That is the only direct evidence we have about the fictional author, the character traits that distinguish him from others, and the idiosyncratic features of his mental life. For the fictional author does not exist outside the fiction. He keeps no private diary in which he records his beliefs (unless it is part of the story that he does); he has no acquaintances who can tell us about him; he leaves no trace upon the world that we can hope to document historically.

But the text alone isn't enough. When we try to build up a picture of someone's belief set we don't proceed mechanically, by listing all the indicative sentences he utters, concluding that his beliefs are exactly the propositions expressed by those sentences. Such a procedure would be misleading for two reasons. First, as we have seen, people sometimes speak nonliterally. In that case the content of the speaker's belief and the content of the sentence uttered are different. Second, we cannot assume that a person will express all his beliefs verbally, even if the belief in question is one relevant to his topic. Speakers often simply assume that, in a given context, some of their beliefs can be inferred. When we infer a person's beliefs from what he says or writes, we do so against a background of assumptions that help us choose between alternative hypotheses – assumptions about what someone *like that* would probably believe. When it comes to interpreting the beliefs of the fictional author, the text itself will be one of the things that gives us clues as to what kind of person he is, and our view of the fictional author will change and deepen as we read more. But the text provides these clues only against a background of assumptions for which there might be no warrant in the text itself. Consider again Borges's endlessly useful story of Pierre Menard. When we read Cervantes's *Don Quixote* we assume that the fictional author has beliefs that are, by and large, those of seventeenth-century Europe. The reader of Menard's work, if he was suitably informed about its origins, would assume that here the fictional author has a radically different belief system that is the product of our own time. Starting from these two quite different initial assumptions, the written evidence, which is the same in both cases, will support quite different hypotheses about the fictional author's beliefs, and hence quite different hypotheses about what is true in the stories. With no prior assumptions about the fictional author we cannot start to interpret the text.

Although the real author and the fictional author are distinct, it is quite likely that the kind of person the fictional author is will depend in some way or other on the kind of person the real author is. Thus the fictional author of the Sherlock Holmes story is not Doyle but seems at least to be a member of the same community as Doyle: a late Victorian in general outlook. When we read a work from a certain period and place, we usually assume we are dealing with a fictional author of that period and place.[32] It will be helpful, then, if the reader can begin his exploration of the fictional author's beliefs by knowing something about the community from which the text actually issues. But we need start with no assumption about the fictional author more powerful than the assumption that he belongs to that community. As we read, the text itself may suggest more specific hypotheses about where to place the fictional author in that community; the matters of which he speaks and the manner of his speaking may betray a certain kind of outlook or a certain kind of knowledge, and so a certain kind of position in that community.

Readers of fiction read with varying degrees of insight and understanding. A reader of Sherlock Holmes might know little or nothing of Victorian England, and I think it will be agreed that such a reader will have at best a very fragmentary

---

32 A modern author who writes a novel set in the Middle Ages may succeed in placing within the novel a fictional author who has the beliefs that medieval people tended to have. In that case, what will be true in the novel will reflect medieval belief. More likely, his fictional author will display beliefs and attitudes that are distinctly modern. In that case, what is true in the novel will have little to do with the overt beliefs of medieval times.

2.6. Fictional author and informed reader

understanding of the story. (Imagine our own predicament if we had to interpret a Martian novel, knowing nothing of Martian society.) We need, then, the concept of an *informed* reader, a reader who knows the relevant facts about the community in which the work was written. The informed reader, unlike the fictional author, is not a fictional entity. A real reader can be an informed reader, although not every real reader is. What are the relevant facts the informed reader knows?

Remember that the reader's task is to work out what the fictional author believes. What is relevant to working this out is a knowledge of what people in that community tended to believe. Since we don't identify the fictional author with any particular member of that community, we don't need to associate beliefs with particular individuals; patterns of belief in the community and in its subcommunities will do. Also, we do not, strictly speaking, need to know what is or was *true* in the relevant community. Of course, what is true is often a good guide to what people believe, but if the truth is controversial or obscure it may not be believed. In the Sherlock Holmes story a certain kind of morality is part of the appropriate background. What makes it part of this background is not its being true (if moral propositions can be true) but its being believed quite widely in Victorian society. And in the same story the planet Pluto does not exist undiscovered. It does not exist at all, since no one believed in it at the time.

One should not conclude from these remarks that the method of interpretation I describe will lead always to the conclusion that the fictional author's beliefs are maximally conventional – the method would not be very useful if it did. The text itself may provide evidence that the fictional author's beliefs are unconventional in one way or another. Conventionality of belief is our starting point, from which we move as the text dictates. The only thing our reader knows in advance about the fictional author is that he belongs to a certain community. The best strategy for him to pursue in trying to infer the beliefs of the fictional author will be to assume that his beliefs are conventional unless the text indicates that they are not. The ways in which deviations from conventionality are to be inferred can be rather complicated. If the text indicates a belief on the fictional author's part in dragons, it may be reasonable to infer also that he believes in unicorns, even though there is nothing said about unicorns in the text. Thus it won't do to adopt the very simple strategy: assume that the fictional author's beliefs are as close to being conventional as the explicit content of the text will allow. I have no rules to substitute for this one, but I take it there would be considerable agreement in practice about how such inferences as this ought to proceed. We shall examine some of these inferences in the next section.

Let us now state the proposal for the truth conditions of statements of the form "$F_s(P)$", where S is the story in question:

(3) "$F_s(P)$" is true iff it is reasonable for the informed reader to infer that the fictional author of S believes that P.

As readers, our make-believe is that we are reading a narrative written by a reliable, historically situated agent (the fictional author) who wants to impart certain information. Historically situated as he is, the fictional author speaks to an audience of his own time and, most likely, of his own culture. He cannot, of course, tell us everything he knows that is relevant to his story – it would take too long and the attempt would dissipate our interest. But he knows that he does not need to tell us everything. He can rely upon a shared background of assumptions, telling us only those things that deviate from or supplement that background, or those things that belong to background and that he feels a need to emphasize. Because the teller – the fictional author – is a fictional construction, he has no private beliefs, no beliefs that could not reasonably be inferred from text plus background. His beliefs are not discovered by a reading (a rational and informed reading) but *constructed* by it.

The proposal has some affinities with Lewis's (2). According to (2), fictional truth is the product of two factors: what the text says, and what is overt belief in the author's community. But the overt belief condition is rather strong. Something is overt belief if almost everyone believes it, almost everyone believes that almost everyone believes it, and so on. Many beliefs we think of as important or characteristic of Victorian society would not count as overt beliefs in Lewis's sense, for instance, the belief in spiritualism. But this belief might well have to be taken as part of the unspoken background of a Victorian story (though not, of course, of every Victorian story). On my view, the informed reader must know more than what was common knowledge in the community; he must know what beliefs were to some degree or other prevalent, and to some degree or other acknowledged to be prevalent.[33]

2.7. STRATEGIES OF INTERPRETATION

To give substance to this so far rather abstract discussion it will be useful to see how the method operates in practice. I begin with a real-life example of uncertainty about the meaning of a text. Then I test the proposal against some hypothetical problem cases which I take over from David Lewis.[34] Resolving such problem cases will give us additional reason for believing that the proposal is on the right lines. And let us assume, temporarily, that we are dealing with a fiction that contains no contradictions, hidden or otherwise.

An interesting example of the way in which judgments about what was believed in the author's community affect

33 I have said that a competent reading of fiction requires us to postulate a fictional character (the fictional author) who is telling the story as known fact. Perhaps we could define fictional works as just those narratives that involve such a character. (A suggestion made by Laurent Stern, "Fictional Characters, Places and Events," *Philosophy and Phenomenological Research* 26 [1965]: 202–15.) But although it is true that a work is fictional just in case it involves a fictional author, we cannot use this as a *definition* of fiction. To understand what a fictional author is we must first understand what fictional characters in general are. To understand fictional characters we must first understand "fiction," just as we must understand "cause" before we can understand "causal antecedent." Recognizing this priority, fictional characters will have to wait their turn in Chapter 4.

34 Again, references in the text of this section are to the reprint of "Truth in Fiction" in *Philosophical Papers*, vol. 1.

2. *The structure of stories*

our judgments about what is true in the work is the debate about the status of the Ghost in *Hamlet*. Is it part of the story that the Ghost of Hamlet's father appears, or might it be that Hamlet is deluded by supernatural and evil forces into committing a great wrong? When Hamlet says

> The spirit that I have seen
> May be a devil – and the devil hath power
> T'assume a pleasing shape
> (2.2.551–53)

is this procrastination or genuine doubt? Probably, we shall never know Shakespeare's intentions in this regard, nor would finding out about them help us to resolve the ambiguity (if ambiguity it is rather than genuine indeterminacy in the plot[35]). Instead we should look, as interested scholars have looked, at the background of community belief concerning the explanation of spiritual phenomena. Philip Edwards, in a recent introduction to the play, summarizes the present state of the debate. The summary is worth quoting at length for its sensitivity to the relation of the play's structure to the shape of Elizabethan belief.

> [John Dover Wilson's] conclusion that there were three degrees of scepticism [about ghosts], with Catholics being less sceptical than Protestants, has proved too much of a simplification . . . It is impossible to ignore, in considering *Hamlet*, the deep caution and scepticism with which Shakespeare's contemporaries, whether Catholic or Protestant, viewed ghosts and reports of ghosts. They might be hallucinations, or angels, or demons out to ensnare one's soul. That a ghost might be the soul of a dead person revisiting earth was a very remote possibility. Hamlet's early affirmation of the Ghost's genuineness has come to look more questionable than his later doubts, and the confidence of generations of critics . . . that Hamlet's profession of scepticism in 2.2, with his plan to test the Ghost, is mere procrastination now seems insecurely founded. Not many would go as far as Eleanor Prosser in

35 An ambiguity arises when we are unsure whether P is true in the story or whether Q is. An indeterminacy arises when P or Q is true in the story but neither P nor Q is.

2.7. Strategies of interpretation

holding that the Ghost *was* a demon. But one of the important achievements of modern scholarship is to have unsettled the Ghost and made it impossible to accept his credentials and authority as a matter of course and without question.[36]

Our situation as Edwards describes it is one in which our knowledge of what was believed in Elizabethan society enables us to attribute to the fictional author a disjunctive belief – either the Ghost is genuine or it is a demoniacal attempt to mislead Hamlet about his duty – but in which we are unable to attribute to him a belief in either disjunct. So we are in a position where our current knowledge leaves the play ambiguous on this score. And, as Edwards suggests, if we knew more about Elizabethan belief, or knew differently, we might be able to attribute to him a stronger belief and so disambiguate the play. To see *Hamlet* as the product of a society prone to regard ghostly appearances as false representations rather than as dead souls is to be more receptive to the idea that the lines quoted were intended to be understood as an expression of genuine doubt, and written with the expectation that such doubts would find a ready response in the audience. It would not matter if Shakespeare actually had no such intentions and expected no such response (he might have been out of step with contemporary thought). What matters is whether it would be reasonable, given community belief, to see in these lines the evidence of such an intention. If so, they add weight to the hypothesis of at least an indeterminacy in the plot concerning the Ghost's real nature.

I have said there is more in a fiction than is stated in or implied by the text. Lewis gives an example:

> I claim that in the Holmes stories, Holmes lives nearer to Paddington Station than to Waterloo Station. A glance at the map will show you that his address in Baker Street is much nearer

---

36 Introduction to *Hamlet* (Cambridge: Cambridge University Press, 1985), p. 39. Hamlet is not a work of prose fiction but a work intended to be performed. This may be thought to introduce a complication that the present proposal concerning fictional truth cannot deal with. But see Section 2.9.

83

to Paddington. Yet the map is not part of the stories; and so far as I know it is never stated or implied in the stories themselves that Holmes lives nearer to Paddington. There are possible worlds where the Holmes stories are told as known fact rather than fiction which differ in all sorts of ways from ours. Among these are worlds where Holmes lives in a London arranged very differently from the London of our world, a London in which . . . Baker Street is much closer to Waterloo Station than to Paddington. ("Truth in Fiction," p. 268)

Lewis's analyses (1) and (2) can cope with this; so can my theory. I claim it would be reasonable for the reader to suppose that the fictional author believed that Baker Street is closer to Paddington than to Waterloo. The inference would proceed like this: He writes about events he is acquainted with, many of which take place in London and into which many of London's actual buildings and other landmarks are incorporated. Someone who knew these things would probably also know the locations of the main railway termini. So it is reasonable to conclude that he believed Baker street to be closer to Paddington than to Waterloo. So it is true in the stories that it's closer to Paddington than to Waterloo.

It is instructive to compare this case with another. Suppose Holmes's adventures had taken him briefly to Minsk, but that Minsk itself is not described in the story. Would we say that the location of Minsk's major buildings constitute part of the story in the same way that the location of London's major buildings obviously do? I think not. And the reason is clear: We would have no confidence that the fictional author of this story had any knowledge of the layout of Minsk.

Lewis discusses another example, which leads him from (1) to (2). In "The Adventure of the Speckled Band," Holmes solves the mystery by showing that the victim was killed by a Russell's viper that escaped up a bell rope. As a matter of scientific fact, a snake of this kind cannot climb a rope. The story does not actually say that Holmes's solution is the correct one. So on definition (1), Holmes bungled the case (p. 271). Definition (3) offers a satisfactory resolution. The reader may reasonably infer that the fictional author believes a Russell's viper can climb a rope (this, after all, is what he says, and there is no indication that he is speaking nonliterally at this point). The reader may reasonably suppose that if the fictional author thought Holmes had bungled the case he would have said so, and if he thought this particular snake was some amazing exception to the general inability to climb ropes exhibited by members of that species, he would have said that too. So it is reasonable to attribute to him the (erroneous) belief that Russell's viper is the kind of snake that can climb a rope. So this is true in the story, as it should be.

Now we come to some ingenious cases that Lewis presents as difficulties for both his (1) and (2). I think my theory gives the right results in these cases.

> In the *Threepenny Opera* the principal characters are a treacherous crew . . . . There is also a street singer. He shows up, sings the ballad of Mack the Knife, and goes about his business without betraying anyone. Is he also a treacherous fellow? The explicit content does not make him so. Real people are not so very treacherous, and even in Weimar Germany it was not overtly believed that they were, so background does not make him so either. Yet there is a moderately good reason to say that he is treacherous: in the *Threepenny Opera*, that's how people are . . . everyone put to the test proves treacherous, the street singer is there along with the rest, so doubtless he too would turn out to be treacherous if we saw more of him. (p. 274).

How ought we to reason out the case in terms of my proposal? We have a story in which it's plain that everyone tested turns out to be treacherous. So on my theory it is a story, the fictional author of which believes that everyone tested has turned out to be treacherous. When someone believes that everyone tested has turned out to be treacherous, we know there is, as Lewis puts it, "moderately good reason" to suppose he believes that those as yet untested are likely to be treacherous too, unless he gives some explicit indication that he does not believe this. In this case the fictional author gives no such explicit indication. We can infer, then, that he believes the singer to be treacherous. So that is true in the story.

Here is Lewis's other example:

> Suppose I write a story about the dragon Scrulch, a beautiful princess, a bold knight, and what not. It is a perfectly typical instance of its stylized genre, except that I never say that Scrulch breathes fire. Does he nevertheless breathe fire in my story? Perhaps so, because dragons in that kind of story do breathe fire. But the explicit content does not make him breathe fire. Neither does background, since in actuality and according to our beliefs there are no animals that breathe fire. (It just might be analytic that nothing is a dragon unless it breathes fire. But suppose I never *called* Scrulch a dragon: I merely endow him with all the standard dragonly attributes except fire-breathing.) If Scrulch does breathe fire in my story, it is by inter-fictional carry-over from what is true of dragons in other stories. (p. 274; italics in the original)

The point of Lewis's last quoted remark about interfictional carryover is that sometimes what is true in one fiction depends on what is true in some quite different fiction, rather than on what is actually true or actually believed to be true. I think there is something like interfictional carryover at work in this case, and no doubt in others as well, but I also think that interfictional carryover operates only via the kinds of inferences about the fictional authors beliefs that I have described. Many of us have, I suppose, encountered people whose beliefs seem to be influenced by myth and legend, and often a working knowledge of the myths and legends involved would enable one to predict some of what these people believe. If someone described to me, in all seriousness, his encounter with a dragonlike creature and if, as Lewis puts it, his story was "a perfectly typical instance of its stylized genre," I should be disinclined to believe him. But I *would* be inclined to ascribe to him the belief that his creature breathed fire. So I think it is quite reasonable, in the case Lewis describes, to infer that the fictional author believes that the creature breathes fire, and so that is true in the story.

2.7. Strategies of interpretation

How does my theory handle the various kinds of impossible fiction? Suppose the inconsistency is a minor one: the location of Watson's wound from the Afghan campaign. Suppose there are a number of occasions in the text where the wound is referred to; on one occasion it is said to be in the shoulder, on the others it is said to be in the leg. The reader will reasonably assume that the fictional author believes it to be in the leg (one slip being more likely than several). This will be what is true in the novel. If references to the shoulder and the leg are about equal in number and significance and there is nothing in the text to indicate which hypothesis was actually believed by the fictional author, no inference can be made, and it will be true in the story neither that it is in the leg, nor that it is in the shoulder. It will, however, be true in the story that it is in one or the other, for it is reasonable to infer that he believes it to be in one or the other. These, I take it, are the intuitively desirable results.

Suppose the fiction is about a circle squarer or Gödel refuter, it being central to the story that the main character actually does one of these impossible things. Elimination of the contradiction would destroy the story altogether. We need to distinguish a case of this kind from a case of the previous kind (where we suppose the fictional author to have made a mistake), on the grounds that here the text suggests that he does actually believe the contradictory thing. Because the story is built around the idea that someone squares the circle it is just not plausible to suppose the idea got into the narrative by way of some momentary inattention or confusion on the fictional author's part. So we have to attribute to the fictional author a belief in the falsity of Gödel's theorem, or in the possibility of circle squaring (or incoherent time travel, or whatever). It's quite common for us to attribute to people beliefs of this kind, but when we do we do not usually attribute to them a belief in any of the explicit contradictions that follow from these things. When people believe in the possibility of circle squaring they do so partly because they fail to see the contradictory consequences of their belief. So nothing manifestly contradictory – no proposition of the

87

form $P\&{\sim}P$ – will be true in the story. And, certainly, not every proposition will be true in the story.

Now, a story may contain an *explicit* contradiction of this irremediable kind. A time-travel story may have it that a certain event did occur at a certain time and that it did not, and other events in the story may crucially depend upon both these things being the case.[37] Reading the story, we shall infer that the fictional author believes the event occurred and that he believes it did not. We shall conclude that he believes contradictory things. And it may happen that we attribute to someone a belief in a proposition and a belief in its negation, although it would be unusual to do so. Why did Mr. Smith go out without taking his house key? He went out believing he was due to meet his wife; he left without a key believing his wife was at home to let him in. (I have found myself in situations not unlike this.) It seems we must attribute contradictory beliefs to Mr. Smith. So it is with the beliefs of the fictional author in the case of our time-travel story, and it will be the case that contradictory propositions are true in that story. But, as before, it by no means follows that everything is true in our story, for people do not believe all the consequences of what they believe.

Supposing that truth in fiction goes by belief sheds light on a phenomenon that would otherwise be rather hard to explain. In a time-travel story of the kind I described just now we are told in one place that event E occurred and in another place that it did not. But suppose we are told, in a single sentence, that E both occurred and did not occur. I think readers will find this much harder to cope with. Why? Because to integrate it into the story the reader will have to conclude that the fictional author believes a manifest contradiction, that he believes something that he himself describes as being of the form $P\&{\sim}P$. This time the reader could not explain such a belief by saying that the fictional author is sheltered from the

---

37 Ray Bradbury's "A Sound of Thunder" is a story of this kind. It is mentioned in John Heintz, "Reference and Inference in Fiction," *Poetics* 8, (1979): 85–99. William Tenn's "Brooklyn Project" prefigured Bradbury's theme, as Charles Pigden pointed out to me.

contradictory nature of his belief by deductive ignorance or psychological partitioning: believing, as with our confused Mr. Smith, that P "in one part of his mind" and that not-P in another.[38] Apparently the fictional author has a single belief that is manifestly contradictory, and this is very hard to make sense of. We would try just about any interpretative strategy rather than conclude that someone did believe such a thing – supposing him to be equivocating, speaking nonliterally or misunderstanding his own words. That we are equally puzzled by a text that contains an explicitly contradictory statement, that we try in similar ways to reinterpret the statement, is evidence of a strong connection between the way we figure out belief and the way we figure our fictional truth.

The examples I have given are examples of quite straightforward procedures for working out what is true in fiction. Of course, there will be cases that are much more difficult to calculate. For example, it isn't always clear whether or not, or to what extent, a certain belief is to be counted as prevalent in the community of the author. And so there will be cases in which it is correspondingly unclear what belief to attribute to the fictional author. The notion of prevalence I am working with here is vague in ways it would be difficult to remedy. But vagueness in our explication of fictional truth may not be a disadvantage, for it is likely that the concept of fictional truth is itself vague in ways that mirror the vagueness inherent in any reasonable method of belief attribution. In that case we are explicating one vague notion in terms of another. As Lewis puts it, "Two imprecise concepts may be rigidly fastened to one another, swaying together rather than separately, and we can hope to be precise about their connection."[39] This very well describes the relation between fictional truth and the beliefs of our fictional author.

---

38 For an account of inconsistent believing that makes use of this idea, see Robert Stalnaker, *Inquiry*, chap. 5.
39 "Counterfactuals and Comparative Possibility," *Journal of Philosophical Logic* 2 (1973): 418–46, reprinted in *Philosophical Papers*, vol. 2. The quotation is on p. 6 of the reprint.

2. The structure of stories

2.8. FICTIONAL TO A DEGREE?

Arguably, the vagueness of truth in fiction does not distinguish it from truth. If the boundaries between concepts are vague, the truths generated by application of these concepts shade off into falsehoods, with a gray area in between. But although truth may be vague, there are not degrees of truth. What lies in the gray area isn't true (or false) to a degree. And verisimilitude is not degree of truth: it is the distance of a false proposition from the truth. Up to this point I have been assuming that truth in fiction is like truth in this respect, that it does not admit of degree. But there is reason to think it does. Consider the following propositions about Sherlock Holmes:

> Holmes was a detective.
> Holmes had a full set of fingers and toes.
> Sometime in his early life Holmes suffered a severe illness.
> Holmes had a full set of teeth.
> Sometime in his early life Holmes suffered from diphtheria.
> Sometime in his career Holmes visited Minsk.
> Holmes was moonlighting as a gentleman cracksman in the
> style of Raffles.[40]

The ordering here given corresponds, I think, to the ordering most people would give if they were asked to rank these propositions in decreasing order of plausibility, relative to the story. If asked simply to distinguish between those that are true in the story and those that are not, I'm not sure where I would make the cut. And I would suspect the cut, if I made it, of being arbitrary. (I'm assuming here, reasonably, I think, that my indecision, or some of it, would remain even if all the vagueness attaching to the relevant parts of the text and to relevant background knowledge were removed.) An ordering such as the one above certainly seems a more natural way of locating these propositions in relation to the story than does a bifurcation into true-in-the-story and not-true-in-

40 For the career of A. J. Raffles, see E. W. Hornung, *The Collected Raffles* (London, J. M. Dent, 1985).

90

the-story. And even if you think there is a natural cutoff point, you may still agree that some of the propositions above the cut are *more* true in the fiction than some others; similarly for those below. This strongly suggests that our intuitive notion of truth in fiction is the notion of something that admits of degree.

You might object that, although the ordering reflects a difference between these propositions in relation to the Holmes story, it is merely an *evidential* difference. There is better reason for thinking that some of these propositions are true in the stories than for thinking that others are. But to talk like that is to be seduced by the picture of a determinate fictional reality to which we have greater or lesser epistemic access. When it comes to truth in fiction there is no distinguishing an epistemic from an ontological difference. There is no sense to the suggestion that although total evidence may leave the question undecided, a proposition is either true in the story or not.

It is an advantage of my theory that it can easily accommodate the idea that truth in fiction admits of degrees. The right-hand side of our definition (3) of truth in fiction speaks of reasonable inference – an inference conducted within the scope of the make-believe that the fictional author tells that of which he knows. And when it comes to inferences about what people believe – inferences of a nondemonstrative kind – it is often difficult and to some degree arbitrary to distinguish the reasonable from the unreasonable, but easier and more natural to judge that one such inference is *more* reasonable than another (in light of the same body of total evidence). Since reasonableness in inferring is a matter of degree, and truth in fiction is defined exactly in terms of reasonable inference, we can expect truth in fiction to be a matter of degree also. And that is, as I have argued, the result we want.

To indicate that truth in fiction admits of degree we can supplement our operator **F** with a parameter r taking real values in the unit interval, and represented by "$F_{s_r}(P)$" – to be read: "P is true in S to degree r." The value of this parameter is determined, in particular cases, by the value of the corresponding parameter that occurs implicitly on the right-hand side of (3): the parameter that measures reasonableness of inferring. Thus we might modify definition (3) as follows:

(3*) "$F_{S_r}(P)$" is true iff it is reasonable to degree r for the informed reader to infer that the fictional author of S believes that P.

It would not be easy, on the other hand, to adjust Lewis's theory in a similar way. Recall Lewis's first definition:

(1) "$F_S(P)$" is true iff there is an S_P-world closer to @ than any $S_{\sim P}$-world.

The right-hand side specifies a condition that simply holds or fails to hold, not a condition that holds to a greater or a lesser degree. There is thus no quantitative variability on the right-hand side that could be exploited to explain the variability we detect within $F(P)$ and which our parameter r makes explicit.

Assignments of point values to r must not be taken too seriously. At best they have only ordinal significance, and even then they will have to give way under pressure from vagueness and indeterminacy. But once again, vagueness and indeterminacy need not bother us if their occurrence on the left side of (3*) is matched by their occurrence on the right.

We say that an inference is reasonable when it has a relatively high degree of reasonableness, unreasonable when its degree of reasonableness is very low. I shall continue to speak of propositions being true in the fiction and false in the fiction, meaning that their place on the truth-in-fiction scale is, respectively, very high or very low.

2.9. FICTIONS IN VISUAL MEDIA

There is a problem for my account of fiction if it is intended, as I do intend it, to be applicable to works in all media. The problem arises when we consider media where the story is presented in a visual form instead of, or possibly as well as, in a linguistic form. When we watch a play or a movie we seem to be in direct, unmediated contact with the characters and events. While watching the movie we don't just learn about what Indiana Jones did, we watch him doing it. Of course, we don't really see him, because Indiana Jones does not exist. But surely we do make believe that we see him; we don't make believe that we are being told about him. In movies and plays there is sometimes a narrator, but the narrator cannot function as the fictional author in my sense. The narrator in a film or play can do no more than supplement the images and sounds with commentary and additional information. The rest of the visual and auditory information we get is not derived from him.

I think this plausible model of fiction in visual media – let us call it the direct presentation theory – is wrong. Part of the reason I am inclined to reject it is, of course, that it's inconsistent with my theory of fiction. But I have another, independent, reason for thinking it wrong. For the model has some very awkward consequences. It is, in fact, quite out of keeping with at least most of our experience of visual media that we should make believe we are actually watching the events and characters depicted. This is particularly obvious in film, where a single scene may be divided into many shots from different perspectives. As shots succeed one another we don't have any sense of changing *our* perspective on the action. Those familiar with the conventions of cinema hardly notice the cutting as the camera moves from one face to another. Many camera perspectives would be difficult or downright impossible for the viewer to achieve; viewing the Earth from deep space one minute, hanging from the ceiling in a drawing room the next. In some films what we would have to make believe in order to make sense of our being observers of the scene would be wildly at variance with the conventions of the story. For example, in *The Lady in the Lake*, a film of Raymond Chandler's detective story, the action is depicted through the eyes of Philip Marlowe. If we are to make believe that we are literally seeing events through Marlowe's eyes, the story would seem to have become a science fiction fantasy. This is not the impression created in the viewer's mind while watching the film.[41]

It might be suggested instead that our make-believe is that we are watching a filmed record of events that have happened, rather than watching the events themselves. Kendall Walton seems to be taking this view when he says, "the viewer seems to be seeing [the depicted] events via the film"; when a fictional killing is shown on the screen it seems "to the viewer that he is seeing an actual killing *via a photographic film* of it."[42] But this is hardly an improvement. First of all, it's quite unclear how we could be watching a film taken through Marlowe's eyes, so the *Lady in the Lake* problem remains unsolved. And we would in general have to make believe that there is a film crew following the characters of the film about. But the only kind of film for which this is a plausible assumption would be a film in which it is part of the story that the film itself is a documentary – as with Rob Reiner's *This Is Spinal Tap*.

It is less easy to find forceful illustrations of this point in connection with theater, where visual perspective is determined by the position of the viewer and does not jump about in a discontinuous way. But it would be odd to say that we make believe we are somehow witnesses to intimate scenes between characters that depend for their dramatic force on the assumption that no one else is there. And when I move my seat because the man in front is obscuring my view, is it part of my make-believe that I change my position relative to Othello?

Instead of trying to live with these awkward consequences of the direct presentation theory, I suggest we reject it and regard visual media as presenting fictions of structurally the same kinds as novels and other narratives. Reading the novel, we make believe that the fictional author is presenting us with information he knows to be true. He is presenting that information verbally. And in the play or film it is simi-

---

41 I owe this example to David Lewis. But I don't know whether Lewis would agree with my analysis.
42 See Walton, "Transparent Pictures: On the Nature of Photographic Realism," *Critical Inquiry*, 11 (1984): 246–77. The quotation is from p. 258.

larly make-believe that the fictional author is also presenting us with information he knows to be true. The difference is in the mode of presentation of the information. Imagine the ways in which a storyteller might tell his story. He might describe the events in words. But instead (or in addition) he might act out a shadow play with his hands. Going further, he might use glove puppets and then marionettes. Extending his resources still further, he might rope in others to assist, telling them what movements and sounds to make. From there it's a short step to the conventions of theater and cinema. Through the successive extensions the teller tells his tale – he simply uses more and more elaborate means to tell it. What happens when we watch *The Lady in the Lake*? We make believe, not that we are looking at the world through Marlowe's eyes, but that we are being informed about how things looked to Marlowe.

One might object that this account of theatrical and cinematic experience makes it hard to explain the intensity that experiences of this kind can have, and which seems to arise out of the make-believe that the audience is in unmediated contact with the characters. Thus it is surely part of my make-believe when I watch the movie that I'm watching Indiana Jones as he is about to be crushed by a huge boulder; it is not part of my make-believe that I'm watching a re-creation of that event. If that were the content of my make-believe, it would be hard to explain the feelings, tensions, and anxieties aroused by the images on the screen. But the response to this is straightforward. When I read a novel I may become intensely involved with the characters, the things they do, and the dangers they encounter. Yet I don't adopt as part of my make-believe the idea that I am present at the action, that I hear and see the characters described. My make-believe is rather that I am reading a true account of their actions and sufferings. If the intensity of our experience in the theater or cinema were an objection to my account of fictions in visual media, it would also be an objection to the most plausible account of make-believe in literary fiction.

There is a theatrical phenomenon that seems easier to

explain on the theory of direct presentation than on mine. Sometimes the actors speak directly to the audience; in unconventional theater they may physically interact with the audience. How can the audience make sense of such interaction unless it is part of their make-believe that they really are present to be interacted with? In Brechtian theater the interaction isn't supposed to be incorporated into the make-believe but is used for didactic purposes or to inhibit the make-believe. In other cases, though, it is intended to be incorporated. In these cases I think the members of the audience come to play a dual role. They are both spectators *of*, and actors (or sometimes merely props) *in*, the production. They play characters participating in the action and it becomes make-believedly true that they are those characters. But they are still members of the audience, and as such they observe themselves playing these roles. As members of the audience they are to make believe that they are taking part in a *representation* of actually occurring events, not that they are participants in those very events. In fact cases of actor–audience interaction are really rather difficult to explain on the direct presentation theory. For if it were part of our make-believe that we directly confront the action, it would be quite natural, within the context of such a make-believe, for the characters onstage to address remarks to us or call on us for help. But we don't find these things in the least natural; it's because we find them surprising and even shocking that writers and directors are tempted (perhaps too often tempted) to employ them.

I have tried to explain the fictional character of movies, photographs, and paintings in terms of make-believe. Can we explain their representational character in the same way? Can we explain how it is that Goya's picture depicts the Duke, or how it is that in the movie a menacing villain is depicted, by appealing to facts about what we do or might make believe when we look at the pic-

2.9. Fictions in visual media

ture or watch the movie? Kendall Walton thinks we can.[43]

According to Walton, depictions are props in games of make-believe, and what they depict depends upon their role in the game. Thus, a picture depicts the Duke of Wellington if it serves as a prop in a game in which looking at the picture counts, within the game, as looking at the Duke. It is make-believedly true, of a person who looks at the picture, that he is looking at the Duke.

We might wonder whether this account makes the depictive qualities of a picture audience-relative in an undesirable way. If Goya's picture is used, as it might be used, in a game of make-believe in which looking at the picture counts as looking at Napoleon, does that mean that the picture then depicts Napoleon? This would be an awkward consequence. We could adjust the theory so as to make it artist-relative rather than observer-relative. We could say that the picture represents whatever we are intended by the artist to make believe, rather than what we are apt to make believe. This would be an improvement, in my view.

One can certainly imagine Goya's picture being used as a prop in a game of make-believe, and being intended to be so used. The question is whether its role in such a game is explanatory of its depictive qualities. It seems to me that things are quite the other way around. The picture would serve very nicely in such a game exactly because it depicts the Duke. A picture that depicted a bowl of fruit would not serve so well in such a game. Our recognition that it depicts the Duke (or at least that it depicts a man in military attire) precedes our employment of the picture in any such game.

Walton's thesis also has the drawback that it obliterates the distinction between fictional and nonfictional depictions.[44] Fictional pictures are just those intended to be used in games of make-believe, as we are intended to make believe that

---

43 See "Pictures and Make-Believe," especially sec. 6, "Analysis of P-Depiction," and *Mimesis as Make-Believe*, chap. 8.

44 Walton acknowledges that his account leaves no room for nonfictional depictions (see *Mimesis as Make-Believe*, sec. 8.8).

there are strange and disturbing hybrid creatures when we look at Fuseli's *Titania and Bottom*.[45] Maps (except those like the maps that accompany *Lord of the Rings*), most photographs, and Goya's portrait of the Duke are not to be counted as fictional by this criterion – and rightly so. If we try to explain depiction in terms of make-believe, we shall not be able to make this distinction.

If this is right, we shall need an account of depiction that does not appeal to the idea of make-believe. Recent work suggests we may find the answer in terms of a certain kind of experienced similarity.[46] But work on this program is not to be undertaken here, since I am concerned with problems that arise only in the context of fictional works. The nature of depiction is a problem that arises for fictional and nonfictional works alike.

I now summarize what I have claimed about the fictionality of works in visual media. There is a distinction, for all kinds of visual media, between works that are fictional and works that are not. And the question whether a work belonging to a visual medium is fictional or not is to be answered in just the same way as it is to be answered for literary works. The kind of make-believe that is appropriate to works in visual media is of just the same kind as that for literature: we make believe that a story is being told as known fact. The difference between visual and nonvisual fiction lies only in the manner of the telling, as that manner is dictated by the medium itself. And we cannot use the idea of make-believe to explicate the idea of representation in visual media, because the notion of representation is prior to that of make-believe, and because any attempt to proceed in this way destroys the distinction between works in visual media that are fictional and works in those same media that are not.

---

45 We are intended to make believe, not that the depiction itself is what is depicted (as Walton would have it), but that the depiction is a depiction of real hybrid creatures.

46 For a recent account of depiction along these lines, see Christopher Peacocke, "Depiction," *Philosophical Review* 96 (1987): 383–410.

Chapter 3

Interpretation

In this chapter I make some applications of the theory of truth in fiction developed in Chapter 2. These applications concern questions about the nature of interpretation: Is there an irremediable relativism involved in interpretation? Is there an "intentional fallacy" one can commit in deciding what is fictionally true? What is the relation between fictional truth and literary style? Finally, I discuss a couple of problems raised by the use to which I have put the idea of a fictional author.

3.1. RELATIONALISM AND RELATIVISM

When we decide that Holmes is a human being, we don't decide that it's literally true that he is; we decide that it's true in the story that he is. We decide that F_H(Holmes is human). But we are, at one remove, deciding about literal (not literary!) truth; we decide that it's true that F_H(Holmes is human). According to my definition of truth in fiction, $F(P)$ is true just in case it is reasonable to infer that the fictional author believes that P.

We do not make these inferences piecemeal. We do not pair off one sentence of the text with a proposition that we decide is true in the story and then move on to the next sentence. Judgments about what is true in the story are dependent upon the overall impression the text makes. We move back and forth, changing our minds about earlier hypotheses in the light of later evidence, relying on the overall tone of the

99

work in order to decide what is to be taken literally, what as irony, and so on. As we read we have to resolve clashes with background assumptions. If the work turns out to be some kind of fantasy, we might be left at the end with little of the real world of the author's community.

As I remarked earlier, interpreting a work of fiction is much like interpreting a person (as we would expect, on the hypothesis that interpreting a story is a matter of interpreting the fictional author). We do not, except where the demands of practical life rule out a broader view, pair off items of a person's behavior with individual beliefs and desires. We must have regard to the overall coherence of the picture we construct of that person's mental life. In the same way, claims about what is true in the story are not to be thought of as corroborated individually by the text, but only as they belong to a system of such claims. The reasonableness of one assumption about what is true in the story depends on its place in a system of such assumptions that make good overall sense of the story. Within a given set of interpretative hypotheses, a single claim might be poorly corroborated, yet well corroborated within another such set. Consider the claim that it's true in *The Turn of the Screw* that the governess is mad. Whether this is to be regarded as corroborated by the text depends very much on what other interpretative assumptions we are prepared to make about the story (that there are no ghosts, that the children are innocent, etc.). Of course, there will be some interpretative claims that will not be well corroborated whatever other assumptions we make: that the governess is a figment of Mrs. Grose's imagination might be an example of this.

If P is true in the story (that is, if $F(P)$ is true), that's because P is one of a larger body of propositions that constitute an overall interpretation of the text, a larger body of propositions that it is reasonable to suppose the fictional author believed. The text, together with relevant background assumptions, confirms the propositions that go to make up an interpretation only when they are taken together. (In Chapter 4 we shall see grounds for a more radical holism about interpretation. For if I am right in what I say there about the semantics of fictional names, it turns out that a fictional story is not a set of distinct propositions but one big proposition. Thus holism of confirmation is accompanied by holism of meaning, though the latter is not derived, as it sometimes is in other contexts, from the former.)

Now, it is possible both in the case of interpreting behavior and in the case of interpreting fiction that there are competing systems of interpretation with nothing to chose between them. Although they conflict, each interpretation makes good (in fact equally good) sense of the work, and nothing else makes better sense of it. Thus my theory of interpretation implies the possibility of nonequivalent, maximally good interpretations. (Perhaps the ghost story interpretation and the delusion interpretation of *The Turn of the Screw* are examples of this.)[1] Now, a theory with this sort of consequence is apt to be accused of two things: of being antirealist, and being relativistic. I admit the first charge but not the second. Let us take them in turn.

One way to characterize realism is in terms of a gap between evidence and truth. According to the scientific realist an ideal scientific theory – a theory that meets all the determinable constraints we could impose on it, like conformity to all the observable data – might still be false. The scientific realist conceives of the world as transcending our sensory capacities, while he supposes our theories to be capable, in principle, of corresponding to that transcendent reality.[2] If realism is correct, we could not be certain our theory was true, even if we knew it was supported by *all* the evidence (past, present, and future). The antirealist, by contrast, will not grant any coherence to a conception of truth that transcends all possible criteria of rightness we can apply, and will insist that truth is nothing more than the limit of conformity

---

1 My own view is that the delusion interpretation is inconsistent with the text. I ignore this for the sake of the argument.
2 This is Hilary Putnam's characterization of realism. See his "Realism and Reason," in *Meaning and the Moral Sciences* (London: Routledge & Kegan Paul, 1978), p. 125.

to the data. In matters of science I incline to realism. But I have no such inclination concerning fiction. As a realist about science I believe the truth about the physical world transcends our powers of observation. But I can make nothing of the idea that the truth about a *fictional story* might be beyond the reach of our best interpretative methods.[3] By holding certain patterns of rational inference to be constitutive of what is true in the story, we close the gap between evidence and truth, and the possibility of a best supported but incorrect interpretation disappears. In literary interpretation there is no truth beyond the ascertainable truth.

We can take the analogy with scientific theories further. If two competing scientific theories are maximally supported by the total evidence, they both count, for the antirealist, as true. Truth for an antirealist just is conformity (in the limit) to the data. Suppose we say that maximally supported interpretations of the fictional work are both true. What, then, if we have maximally supported interpretations that contradict one another, as with our two interpretations of *The Turn of the Screw*?

The contradictions might need some teasing out. Even if F(P) is part of one maximal interpretation and F(~P) is part of the other, we don't yet have a contradiction between the two interpretations. For that we need both F(P) and ~F(P). F(~P) does not entail ~F(P) because, as we have seen, it is possible for a correct interpretation to have it that both F(P) and F(~P). But if we are dealing, as we often are, with interpretations that do not make contradictory things true in the story, we may well have F(P) according to one and ~F(P) according to the other.[4] Relative to the supernatural reading

---

3 In practice, of course, we may be unable to interpret a story because we lack the relevant evidence. What I deny is that something other than total evidence might determine the correctness of an interpretation. It is at this point that the analogy between interpreting a story and interpreting the beliefs of a (real) person breaks down. For it does make sense to suppose that there is a determinate *mental* reality beyond the reach of our best interpretative methods.

4 Strictly speaking, we ought, in light of the results of Section 2.8, to say that these interpretations contradict each other concerning the degree to which P is true in the story. But this is a complication we may ignore here.

of *The Turn of the Screw*, it is reasonable to suppose the fictional author believes the ghosts to be real; relative to the psychological reading it is not reasonable to suppose the fictional author believes this. Assume that both these readings are, when each is taken as a whole, maximally well supported. Let P represent the proposition that the ghosts are real. My theory of fictional truth has it that both $F(P)$ and $\sim F(P)$ are true. But this is not an acceptable consequence.

We could get around the problem posed by competing interpretations by always uniting readings that clash and which are all maximally good readings into a grand, disjunctive reading. Where the readings overlap – and they probably will overlap to some degree – we take their common part. Where they contradict one another we disjoin contradictory elements. If the maximally good readings of *The Turn of the Screw* are the supernatural and the psychological ones, we could then say that the unique best, and therefore true, interpretation is one in which it is true in the story that either the governess really sees ghosts or she suffers delusions and does not really see them, but in which neither disjunct taken by itself is true in the story.

The process of disjoining might get rather complicated. We might need to disjoin not only propositions that contradict one another, but propositions that are in tension to some degree. Consider two maximal interpretations, A and B, of a single story. They contradict each other in various ways, and here we disjoin. But also, according to A, the hero habitually helps old ladies across the street, whereas according to B, he mugs them for their social security checks. No contradiction here, but we might not want it to be the case, according to our grand disjunctive interpretation, that he does both. Better to disjoin and say that it is true in the story that he does one or the other, but not true in the story that he does the one, nor true in the story that he does the other. The rule is: When in doubt, disjoin.

It won't do to object against this proposal that disjunction produces a gerrymandered result that no one would intuitively regard as an interpretation. For we have already seen

103

that disjunction is a common feature of fictional stories.[5] Does Holmes have an even number of hairs on his head at the moment of his struggle with Moriarty at the Reichenbach Falls? Assuredly it is true in the story that he either does or does not; Doyle did not write stories in which the law of bivalence is up for grabs! But clearly, it is not true in the story that the number is even, nor true in the story that the number is odd.

The problem with this proposal is not that disjoining always leads to undesirable results, but that it sometimes does. The supernatural interpretation is *one* interpretation, the psychological interpretation another. Their disjunction is exactly that – a disjunction of interpretations. It is not an interpretation. If there is a resolution to be had, we must look somewhere else for it.

We find the beginnings of a solution in an analogy. One person may claim that an object is moving with a certain velocity, and another may claim that the same object is moving with a different velocity. These claims sound as if they contradict one another, but perhaps they do not. They will contradict each other only if they are judgments of velocity made relative to the same frame of reference. Velocity is not a monadic property of objects but a two-place relation between an object and a frame of reference. If the two judgments of velocity are made relative to different frames of reference, they don't contradict each other, for they are not to be understood as disagreeing about whether the object has a certain property. Rather, one party says the object stands in a certain relation to another object, and the other party says the objects stands in another relation to yet another object. So it is with statements about what is true in a fiction. The statement that P is true in the fiction is like the statement that the object has a certain velocity: both are incomplete until something else is specified. In the case of the statement of velocity it is a set of coordinates that must be specified; in the case of

---

5 See feature (D) on my earlier list of similarities between truth in fiction and belief, Section 2.5.

3.1. Relationalism and relativism

the statement of fictional truth it is an overall interpretation that must be specified.

So the theory I have offered in the preceding chapter is subject to this much correction: It is a theory of the truth conditions for *relational* statements of the form F(P,I). It tells us that the statement "P is true in the fiction relative to interpretation I" is true just in case P is a member of a set of propositions I, and it is reasonable to infer that the fictional author believes I. If we frequently suppress a reference to a particular interpretation when we are asserting that some or another proposition is true in the story, that's because many such propositions would count as true in the story under *any* acceptable interpretation, and can therefore be regarded as "coordinate free." Thus it is likely, I suppose, that any acceptable interpretation of *The Turn of the Screw* will have it that the governess is a young lady whose father is a clergyman, that Miles and Flora are orphaned children and that Mrs. Gross is their housekeeper. An interpretation of the story that tried to overthrow these judgments would simply encounter so much hard textual evidence working against it that it would never seem plausible.

Relationalism is the doctrine that fictional truth is relational; what is true or false is always a statement of the form F(P,I), and never anything of the form F(P). What, one might ask, is antirealist about this doctrine? If someone were to propose a comparable doctrine concerning scientific theories rather than literary interpretations, it would be clear that the proposal was an antirealist one. If it were said that a statement about the world is not, straightforwardly, either true or false, but always true or false relative to some theory about the world, and that a statement may be true of the world relative to one theory and false relative to another, it would be clear that realism had been abandoned.[6] To think of the truth about the world as theory relative is to think of the world as not constituting a determinate reality independent of us. To

6 Nelson Goodman seems to be proposing such a doctrine (he calls it "irrealism") in *Ways of Worldmaking* (Indianapolis: Hackett, 1978).

105

think similarly about fictions is to think antirealistically about them. And that, it seems to me, is the correct way to think about them.

The doctrine just announced is the doctrine that fictional truth is *relational*. Theorists of literature often seem to embrace, or at least to flirt with, some form of *relativism* about interpretation. The kind of relationalism I have been advocating might be thought hospitable to relativism. I shall argue that it is not.

Interpretative relativism is best understood in opposition to interpretative objectivism: the view that there are objective standards for judging interpretations. An extreme relativism is this: because a text has no meaning in itself, any interpretation of it is as good as any other. A less extreme view is that correctness of interpretation is not a matter of conformity to the meaning of the text (for there is no such thing) but rather of conformity to current community-wide standards of interpretation. This is the sort of picture Stanley Fish presents us with; it gives the critic a narrower range of interpretative options than does the first, "anything goes," version of relativism, but it does not allow us to say there is anything wrong with a given interpretation other than that most critics do not like it.[7]

7 See Stanley Fish, *Is There a Text in This Class?* (Cambridge, Mass.: Harvard University Press, 1980). Fish is always keen to deny that his theory has unwelcome relativistic consequences. He denies that "anything goes" (ibid., p. 357); "we are," he says, "always 'right to rule out at least some readings' " (ibid., p. 349); "rather than unmooring the subject [Fish's theory] reveals the subject to be always and already tethered to the contextual setting that constitutes him and enables his 'rational' acts" ("Pragmatism and Literary Theory," *Critical Inquiry* 11 (1985): 433–58; the quotation is from p. 440. Note the – appropriate – scare quotes around "rational"). Sometimes Fish's apologetic borders on the incoherent: "I may, in some sense, *know* that my present reading of *Paradise Lost* follows from assumptions that I . . . may not hold in a year or so, but that 'knowledge' does not prevent me now knowing that my present reading of *Paradise Lost* is the correct one" (*Is There a Text in This Class?* p. 359).
Fish's position, and his defense of it, are strikingly similar to the views of Thomas Kuhn on scientific theories (see especially Fish's discussion of paradigms in *Is There a Text in This Class?*, p. 362–3). Fish and Kuhn are not "epistemological anarchists" in the style of Paul Feyerabend; they do not believe that anything

3.1. Relationalism and relativism

Views like this have little connection with the relationalism argued for above. Relationalism says that a statement to the effect that something is fictionally true is at least implicitly relational, in much the same way that a statement of velocity is. And it would be a complete misunderstanding of relationalism about velocity to say that, on this view, it's up to us to decide what velocity an object has. Velocity is a perfectly objective relational feature of an object. That is, given a choice of object and coordinate system, the object's velocity relative to that coordinate system is decided quite independently of what we think or choose. In fact, there is an aspect to the objectivity of interpretative statements not captured in the analogy with velocity. For any given velocity, it is always possible to find a frame of reference relative to which it is (objectively) true that the object is traveling at that velocity.[8] But it is not the case that, for any proposition P, we can find an acceptable interpretation of the story to which P belongs. There is no acceptable interpretation of the Holmes story that would have it that Holmes is a Martian in disguise. Given the sorts of theories currently fashionable in the critical community, this is perhaps a view that would need to be argued for rather than merely stated as an obvious truth. But I don't intend to argue for it here. My point is only that it doesn't *follow* from relationalism about interpretation either that what is true in the fiction depends upon the reader's or the critic's personal preference, or that any old interpretative claim, however bizarre, will find a home in some acceptable overall interpretation of the work. The kind of relationalism I advocate makes only one concession to relativism, and it is a

goes. But they do believe – however often they speak of standards of rightness and wrongness – that the standards that inform their disciplines have no "transcendent" justification. They have only the force of authority. Fish's picture is more complex and pluralistic than Kuhn's. Whereas Kuhn paints a picture of science as dominated by one reigning paradigm, Fish's interpretative community defines a complex structure of interpretative strategies, some central, some "off the wall," and some, no doubt, in between. But Fish and Kuhn share the belief that the rightness of an interpretation or scientific theory is determined by nothing more than consensus within the community, a consensus that changes over time.

8 Except insofar as the laws of physics set an upper bound to this.

minor one. It grants that there are *some* interpretations of *some* works such that there is no choosing between them on rational grounds, and it grants, consequentially, that it is sometimes possible to say that *P* is true in the story, relative to one interpretation, and that not-*P* is true in the story, relative to some other interpretation. But to say this is not to abandon the idea that there are objective standards for choosing between interpretations. There may be interpretations between which no rational choice is possible, but rational choice between interpretations is at least often possible.

The sometimes confused debate over whether literary interpretation can aspire to objectivity suffers from a failure to distinguish between two contrast pairs: the objective–relativistic, and the absolute–pluralistic, which cut across one another. What is at stake in the first is the existence or otherwise of objective standards according to which we can say that some interpretations are better than others. The objectivist claims there are such standards; the relativist denies there are. What is at stake in the second is the existence or otherwise of a unique, best interpretation of each fiction. The absolutist claims there is always such an interpretation; the pluralist denies there is.[9] Although objectivism is sometimes confused with absolutism, we can see from this characterization that objectivism is in fact a weaker doctrine. According to the objectivism I'm advocating, there are objective standards of interpretation – they are the standards that ought to (and to some extent do) regulate our interpretation of people's ordinary speech behavior.[10] But these standards don't guarantee a winner in the interpretation stakes. Although there are beliefs it certainly is unreasonable to attribute to the author, there may be distinct sets of beliefs it is equally reasonable to attribute to him, and no other set of

9 For an example of critical absolutism, see P. D. Juhl, *Interpretation* (Princeton, N.J.: Princeton University Press, 1980): "A literary work has one and only one correct interpretation" (p. 198).

10 Grice has gone some way toward articulating the principles that govern our interpretation of speech in his studies of conversation referred to in Section 1.7. Much work remains to be done in this area.

beliefs it is more reasonable to attribute to him. Contrary to what absolutism would have us believe, there is no "hidden reality" that can break such a tie; the limits of reasonable inference are the limits of fictional truth. In particular, the tie cannot be broken by comparing the rivals with what the author actually intended for his work – as we shall see immediately.

3.2. THE INTENTIONAL FALLACY

Not so long ago, just about any theory that connected an author's intentions with the activity of criticism in any way was described as a version of the intentional fallacy. Fortunately that kind of antiintentionalist hysteria is no longer with us. But it is a fallacy to suppose, if anyone does, that something can be true in a fiction just because the author intends it to be. It is true in the Holmes story that Holmes lives close to Paddington Station, even if Doyle never intended that this proposition be part of our make-believe. Indeed, the author may intend a proposition to be true in a fiction without it thereby being true in the fiction. Suppose Doyle had peculiar beliefs about alien beings and their infiltration of our world, and that he thought of Holmes as a fictional representative of this race of aliens. Believing his beliefs to be widely shared by members of his community, he might have intended his audience to take his story of the distant, quirky, and highly intelligent Holmes as a story about one of these aliens (that's how these aliens are, according to Doyle's strange belief system). But even if Doyle's private correspondence revealed this intention, we would go wrong in concluding that it was true in the story that Holmes is an alien being. The reason why is clear from the foregoing discussion: a knowledge of the text together with a knowledge of what was commonly believed in the author's community would not enable someone playing our make-believe game to infer that the fictional author believed this. To make a proposition P true in his fiction the author has to compose sentences that, against the background of relevant community belief, make it reasonable for the reader to infer that the fictional author believes *P*.

There is, then, at least one intentional fallacy. But Monroe Beardsley and William Wimsatt seemed to have some larger and more nebulous doctrine in mind as their target in "The Intentional Fallacy." It is the doctrine that "In order to judge the poet's performance, we must know what he intended." To this they replied, "to insist on the designing intellect as a cause is not to grant the design or intention as a standard by which to judge the worth of the poet's performance."[11]

"The Intentional Fallacy" had the emotional attractions, and the intellectual drawbacks, of a radical manifesto. While it portrayed the opposition as confused by a woolly-minded attachment to romantic expression, its sweeping denunciation and urgent message disguised the gaps and ambiguities in the argument. To consider just one obvious defect: Their reply to the intentionalist quoted above illustrates their own commitment to a fallacy. For we might hold that intentions (of certain kinds) are relevant to a decision about the value of the work without holding that these or any other intentions dictate the norms of criticism.

Beardsley and Wimsatt have been roughly handled by their critics, by and large with good reason. But there is a way of taking at least some of what they say which accords well with my own proposal. They begin by claiming that the poem means what its words and sentences mean, not what its author intended it to mean. The meaning, they say, is *internal* to the text. But what they are prepared to call "internal" ends up including more than just the meanings of words and sentences: "What is (1) internal . . . is discovered through the semantics and syntax of a poem, through our habitual knowledge of the language, through grammars, dictionaries and all the literature which is the source of dictionaries, in general *all that makes a language and culture.*"[12]

---

11 "The Intentional Fallacy," *Sewanee Review* 54 (1946): 468–88, reprinted in W. Wimsatt, *The Verbal Icon* (Lexington: University of Kentucky Press, 1954). The quotation is from p. 4 of the reprint.
12 Wimsatt and Beardsley, ibid., p. 10 of the reprint. My italics.

3.3. Intentional meaning and conventional meaning

I am uncertain what Beardsley and Wimsatt meant by "all that makes a culture," but one way of interpreting the phrase puts their position pretty close to my own. For something that goes a long way toward identifying a culture is the pattern of beliefs expressed within that culture. Doyle's (hypothetical) beliefs about aliens would be considered a mere oddity by the historian of Victorian culture, whose material is prevalent belief, rather than idiosyncratic opinion. Public knowledge is partly knowledge of linguistic meaning, which Beardsley and Wimsatt include as legitimate evidence for an interpretation. But it also concerns matters of nonlinguistic fact – the locations of famous buildings, the characters of famous persons, the means of transport most likely to be adopted in a particular situation, together with perhaps more controversial opinions about the existence of ghosts, the likely motives one may have for acting in a certain way, and so forth. Drop the restriction on public knowledge to "internal" textual evidence, and Wimsatt and Beardsley's claim that what is relevant to interpretation is exactly what is public falls in line with my own – at least when we restrict ourselves to the question of fictional truth (more on this restriction in Section 3.4).

3.3. INTENTIONAL MEANING AND CONVENTIONAL MEANING

The tide of opinion has swung against Beardsley and Wimsatt. Two recent literary theorists, Steven Knapp and Walter Benn Michaels, have offered a very radical defense of authorial intention.[13] Meaning, they tell us, is intended meaning, or there is no meaning – only marks or sounds unrelated to language. Because there is no other kind of meaning, "a text means what its author intends it to mean."[14] In particular,

---

13 See their "Against Theory," *Critical Inquiry* 8 (1982): 723–42, and "Against Theory 2: Hermeneutics and Deconstruction," *Critical Inquiry* 14 (1987): 49–68. See also Knapp and Michaels, "A Reply to our Critics," *Critical Inquiry* 9 (1983): 790–800, and "A Reply to Richard Rorty: What is Pragmatism?," *Critical Inquiry* 11 (1985): 466–73.
14 "Against Theory 2," p. 49.

they claim there is no such thing as *conventional* meaning distinct from intended meaning. To assess their argument we need to have before us a clear picture of what conventional meaning is supposed to be and how it is supposed to relate to intended meaning.

In Chapter 1, I outlined a theory, based on the work of Grice, about what it is for someone to mean something by saying (or, more generally, doing) something. According to that theory, I mean by my utterance of X that P just in case I utter X intending to get you to believe (or to make believe) that P, and intending that one of your reasons for responding in this way will be your recognition of that very intention.[15] This is an account of *intentional* meaning; it is an account of what a speaker means (intends) by his words. To get an account of *conventional* meaning we need first an account of convention, and then a story about what conventions of language might be.

The primary objection to accounts of language in terms of convention has been that conventions of meaning seem to require agreement between members of the language community. But there never was any such agreement, and, indeed, there could not have been; for how can there be agreement about language prior to language? Some years ago, David Lewis developed an account of convention according to which there can be convention without agreement.[16] Lewis's claim is (roughly) that a convention (not necessarily a convention of language) is a regularity of behavior within a group where the regularity solves (and is commonly known to solve) a recurrent problem (a "coordination problem") that members of the group face, and where the regularity is continued because it is known to solve the problem. It is a convention, where I live, to drive on the left because we do regularly drive on the left, because we want to coordinate our driving with that of others, because we realize that by

---

15 This is, of course, a simplification. For greater detail, see Section 1.7.
16 See Lewis, *Convention* (Cambridge, Mass.: Harvard University Press, 1969), esp. chap. 1.

driving on the left we achieve the right kind of coordination, and because this is merely one of several ways we could achieve it. Everyone prefers to drive on the left just in case everyone else does, driving on the left being no more intrinsically desirable than driving on the right.

Conventions of meaning can be similarly analyzed. We want to establish a regularity in the use of signs so as to avoid having to start from scratch every time we try to communicate. We don't care very much what signs are used to communicate what bits of information; we care much more that the same sign be used to communicate the same thing. Knowing that we all know and want the same thing in this regard, a regularity of use is sustained. The regularity becomes a convention. In a language like English there are in fact two kinds of conventions at work: conventions governing the meanings of words, and conventions governing the ways in which words can be combined to make meaningful sentences. Thus, it's a convention with us to use the word "red" to refer to the property of redness. And it's a convention with us that a name of an object followed by the copula followed by a predicate is a sentence that is true just in case the object named has the property named by that predicate. These two kinds of conventions work together to produce the result that, for instance, "Fred is tall" is true just in case Fred is (has the property) tall(ness). That Fred is tall is what "Fred is tall" conventionally means.

Now someone can say, "Fred is tall," and *not* mean by it what that sentence conventionally means. The speaker might be speaking ironically, intending to get the audience to believe that Fred is in fact short. We have already seen that a speaker may, in the right circumstances, reasonably expect the audience to understand, on the basis of their acquaintance with conversational rules, that this is his intention.[17] In that case the speaker speaks contrary to the prevailing conventions of the language. What he means by uttering that sentence is something other than what that sentence conven-

---

17 See Section 1.7.

tionally means. Here conventional meaning and intentional meaning come apart.

Sentences are the primary vehicles of conventional meaning ("C-meaning," as I shall call it) while utterances of sentences are the primary vehicles of intentional meaning ("I-meaning"). Let us say that an utterance has whatever C-meaning the sentence it is an utterance of has. In that case we can say, of any given utterance, what its C-meaning and its I-meaning are, and whether they are the same.

With this – very rough – account of conventional meaning let us go back to the thesis of Knapp and Michaels: A text means what its author intended it to mean. Their first argument is based on a kind of example, now rather familiar, designed to show that language-like marks produced by natural forces or in some other unintentional way, would not be linguistic items at all and would have no meaning.[18] Weather may cause a pattern of cracks in a rock face that look exactly like an inscription of the English sentence "Welcome to Wales." But it won't be an inscription of that sentence unless the pattern was caused by someone who intended the resulting pattern to be an inscription of English.[19]

But the example does not show that there is no difference between I- and C-meaning. It shows merely that marks or sounds cannot have *any* meaning unless they are intentionally produced. If I throw coins on the ground and they form the pattern of the sentence "Welcome to Wales," I have not produced anything meaningful in either the I- or the C-sense. If, on the other hand, I arrange the coins so as to form that sentence, I have produced a sentence that C-means Welcome to Wales. But that may not be what I mean by producing the sentence. If I am a member of a militant Welsh nationalist group, I may intend it to be taken as an ironic warning to English tourists.

Knapp and Michaels consider a case apparently of this

---

18 See "Against Theory," p. 727.
19 See Section 1.10. "Welcome to Wales" is an example of Richard Taylor's that he puts to a rather different purpose. See his *Metaphysics*, 3rd ed. (Englewood Cliffs, N.J.: Prentice-Hall, 1983), pp. 100–1.

latter kind: an ironic utterance of the word "go." Doesn't the speaker here notice a discrepancy between *I*-meaning ("stop") and *C*-meaning ("go")? They say no: "The utterance only counts as ironic if the speaker *intends* that both the conventional meaning and the departure from conventional meaning be recognized. Since both aspects of an ironic utterance are equally intentional, irony in no way frees the meaning of the utterance from the speaker's intention."[20]

Knapp and Michaels are right, more or less, to say that irony (or any other kind of nonliteral speech) depends on the speaker's intending that "both conventional meaning and the departure from conventional meaning be recognized." But we cannot infer from this that the *C*-meaning is nothing different from the *I*-meaning, for in speaking ironically, a speaker intends the audience to *recognize the disparity between* C*-meaning and* I*-meaning*. Nor can we infer the weaker conclusion that *C*-meaning, like *I*-meaning, depends on the speaker's intentions. If the speaker had said "go" thinking that this word conventionally means "stop," he would simply have been making a mistake. Having decided to utter the English word "go," the speaker is not able to determine what the *C*-meaning of that word is, although it is up to him to determine what, on this occasion of use, its *I*-meaning is.

We can see a common thread running through the errors of Knapp and Michaels. It is to suppose that the distinction between *I*- and *C*-meaning can be undermined by observing that every act of speech is in some way or other intentional. Once we are careful to distinguish the different kinds of meaning-related intentions a speaker may have, their argument collapses.[21]

---

20 "Against Theory 2," p. 54. Italics in the original. Note that this remark is hard to square with their rejection of the *concept* of conventional meaning, since they tell us about a speaker who intends the *conventional meaning* of his utterance to be recognized.

21 Knapp and Michaels warn against misinterpretations of their thesis that would commit them to the view that meaning and intention are the same thing. They

3. Interpretation

I have been defending the coherence of the distinction between *I*-meaning and *C*-meaning. Both are kinds of meaning that the text of a fictional work has, and the *I*-meaning and the *C*-meaning of a fictional text – or of any kind of text – will coincide a good deal of the time. But there is a kind of meaning, in perhaps a slightly extended sense of "meaning," that only a fictional text may have. It is the kind of meaning I have been concerned with in this chapter and the previous one. It is the meaning we discover when we decide what is true in the story. Let us call this "story-meaning." One who is undecided between the supernatural and the psychological interpretations of *The Turn of the Screw* and who wonders which to adopt is wondering about story-meaning. Story-meaning depends partly on *C*-meaning; if the words of the text had different *C*-meanings, different things would probably be true in the story. My antiintentionalism consists in the thesis that story-meaning does not depend on what the author meant by his words. But in working out story-meaning we still need recourse to the concept of *I*-meaning. We have seen that working out what is true in the story is a matter of working out what the fictional author believes. In deciding what the fictional author believes we take the text as the expression of his beliefs. But we do not always assume that the text expresses literally what he believes. The fictional author expresses himself – so we make believe – by using language in the way a real person does: sometimes literally and sometimes not. Working out what the fictional author believes may involve us in judging – again, as part of our make-believe – that his description of a character is meant ironically, or metaphorically, or in some other nonliteral way. Thus we employ the concept of *I*-meaning as well as *C*-meaning when we decide what is true in the story. But in applying the concept of *I*-meaning we do not seek to decide how the real author intended his words to be taken.

note that "not all intentions are intentions to mean" ("Against Theory 2," p. 49, note 2). My claim is that they are, in fact, subject to a slightly less obvious confusion: supposing that all intentions *concerning meaning* are intentions to mean.

3.4. *The return of the author*

3.4. THE RETURN OF THE AUTHOR

All this sounds, no doubt, like an anglophone version of Roland Barthes's "death of the author."[22] But the intentions of the real, rather than the fictional, author do play a role in those interpretative strategies that take a broader view of their textual object than the view we have so far considered in this chapter and the last. There is more to interpreting a text than just finding out what story it has to tell, and there is more to the experience of fiction than is explicable in terms of make-believe.

When critics talk about the objectivity of meaning and the role of authorial intention in determining it, they often do not distinguish clearly between the various kinds of meaning that can be ascribed to a text. For them, "meaning" seems to mean any aspect of the work, broadly connected with its language, that can be investigated by the critic. This chapter is mostly concerned with one narrow and perhaps pedestrian sense of "the meaning of the text": what I have called story-meaning. In fact, critics often ignore this aspect of meaning in their theoretical discussions and concentrate instead on questions about the work's genre, its symbolic elements, its underlying moral and aesthetic vision. My primary interest is not in these things, and I have no developed theoretical framework for dealing with them. What I have said about the notion of fictional truth allows no ready generalization to cover these other aspects. I have concentrated on story meaning here partly because it is the most tractable element in all that can' be called, in the broad sense just indicated, the meaning of a fictional work; it seems to be that aspect most likely to yield to an analysis of some precision. Another reason is that story meaning is basic to our understanding of these other, perhaps more glamorous,

---

22 See Barthes' "The Death of the Author," in *Image–Music–Text*, essays selected and translated by Stephen Heath (London: Fontana, 1977). See also Michel Foucault, "What is an Author?," in D. Bouchard (ed.), *Language, Countermemory, Practice* (Ithaca, N.Y., Cornell University Press, 1977).

kinds of meaning. If we have no firm grip on the story the work has to tell – if we are confused about what is true in the story – we are likely to go wrong in our probing of its symbolic or metaphysical content. A final reason for concentrating on story meaning is that it is a kind of meaning peculiar to fictional works, and it is with fiction that we are concerned here.

Since there are important aspects of the work not analyzable in terms of story-meaning, and since our response to and judgments about the work depend crucially on our perception of these aspects, it follows that there is a great deal in our response to the work that is not analyzable in terms of make-believe. Our response to a work will depend not only on the structure of the story but upon the *purpose* we perceive that structure to have, upon our *expectations* about the way in which the story will develop as we read, and upon our perception of certain elements as having a certain kind of *salience* within the story. And our perception of these things depends crucially on assumptions we make about the author's intentions. The purpose of a work is, after all, the purpose it was intended to have. McGonagall's poetry is funny partly because it was seriously meant, and Fielding's *Shamela Andrews* would be a mystifying work if we did not know it was intended as a travesty of Richardson's *Pamela*.[23]

Perception that the work belongs to a certain genre will influence our expectations about plot development and our recognition of certain elements within it as having salience. Suppose I'm reading a detective novel, a novel that appears to have all the features standard for the genre. Awareness of the work's genre will create in me all sorts of expectations about what is likely to happen later in the work (it will be the least likely suspect who will be revealed to have done it) and about what things are relevant to the outcome (the appar-

---

23 P. D. Juhl gives an interesting example of a poem that might be thought to parody racist sentiment but that was actually intended to endorse it. See his *Interpretation*, pp. 121–2.

ently least relevant thing will be the vital clue). But these sorts of expectations – often an integral part of our response to the work - are not produced within the make-believe framework. It is part of the make-believe adopted by the reader that the text is assertively uttered, and within that make-believe he cannot suspect the least likely character *just because* he is the least likely one. (It is not true in the story that the unlikely always happens; a detective novel in which that was true would be an attempt to subvert the genre.) And genre membership is, at least in part, a matter of authorial intention. A work belongs to a genre not merely in virtue of having features characteristic of that genre but because it was intended that the audience should recognize those features as significant in a certain way. It is possible, as James Thurber so hilariously showed, to interpret *Macbeth* as a murder mystery, because one can find within it elements characteristic of the genre. Its not being one is a matter, in part, of those elements not being intended to have the salience they would have in a genuine murder mystery.[24]

All this has little to do with make-believe. If one's response to a fictional work were nothing more than a make-believe engagement with the beliefs of the fictional author, considerations about the intentions of the real author would not be able to affect our response to the work. But clearly they do affect it. The response to fiction is a complex product of make-believe and judgments about the work that do not occur within the scope of the make-believe at all.

3.5. THE TEXT

There is another important aspect of the work determined by the author's intentions: the text. The text of the work is *the text the author intended it to have.* I don't mean by this that if the author merely intended the text to be better than it turned out to be, there is a nonvisible text that is the real text of the

---

24 See James Thurber, "The Macbeth Murder Mystery," in *The Thurber Carnival* (New York: Random House, 1957).

work, better than the written text. The text of the work is determined not by the writer's general, unspecific intentions to produce a text that is, say, powerful in a certain way; it is determined by the author's *lexically specific* intentions. The author has a lexically specific intention when he intends to write a certain word or sequence of words, spelled in a certain way. When the author has such an intention his act of writing may fail to embody that intention. He may, through oversight, write something that does not correctly mirror his intentions. If he does, the text he inscribes will deviate in some way from the text of the work.

Editors routinely correct the manuscripts of authors, sometimes, no doubt, referring their corrections back to them for authorization. But where the author is not available for comment such corrections are still frequently made. What principles may guide us in such a case? We might suppose that a change is judged allowable simply if its brings the text into line with correct spelling conventions. But we see on reflection that a spelling change is allowable only if there is reason to think the change brought the spelling of the text into line with the spelling the author intended, and not allowable merely on the grounds that the change amounts to a correction in the above sense. A copy editor who "corrected" the spelling in an anthology of poems by e. e. cummings would not keep his job long. The reason we would deplore such a change is that we have reason to believe that cummings intended his poems (like his name) to be spelled in a nonstandard way. Faced with a text that shows no signs of having been produced with such an intention, we correct the occasional misspelling with a good conscience. But when doubts about the author's intentions creep in, we hesitate.

It might be argued that whatever our editorial practices may be, the principle I offer as a rationalization of them has an unacceptable result: that where the author has false beliefs about how a word is spelled, those beliefs will feed into intentions that will set his mistakes in concrete. If the author intends to spell "cat" "c-a-t-t" because he thinks that's how it's correctly spelled, then the intentionally determined text will have all occurrences of "cat" misspelled. And this would be a gratuitous multiplication of error. But in these cases of error based on ignorance the author has conflicting intentions. He intends to spell "cat" correctly, and because he believes that it's spelled "c-a-t-t" he intends to spell it like that. In such a case the intention to spell the word correctly dominates the intention to spell it any particular way. If the error were pointed out to the author, he would abandon the intention to spell it that way. (If he did not abandon it, and insisted in a cummings-like way on the misspelling, the misspelling would have to prevail.) So we let the dominant intention determine the text at this point. This shows that we cannot understand the phrase "lexically specific intentions" to apply narrowly to intentions to write a certain series of letters in a certain order; to do so would be to rob ourselves of the opportunity to solve the kind of problem we are considering here by allowing the intention to spell the word *correctly* to dominate. Lexically specific intentions are intentions to write words spelled in the manner *F*, where "the manner *F*" might be "c-a-t-t" or "the correct sequence of letters for spelling 'cat.' " On the other hand, merely intending to spell the word the way it would be spelled by someone who was a bad speller would not count as a lexically specific intention; there is no unique way that a bad speller would spell "cat," and "the way a bad speller would spell 'cat' " is an improper description.

3.6. STORY AND STYLE

There is a temptation to suppose that what is true in a fictional story has little to do with the style in which it is written. After all, two works of fiction may tell the same story but be stylistically quite different, and works may be written in the same style and tell quite different stories. Story and style are indeed logically independent in this sense, but nonetheless there are important relations between them. In particular, the style of the work may contribute to the determination of what is true in it.

3. Interpretation

The somewhat obscure concept of style has been significantly clarified by Jenefer Robinson, who argues that individual style – as opposed to the style of a group or period – is the way in which the author expresses a personality through the text.[25] Stylistic elements are just those aspects of the text that contribute to the expression of that personality. Robinson makes a distinction, as I do, between the real and the fictional author, although she does not use my terminology. The personality expressed through the text may not be the real author's own. That personality may be pessimistic or misogynistic, rigidly conventional or sternly moralistic, without the real author being any of these things. But if that is the personality the style suggests, that is the personality the fictional author has.

Robinson's thesis has a number of interesting implications. For instance, she notes that works sharing certain formal features may be quite different stylistically because the formal quality may contribute to the expression in each work of a very different personality. For example, euphony is a significant feature both of Swinburne's *Garden of Proserpine* and of *Paradise Lost*, "but the personalities expressed in the individual style of these two works are very different. In the Swinburne poem the gentle, musical sounds help to express the implied author's sense of world-weariness, melancholy and resignation, whereas the famous Miltonic melody generally serves to help express the implied author's sense of the dignity and grandeur of his theme."[26]

If we combine Robinson's hypothesis with what I have said in Chapter 2 about fictional truth, we can see a close connection between the individual style of a fiction and what is true in that fiction; stylistic features will be crucial determinants of what is true in the story. Inferring the author's beliefs will require us to make all sorts of assumptions about what kind of person he is. Is the author cynical or idealistic,

25 See Jenefer Robinson, "Style and Personality in the Literary Work," *Philosophical Review* 94 (1985): 227–47. See also her "General and Individual Style in Literature," *Journal of Aesthetics and Art Criticism* 43 (1984): 147–58.
26 "Style and Personality in the Literary Work," p. 240.

credulous or skeptical? Two authors may write superficially similar stories, but stylistic features of their work may indicate very different personalities. If they do, there may be only a narrow area of intersection between what is true in the two fictions, because there is only a narrow intersection between the belief sets of their fictional authors. Thus we see why style is so very important in fiction. It is not just a matter of literary elegance, it is a matter of the very identity of the fictional story itself. Style and content are thus not independent features of a fictional work.

In at least a good deal of nonfiction it is easier to separate style and content. When it comes to assessing, say, a scientific treatise, we want to distinguish between what the author said and the style in which he said it. Presumably Einstein could have given us exactly the same theory in his 1905 paper on relativity even if he had adopted a different style. Certain stylistic devices, if adopted by scientific or technical writers, can very often obscure the content of their writings. But in fiction a style, even an obscure style, is a partial determinant of the story's content. Thus it is with Henry James, whose convoluted style is an important clue to the fictional author's belief in the endless complexity of human motivation.

3.7. FICTIONAL AUTHOR AND NARRATOR

Some fictions have explicit narrators, as Watson is the narrator in the Holmes story. Watson is a character named and described in the text and his actions form part of the story's explicit content. Sometimes works have a number of different narrators of this kind, as in certain epistolary novels. Sometimes the narrator is someone who has come to know about the story but takes no part in it except in its telling. Sometimes the text signals no explicit narrator and seems to be written from no particular perspective at all. Here it is only the fact that the story is being told that signals the existence of a teller. Shall we identify the fictional author with the explicit narrator if there is one and postulate an unobtrusive narrator if there is not? Such a strategy would lead to trouble.

3. Interpretation

Explicit narrators are notoriously unreliable. It is true in the Holmes story that Watson is less intelligent than he thinks he is, but we could not work this out be inferring that Watson believes himself to be less intelligent than he thinks he is. In Nabokov's *Pale Fire* the narrator Kinbote is either lying or deluded (or both) about his relations to the poet John Shade, whose life he chronicles. Where there are several narrators, their perceptions of the facts may clash – an extreme example of this is Kurosawa's film *Rashomon*, in which we are presented with four equally credible accounts of a purported crime.[27] Some explicit narrators show every sign of being reliable, but this isn't something we can count on. What the explicit narrator believes and what is true in the story can always come apart. The reader must decide, as his reading progresses, whether to put his faith in the explicit narrator. When we decide that the explicit narrator cannot be trusted we move to the level of an unobtrusive narrator who, by putting words in the mouth of the explicit narrator in a certain way, signals his skepticism about what the explicit narrator says.

To say we postulate a teller when no teller is apparent may seem an ad hoc move in defense of a theory which has it that there must be a teller. In fact, there is nothing very implausible about the suggestion. Suppose Nabokov's utterance (his fiction-making utterance) of *Pale Fire* had not consisted in an act of writing but rather in a verbal utterance of the text to his assembled admirers. Quite probably the audience would understand that the performance was in a certain sense *ironic*, that they were not to take the utterances as issuing from an intention on the speaker's part that they make believe what is literally uttered. The audience, if its members had the right kind of sensitivity, would recognize the intention that we make believe the utterances are those of someone called "Kinbote," and that these utterances are not always in conformity with what is true in the story. By his manner of uttering, the speaker indicates to us that the

27 Martin Ritt's film *The Outrage* is an English language version of the same story.

124

words he utters are really those of someone whose picture of himself and of his relations to the world is distorted. In that case the audience would see the speaker at one remove from the character Kinbote, even though Kinbote's words issue from the speaker's mouth in first-person form. They would see that the speaker's perspective on the story is different from Kinbote's, and they would see the speaker's perspective as the reliable guide to what is true in the story. This is what happens, I claim, when we read Nabokov's story.

It might be claimed that I have fallen here into an error I have urged us to avoid: the error of identifying the fictional author with the real author, in this case Nabokov. It is Nabokov, after all, who is uttering the story. But the teller of the tale, the one who tells it as known fact, is not Nabokov. The teller is a character in the game of make-believe played by the audience. Nabokov, as he reads, plays the part of the teller; in the game he is taken to be someone who is telling the story as known fact. Whatever members of the audience know about Nabokov's own beliefs will not enter into their calculations about what is true in the story, for they know that Nabokov is not telling the story as known fact. Instead they imagine themselves in the presence of one who tells a story he knows to be true by speaking with the voice of one of the (unreliable) characters in the story.

I have said that reading a work of fiction always involves the assumption that the text is uttered as known fact by someone who may not appear as a character in the work, and whose presence may not even be signaled by the use of "I" or any similar device. But another objection may now be put. Some works of fiction seem to preclude the possibility that they could be told as known fact. Suppose a fiction has it that there is no intelligent life. (I shall call this genre "mindless fiction"). How can it be sensible to suppose that the story is being told as known fact, when it is part of the story that there is nobody there to tell it?

On my theory mindless fiction generates a game of make-believe in which we are called upon to make believe contradictory things: that it is told as known fact and that there is no one there to tell it. This doesn't mean, of course, that such a game is impossible, or trivial, or indistinguishable from any other game in which there is a conflict within our make-believe. As we have seen, there are time-travel stories that generate games of make-believe in which we are called upon to make believe that P and to make believe that not-P. Let us call games of make-believe with this feature "flawed games." Those who claim that reading fiction does not require the reader to invoke a fictional author will argue, no doubt, that works belonging to the genre of mindless fiction do not, at least not always, generate flawed games. They will argue that mindless fiction is as easy and natural a genre as any other – that it's only my theory that gives mindless fiction a problematic structure.

I believe they are wrong. There is independent evidence – evidence that comes from considerations quite unrelated to the explanation of truth in fiction – for the idea that fiction reading requires us to postulate a fictional author, even in the case of a mindless fiction. The argument depends upon some results presented in the next chapter. So we must see the results before we see the argument.[28]

28 See Section 4.7.

Chapter 4

The characters of fiction

Fictional characters begin their lives in fictional stories. They may have antecedents in real life or in mistaken accounts of real life, but we can properly say that we have a fictional character only when we have a fictional story, however imprecise, that enfolds the character. We might think fictional characters capable of transcending the fictions they arrive in. Faust, Holmes, and others appear in a variety of works in a variety of media, with different authors contributing their own perspectives. Or so we say. I shall argue that we ought not to say such things, or at least that we ought not to take such things seriously when we do. But even if one thinks of fictional characters as thoroughly promiscuous in their relations to fictional works, it is hard to believe that we can learn anything about them by casting aside the stories in which they appear and searching for the characters themselves. I am very far from believing that we can, in general, think about the world only by thinking about the language we use to describe it. But with fictional characters there does not seem to be any other way. Accordingly, my focus in this chapter will be on the ways in which we describe fictional characters and, in particular, on the ways in which we use expressions that purport to be names of them. Expressions of this kind, expressions like "Sherlock Holmes," I call *fictional names.*

Holmes, so the story goes, is a human being. There are other kinds of fictional characters: fictional places, horses,

swords, substances. Not all of them have names in the stories
in which they occur and in some of these stories there are
mystical reasons why they could not have names. There is
nothing special about a fictional character because it gets a
name in the fiction, and a general account of fictional characters should be an account of the named and the unnamed.
Mine will be such an account. But the names of fictional characters are a good place to start.

4.1. FICTIONAL NAMES AND PROPER NAMES

We should not start by assuming that fictional names are
genuine proper names. We need to know more about fictional names and proper names before we can decide
whether they are. To suppose it uncontroversial that fictional
names are proper names is to confuse what is true in a story
with what is true. It is certainly true in the Holmes story that
"Holmes" is a proper name – the name, in fact, of a great
detective. But what is true in a fiction need not be true. Let
us try, therefore, to characterize fictional names in such a
way as to leave it an open question whether they are proper
names. A fictional name will certainly be an expression of
which it is true in the story that it is a proper name. But there
is more to being a fictional name than this, if fictional names
are to be tied closely to fictional *characters*. Napoleon is a character in *War and Peace*, but not a fictional character, and so we
shall not count "Napoleon," as used by Tolstoy, as a fictional
name. Although it is true in *War and Peace* that "Napoleon"
is the proper name of Napoleon, that name is not a fictional
name because there is someone – an actually existing person
– of whom it is true in the story that "Napoleon" is his name.
By contrast, although it is true in the Holmes story that
"Holmes" is a proper name, there is no existing person of
whom it is true in the stories that "Holmes" is his name. Generally: an expression N is a fictional name if it is true in the
fiction that N is a proper name but not true in the fiction of
any existing person or thing that N is a name of that person
or thing.

4.1. Fictional names and proper names

Authors of fiction frequently "have in mind" some real person when they introduce a name into their fictions, but that need not prevent the name from being a fictional name. We know that Lewis Carroll had Alice Liddell in mind when he used the name "Alice" in *Alice's Adventures in Wonderland*. But it is not true in the story that "Alice" refers to Alice Liddell, and "Alice" as used by Carroll in the story is a fictional name. Recall from Chapter 2 that what is true in the story is a matter of what it is reasonable to infer the fictional author believed. Because many of Napoleon's characteristics were common knowledge at the time *War and Peace* was written, and because the description in that book of the character called "Napoleon" comes close to fitting Napoleon, it is reasonable to infer that the fictional author of *War and Peace* intended that "Napoleon" refer to Napoleon, and hence that he believed that it did. Because Alice Liddell was not at all well known at the time of writing, it is not reasonable to infer that the fictional author of *Alice's Adventures in Wonderland* believed that "Alice" referred to her; without identifying the fictional author with Lewis Carroll one would simply never make this inference. As with much else concerning truth in fiction, whether it is true in a story that a name refers to an actually existing person will sometimes be indeterminate, and so it will be correspondingly indeterminate whether the name is a fictional name. From now on I shall assume we are dealing with expressions that are clear cases of fictional names.

I said that it is true in the story that "Holmes" is the proper name of someone. Is "Holmes" really a proper name? If so it is an *empty* proper name, since there is no one that "Holmes," as used in the stories, refers to. Now, fictional names do seem to be meaningful; they contribute to the meanings of sentences in which they occur. If they did not, it would be unclear how we could understand fictional stories. So if fictional names are proper names, we need an account of how empty proper names can contribute to the meanings of sentences in which they appear. It is not generally supposed that an expression must have a reference in order to be meaning-

4. The characters of fiction

ful. Definite descriptions, like "The present king of England" and "Fred's favorite property," are meaningful even though there is no present king of England and Fred has no favorite among the properties. A description theory of proper names has it that proper names are really just disguised or abbreviated descriptions, and so can be meaningful without having a reference. But description theories of naming have come in for harsh criticism. These criticisms are well known, and I shall not rehearse them here.[1] I want instead to examine the problem posed for an account of fictional names by an alternative to the descriptionist view. This alternative is sometimes called the theory of "direct reference."[2]

According to this alternative, the meaning or "semantic role" of a proper name – its contribution to the meanings of sentences in which it occurs – is specified simply by specifying its reference. In the sentence "Walter Scott is famous," "Walter Scott" functions merely to pick out the individual Scott, and that sentence is true in a world just in case Scott is famous in that world. Thus, the possibility of specifying the truth conditions for this sentence depend upon there

1 See, for instance, Saul Kripke, *Naming and Necessity*, 2nd ed. (Oxford: Basil Blackwell, 1980), Lecture 1; and Michael Devitt, *Designation* (New York: Columbia University Press, 1981), chap. 1.
2 The theory of direct reference goes back to Mill and Russell. Recent interest in the theory developed largely out of work on demonstratives and other indexicals done by David Kaplan (see, e.g., "Dthat," in Peter Cole (ed.), *Syntax and Semantics*, vol. 9: *Pragmatics* [New York: Academic Press, 1978)], and John Perry ("The Problem of the Essential Indexical," *Nous* 13 [1979]: 3–21). Recent defenses and elaborations of the theory are to be found in Joseph Almog, "Semantic Anthropology," in P. French, T. Uehling, and H. Wettstein (eds.), *Midwest Studies in Philosophy, Volume IX: Causation and Causal Theories* (Minneapolis: University of Minnesota Press, 1984), "Form and Content," *Nous* 19 (1985): 603–16, "Naming Without Necessity," *Journal of Philosophy* 83 (1986): 210–42; Nathan Salmon, *Frege's Puzzle* (Cambridge, Mass.: MIT Press, 1986); Scott Soames, "Direct Reference and Propositional Attitudes," in J. Almog, J. Perry, and H. Wettstein (eds.), *Themes From Kaplan* (New York: Oxford University Press, 1988), pp. 383–409; Howard Wettstein, "Has Semantics Rested on a Mistake?," *Journal of Philosophy* 83 (1986): 185–209.
  Similar theories are to be found in the work of Gareth Evans (*The Varieties of Reference* [Oxford: Clarendon Press, 1982] and John McDowell ("On the Sense and Reference of a Proper Name," *Mind* 84 [1977]: 159–84). Evans's views are discussed in Section 4.10.

4.1. Fictional names and proper names

being an individual Scott. If there is not – if "Scott" is an empty name – then "Scott" contributes nothing to the truth conditions of the sentence, for the sentence simply has no truth conditions. If fictional names are proper names, not merely in the superficial sense that they are semantically unstructured, but in the deeper sense that they are directly referring devices, then we are obliged to show that they do have reference or admit they are meaningless.[3]

In my view fictional names are not to be thought of as belonging to the category of proper names, so they are not empty proper names and the challenge from direct reference theory can be avoided. But before I lay out my own proposal I want to examine four alternative theories that do take up the challenge. According to the first three we can find a reference for "Holmes" even while admitting that Holmes does not exist. According to the fourth, we can explain our understanding of a fictional story while admitting that "Holmes" is an empty proper name. Although the first two of these theories strike me as untenable, I am far from sure that the third and fourth are wrong. If it turns out that there is something fundamentally amiss with my own account, it will be worth taking a closer look at them.

It should also be noted that there are other problems we must face if we deny that fictional names have reference. For example, some of the sentences in which these expressions occur seem to be true. It is true, for instance, that Sherlock Holmes is a character in a fictional work. How could this be true if "Sherlock Holmes" does not refer to anything? I confront this problem in Section 4.11.

---

3 An expression is semantically unstructured when it does not have independently meaningful parts that contribute to the meaning of the whole. In this sense "Napoleon Bonaparte" is semantically unstructured. Even a name like "Crazy Horse" is semantically unstructured because its parts, although independently meaningful, do not determine that it refers to a (the?) thing that is crazy and a horse.

4. The characters of fiction

4.2. EXISTENT AND NONEXISTENT THINGS

One way to respond to the claim that fictional names don't refer is to make a distinction between what there is and what exists. There are existing things and nonexisting things, and Holmes, along with phlogiston, the planet Vulcan, and a great many other things, is among the nonexisting things (in a once favored vocabulary, these things "subsist"). And the fact that these things don't exist need not stop us referring to them; we can refer to the things that don't exist as well as to the things that do. A view like this is appealing if we want to make sense of the idea that Sherlock Holmes is a smoker, a detective, and nonexistent.[4] But it is open to an objection that is both simple and devastating. Holmes, that nonexistent person, presumably *thinks* he exists. A Holmes who did not would be no candidate for the Holmes of the stories, for it is undoubtedly true in the stories that Holmes thinks he exists. And nothing this Holmes could discover about himself would convince him that he did not exist, for a Holmes capable of being shown that he did not exist would once again not be the Holmes of Doyle's invention. How, then, do we know that *we* exist, since our epistemic situation is just like that of Holmes? What could we ever do to establish that we exist? Nothing, according to those who think that some things are real and some things not. For we would not be able to say, with Descartes, that we know immediately that we exist from the fact of our consciousness; some nonexistent things – Holmes for one – are conscious. This radically extended skepticism might make entertaining fiction in the style of Pirandello, but it is surely not a serious philosophical option. A metaphysics that gives credence to it must be rejected.[5]

4 This view, which goes back to Alexius Meinong, has been developed at length and with great clarity by Terence Parsons (see his *Nonexistent Objects* [New Haven, Yale University Press, 1980]).

5 See David Lewis, *On the Plurality of Worlds* (Oxford: Basil Blackwell, 1986), p. 93. Lewis credits the argument to D. C. Williams (see Williams's "Dispensing with Existence," *Journal of Philosophy* 59 (1962): 748–63).

4.3. Reference fixing and descriptive names

4.3. REFERENCE FIXING AND DESCRIPTIVE
NAMES

A second proposal starts by distinguishing between what exists and what is *actual*. What is actual is what exists in the actual world (@), and that world is just one of many. Things that exist in worlds other than @ are nonactual existents. Could Holmes and his fictional fellows be nonactual existents? Early in this Chapter I confidently asserted that Holmes does not exist, but this was rather like my confident breakfast-time assertion that there is no milk: no milk around here, I mean. My "Holmes does not exist" was really meant, like most statements of this form, as an assertion that Holmes does not exist in the actual world; that, after all, is all you have to claim if you think that no one who has ever lived is Holmes. Holmes's actual nonexistence is consistent with his nonactual existence.

The idea that Holmes is a nonactual existent is not subject to the same objection as the last proposal, for it is not now being denied that Holmes exists. Nor is it subject to a variant objection that substitutes doubt about our actuality for doubts about our existence. If Holmes exists in another world, he is right to think that he is actual, just as we are right to think that we are. "Actual," like "here" and "now," is indexical, depending for its reference on the context of utterance.[6] To say that Holmes is nonactual is like saying that someone in the next room is not here; the person in the next room can say the same thing of us, and Holmes can say of us that we are not actual. That, at least, is the proposal before us.

The proposal may avoid the charge that it lands us in an unintelligible skepticism, but there is another objection to it.[7]

6 See David Lewis, "Anselm and Actuality," *Nous* 4 (1970): 175–88. Reprinted in his *Philosophical Papers*, vol. 1.

7 The objection presented here is similar to one presented by David Kaplan, "Bob and Carol and Ted and Alice," in J. Hintikka (ed.), *Approaches to Natural Language* (Dordrecht: D. Reidel, 1973), pp. 490–518. See also Alvin Plantinga, *The Nature of Necessity* (New York: Oxford University Press, 1974), esp. pp. 155–159; Saul

4. The characters of fiction

The objection parallels our earlier objection to the idea of fictional worlds.[8] For it to be true (that is, true in the actual world) that Holmes exists in a nonactual world w, it must be the case that an inhabitant of w is the reference of the expression "Holmes" *as we use it.* But how can our use of the expression "Holmes" pick out any inhabitant of w who is not also an inhabitant of the actual world (@)? Because Holmes does not exist in @ we cannot identify him by ostension and say "*that* is Holmes in w." All we can do is identify him by description: presumably as the person who does and is all (or some of) the things Holmes is said to do and be in the story. Now if, as we are supposing for the time being, "Holmes" is a genuine proper name – a directly referring expression – "Holmes" cannot merely abbreviate some description extracted from the story. It must be what Gareth Evans called a "descriptive name": a name the reference of which is fixed by description.[9] Thus we might introduce a proper name in the following way: We say "Let us use 'Julius' to refer to the person, if there is one, who invented the zip fastener." Here the description "The person who invented the zip fastener" serves not to give the *meaning* of the name "Julius" but merely to fix its reference. Suppose it was individual A who actually invented the zip fastener. Then, given the way we have introduced the name "Julius," that name refers in each world to A, whether or not A is the person who, in that world, invented the zip fastener. "Julius," so introduced, is a "rigid designator": an expression that refers to the same individual in every possible world. And being a rigid designator is required of it if it's to be a directly referring expression. "Julius invented the zip fastener" is to be true in a world

Kripke, *Naming and Necessity*, pp. 158; and Kendall Walton, "Are Representations Symbols?," *The Monist* 58 (1974): 236–54.

8 See Section 2.1.

9 See Evans, "Reference and Contingency," in *Collected Papers* (Oxford: Clarendon Press, 1985). The example of Julius is due to Evans. The idea of a description's being used to fix the reference, rather than to give the meaning, of a proper name is due to Kripke. See *Naming and Necessity*, pp. 55–8.

just in case it was individual A who invented the zip fastener in that world.

In the example just given, the description fixes the reference of "Julius" because there actually is someone who fits the description. But that's exactly what is not the case with "Holmes." There is no one in the actual world who does and is the things Holmes is said in the story to be and do. Of course, if the description of Holmes in the story is consistent, there are worlds in which there is such a person, since a description possibly true of someone is true of someone in some world. Suppose w_1 is such a world. In w_1 there is an individual, B, who does and is those things. But our reference-fixing activities at the actual world cannot make "Holmes" a proper name of B. For suppose that in w_2 there is *another* individual, C, who does and is those same things. Then the description we have chosen to fix the reference of "Holmes" does not distinguish between B and C. But a genuinely reference-fixing description would have to choose between them. It would have to be a description that made it the case that if "Holmes" refers to B in some world, it refers to B in all worlds; "Holmes" must be rigid if it is to be a directly referring term. We could try to add to the description that fixes the reference of "Holmes" in such a way that the modified description will pick out B rather than C. But even supposing we could do this, which is far from clear, it would be by a purely arbitrary stipulation that we would fix the reference for "Holmes" as B rather than as C. C has as much right to be the reference of "Holmes" as B has, since C satisfies any description we might extract from the story as well as B does. In looking for a reference for "Holmes" we are looking for a reference for "Holmes" *as that expression is used in the story.* From the point of view of the stories, there is nothing to choose between B and C as the reference for "Holmes." Each is a best possible candidate for being the reference, since they both have all the properties ascribed to Holmes in the story. But they cannot *both* be the reference, if "Holmes" is to be a directly referring expression. So neither is. So nobody is.

4. The characters of fiction

4.4. TRANSWORLD IDENTITY AND COUNTERPART THEORY

For the purposes of the argument in the preceding section I have assumed the possibility of "transworld identifying individuals." The argument, briefly put, was that no description to which we may legitimately appeal as a reference-fixing device will make "Holmes" refer to the *same* individual in all worlds.[10] Thus I assume that the same individual exists in many worlds. But this assumption is thought by some to be extremely problematic. Advocates, like David Lewis, of "counterpart theory" prefer to think of individuals as *world bound*.[11] Each world has its own domain of individuals, disjoint from the domains of individuals in all other worlds. But an individual in one world may have a *counterpart* in another. My counterpart, if I have one, in another world w_1 is someone who is pretty much like me in qualitative respects and who is such that no one else in w_1 is any more like me than he is. My modal properties – properties like possibly being the prime minister of England – depend on what my counterparts do in other worlds, not upon what I do in them, for I do not do anything in these worlds. Rather, I am *represented* as doing certain things in worlds where my counterparts do them. I could have been prime minister because there is a world where I am represented as being prime minister; in that world one of my counterparts is prime minister.[12]

We saw just now that someone who believes in strict transworld identification of individuals faces a problem about

10 An expression "*A*" may rigidly refer to an individual *A* even though *A* does not exist in every world. In worlds where *A* does not exist we have a choice. We may say that "*A*" does not refer to anything in that world (Kripke); or we may say that "*A*" refers to *A* in that world even though *A* does not exist in that world (Kaplan). How we choose does not matter for present purposes.
11 Lewis cautions that the expression "world-bound individual" should not be taken to mean "an individual who exists *according to* one world only." On Lewis's view an individual can exist in one world and exist according to another by having a counterpart at that other world. See *On the Plurality of Worlds*, sec. 4.1 and note 11, p. 214.
12 See Lewis, *On the Plurality of Worlds*, sec. 4.1.

identifying a particular individual who is Holmes in many different worlds. There will be different candidates for being Holmes in different worlds, with nothing to choose between them, and so we cannot then speak of *the* Holmes of the story. But counterpart theory offers a more yielding way. Because the relation of qualitative similarity must, according to counterpart theory, replace the (spurious) relation of transworld identity, Holmes is now shown to be in no worse shape than you or I. Identifying Greg Currie in a nonactual world is just a matter of identifying in that world an individual (if there is one) whose qualitative similarity to me is strong, and at least as strong as that of anyone else in the same world. Similarly, identifying Holmes in a world is a matter of identifying in that world an individual whose qualities are close to those described in the Holmes story, and at least as close as those of anyone else in the same world.

But counterpart theory faces a difficulty of its own. How are we to determine the reference of "Holmes" in any given world? We cannot start at the actual world, identify the reference of "Holmes" there, and then seek out his counterparts in other worlds, for there is no actual world reference for "Holmes." We have to start at some other world, presumably by finding, in that world, someone who satisfies the description given in the Holmes story. We then say that *his* counterparts in other worlds are what "Holmes" refers to in those worlds. But it's arbitrary which world we start at; we could have started at another world, with another Holmes look-alike, and then sought out *his* counterparts in other worlds. This arbitrariness won't matter if we get *the same* end result concerning the reference of "Holmes" at each world, whichever world we start at. But will this be the case? For it to be the case, the following would have to be true: that if A in w_1 and B in w_2 both satisfy the Holmes description, then A and B are counterparts. If they are not, we shall get a different end result, depending on whether we start at w_1 or at w_2. Starting at w_1, we shall say that A is Holmes and B is not; starting at w_2, we get the opposite result. But there is no guarantee that A and B will be counterparts. The story may leave

4. The characters of fiction

too much open. Our two world-bound individuals, A in w_1 and B in w_2, judged in terms of overall qualitative similarity, might not be similar enough to be counterparts of one another, although they both satisfy the description of Holmes given in the story. (This will certainly be the case for characters very underdescribed by the stories in which they occur.)

The problem is that counterpartness is determined by overall qualitative similarity – so at least I have been assuming. If we could think of counterpartness as a less exacting relation, we might be able to solve the difficulty. Lewis suggests that we can think of it as a less exacting relation.[13] The idea can be explained in the following way. Macbeth (supposing him to be a real person) sees a dagger when there is no dagger in front of him. Which dagger does he see? To answer that question, consider all those worlds in which Macbeth's current visual state is veridical. In each of those worlds he sees a dagger. Strictly speaking, each dagger is different. But each one can be regarded as a counterpart of the other, not because of overall qualitative similarity between them – they might be very different from each other in various ways – but because they all play the same role in bringing about Macbeth's current visual state. They are counterparts *by acquaintance* for Macbeth.

Now go back to Holmes. I read the stories, making believe I'm getting veridical information from them. In some nonactual worlds – worlds where the Holmes story is told as known fact – I *am* getting veridical information from those stories. In those worlds I'm learning, from a reliable source, about the activities of a great detective. In each such world there is someone whose adventures I learn about. In different such worlds these are different people. But these people are counterparts for me in the same way the various daggers

13 See Lewis, "Individuation by Acquaintance and by Stipulation," *Philosophical Review* 92 (1983): 3–32. Lewis does not explicitly consider fictional characters in this essay; the treatment of fictional characters is suggested by his treatment of the objects of nonveridical seeing. In developing the suggestion of which I shall make further use here, Lewis acknowledges a debt to Hintikka.

in various worlds are counterparts for Macbeth. These people differ in various ways; from the point of ancestry, birth, and childhood, they are, or may be, very different from one another, assuming the stories don't pronounce on the early life of Holmes. But they are counterparts by acquaintance for me. They are alike concerning their epistemic relations to me; they are all of them, in their own worlds, the person about whom I learn when I read that text.[14]

Counterparts by acquaintance as I have explained them are counterparts by acquaintance for a given subject. Two things that are counterparts by acquaintance for me may not be counterparts by acquaintance for you. It would be unfortunate for a counterpart theorist to have to say that my Sherlock Holmes and yours are different. After all, one reason we want a reference for Sherlock Holmes is to establish that we are talking about the same thing when we use the expression "Sherlock Holmes." Lewis (in correspondence) suggests a way out: Consider counterparts by acquaintance for the community rather than for individual members of the community. That is, consider worlds in which members of our community read about the adventures of a real person called "Holmes," and in which this is overtly believed in the community.[15] Identifying those persons called "Holmes" across worlds as counterparts by acquaintance for the community gives us Sherlock Holmes.

There might be a problem for this proposal concerning the interpretation of modal claims about Holmes. According to counterpart theory, the *de re* modal claim "*a* is possibly *F*" is true in world *w* just in case there is in some world a counterpart of *a* that is *F*.[16] But how am I to say that Holmes might not have been a detective? We don't, on the present proposal, have a single Holmes whose counterparts we can now consider. Instead we have a lot of Holmesish individuals in

---

14 Of course, it is strictly speaking my counterparts that do the learning. Lewis notes a serious problem about this (see "Individuation by Acquaintance and by Stipulation"). But the problem and his solution need not concern us here.

15 For the definition of overt belief, see Section 2.3.

16 See Lewis, *Counterfactuals*, p. 40.

different worlds, each a counterpart by acquaintance of the other. Which of these distinct individuals should we pick on in order then to consider *his* counterparts? The choice would be arbitrary. One reply to this is to say that we should count "Holmes might not have been a detective" as true just in case *each* Holmesish individual has a counterpart that is not a detective. This would be a special provision; what makes it true that Holmes might not have been a detective would turn out to be a state of affairs logically different in kind from the state of affairs that makes it true that Dashiell Hammett might not have been a detective. But then fictional beings, if there are any, can be expected to be very different kinds of things from the beings we encounter outside of fiction; perhaps modal claims about them can be expected to have their own peculiarities. Notice that the following would not be a good criticism of Lewis at this point: If we consider counterparts of all the Holmesish individuals, "Holmes might not have been a detective" comes out false because, by assumption, all the counterparts of any Holmesish individual are detectives; they are all alike insofar as they are all detectives about whom I am learning. This objection fails because it fails to notice Lewis's insistence that what we should take to be a counterpart of what depends on context. When we identify who it is I am reading about when I read the Holmes story we consider counterparts by acquaintance for me (or for the community). When we consider whether so-and-so might not have been a detective we consider counterparts determined by some other relation of qualitative similarity; perhaps we consider similarity in ancestry and early development. Counterparts by acquaintance give us Holmes; counterparts by origin give us (some of) his modal properties.

This proposal may or may not suit the advocate of counterpart theory. Like many others I do not accept counterpart theory as a viable alternative to strict trans-world identification of individuals, but this is not an appropriate place in which to decide the issue between them. So I simply leave the proposal in the hands of the counterpart theorists and move on toward my own theory of fictional characters. But before I get there, there is one more proposal to consider.

4.5. DIAGONAL PROPOSITIONS

The theories I have considered so far are theories that attempt to assign reference to fictional names. I shall now consider a suggestion that abandons the attempt, but that purports to combine the view that fictional names are (empty) proper names with an explanation of sentences containing such expressions that does justice to the intuition that such sentences are meaningful.

Robert Stalnaker has suggested that a number of problems in philosophical logic can be solved if we distinguish two different ways in which possible worlds can play a role in semantics.[17] Worlds play a role, first of all, in *determining the truth value* of what is expressed by a sentence. Thus the proposition expressed by "Grass is green" is true in one world and false in another, depending on the color grass has in each world. But worlds may also play a role in *determining what proposition* is expressed by a sentence. Suppose we want to know whether the sentence "Jones smokes" is true. First we must decide what proposition this sentence expresses, and then we must decide whether that proposition is true. Consider the following somewhat restricted logical space, consisting of three worlds. Suppose that in w_1 "Jones" is a designator of individual a, and a is the only person who smokes. Suppose that in w_2 "Jones" designates a again and nobody smokes. Suppose, finally, that in w_3 "Jones" designates a different individual b, the only smoker in that world. This distribution of possibilities trades on the fact that it is a contingent matter not merely whether an individual smokes, but

---

17 See Robert Stalnaker, "Assertion," in Peter Cole (ed.), *Syntax and Semantics*, vol. 9: *Pragmatics* (New York: Academic Press, 1978), and "Indexical Belief," *Synthese* 49 (1981): 129–151. Stalnaker acknowledges a debt to the work of Hans Kamp and Frank Vlatch. The account of fictional names that I develop here is based on ideas of Stalnaker, but his own very brief remarks on fictional names at the end of "Assertion" suggest a somewhat different approach.

also whether he gets one name rather than another. There are worlds in which I'm called "John Smith" and in which someone else is called "Greg Currie." The following matrix represents the relation between the three possibilities described above and the sentence "Jones smokes":

	w_1	w_2	w_3
w_1	T	F	F
w_2	T	F	F
w_3	F	F	T

The rows of the matrix represent propositions as functions from worlds to truth values, the ith row representing the proposition expressed by an utterance in world i of "Jones smokes." Notice that rows 1 and 2 represent the same proposition: that a smokes. What an utterance of our sentence expresses in w_1 and w_2 is the same, it just happens to be true in w_1 and false in w_2. Row 3 represents a different proposition: that b smokes. Thus the sentence "Jones smokes," as uttered in either of w_1 and w_2, expresses the same proposition, since "Jones," as used in either world, refers to the same individual. As uttered in w_3, the sentence expresses a different proposition, because in that world "Jones" refers to a different individual.

Now suppose Smith hears an utterance of our sentence but does not know who is being referred to as "Jones." Not knowing who "Jones" refers to, Smith does not know what proposition is expressed. But Smith may still have reason to believe that what is said is true (the utterer being known to Smith as reliable). He believes that whoever is called "Jones" is a smoker, and what he believes is true in w_1 and in w_3 but false in w_2. Thus he assigns truth values to the utterance in the following way: He assigns it the value T in w_1, F in w_2, and T in w_3. These assignments of truth values determine, relative to our restricted logical space, a proposition: the proposition believed by Smith. This proposition is not any of the propositions represented in the rows of the matrix, but the *diagonal* proposition, the proposition represented by the leading diagonal of the matrix. This proposition can be represented by the sentence "What is said in this utterance of 'Jones smokes' is true," where "what is said in this utterance of 'Jones smokes' " is a nonrigid designator of propositions; what is said differs from one world of saying to another. Let us say that the diagonal proposition is the proposition *associated with* the sentence that generates the matrix.

The importance of this idea is that it suggests how, when someone hears a sentence he does not fully understand, he can end up believing a proposition intimately related to that sentence.

We can apply this method to the problem of fictional names in the following way. Suppose that in "Holmes smokes," as uttered by Doyle, "Holmes" belongs to the semantic category of directly referring expressions. Because it designates nothing, no sentence in which it occurs expresses a proposition. But if things had been different (if another world had been actual), Doyle's utterance would have expressed a perfectly good proposition. Suppose Doyle had been writing a biography of a man named "Holmes." Then Doyle's utterance would have expressed a proposition true in worlds where that man smokes. Now consider three worlds: w_1 (it might be the actual world) in which "Holmes" as used by Doyle is empty, w_2 in which Doyle is writing a biography of a man m_1 who smokes, and w_3 in which Doyle is writing a biography of a different man m_2, again a smoker. "Holmes smokes" as uttered by Doyle in w_1 expresses no proposition, but as uttered in w_2 and w_3 it does express a proposition – a different one in each. Thus we get the following matrix:

	w_1	w_2	w_3
w_1	X	X	X
w_2	F	T	F
w_3	F	F	T

I have written X's in the first row to indicate that there is no proposition expressed by the utterance at w_1. "Holmes smokes" as uttered at w_1 has no truth value at any world. At

143

w_2 and w_3, however, a proposition is expressed – a different one at each. *Now, suppose Smith were to read Doyle's text* (or just the part that reads "Holmes smokes"), and take it for a true account of the activities of someone called "Holmes," otherwise unknown to Smith. He does not know what is said in this text because he does not know which individual it is about, but he believes it to be true. He believes the diagonal proposition generated by our second matrix. This proposition, expressed by the sentence "What is said in this utterance of 'Holmes smokes' is true," fails to take any value in w_1 because in w_1 nothing is said by such an utterance. In w_1 and w_2 it takes the value true.

Now, the ordinary reader of fiction does not take the story to be known fact, but he does make believe that it is. The suggestion is, then, that although the reader of the story cannot make believe the propositions expressed by the sentences of the story, since there are no such propositions, he can make believe the propositions associated with the sentences of the fiction he reads. If this is correct, we can treat fictional names as empty designators, admit that no propositions are expressed by the sentences of the story, and hold that the reader engages with the story by taking the make believe attitude toward certain propositions. And it's the propositions associated with the sentences of the story that are true in the story, not the propositions expressed by those sentences, for they express no propositions. This proposal explains the intuition that sentences in which fictional names occur are meaningful. It tells us that the reader who reads such a sentence unthinkingly makes the transition from the sentence he reads, which actually expresses no proposition, to the associated diagonal proposition, naturally but mistakenly supposing that the sentence expresses that diagonal proposition.

This proposal is interesting and I see no knockdown argument against it. But the account of fictional names it gives us is less satisfactory than the account I present farther on. On the view just outlined, the way in which "Holmes" is used in the story ensures that a sentence of the story containing it literally expresses no proposition. There is no such thing, then, as understanding that sentence. What we then get is an account of our understanding of the story in terms of our grasp of a proposition (the diagonal proposition) expressed by some *other* sentence. In the kinds of case where Stalnaker puts his method to good use the one who grasps the diagonal proposition is one whose understanding of the sentence in question is deficient as measured against the understanding of his more enlightened fellows: enlightenment consisting, in the kinds of cases we are imagining, in a knowledge of the referent of a proper name.[18] But in the case of sentences of fiction containing fictional names there is no comparable contrast between an enlightened and an unenlightened use; there is no proposition expressed by "Holmes smokes" that might be grasped by someone who knew the referent of "Holmes." There is only the "deficient" understanding of that sentence, which consists in a grasp of the corresponding diagonal proposition. But if that's the *only* understanding we can have of the sentence, it cannot be deficient. It would be better, therefore, if we could explain the use of "Holmes" in such a way that the proposition a reader nondeficiently grasps on reading the story is the very proposition expressed by the sentence in which "Holmes" occurs. The theory I shall develop will tell us what that proposition is.

Notice that the account just outlined can work only if we treat sentences containing nondenoting definite descriptions like "What is said in this utterance of 'Holmes smokes' " as truth-valueless. Only in this way does the proposition expressed by "What is said in this utterance of 'Holmes smokes' is true" correspond to the proposition determined by the leading diagonal of the second matrix above. If we treat such expressions along the lines recommended by Russell's theory of descriptions, our sentence will express the proposition that is *false* (rather than truth-valueless) in w_1 and true in w_2 and w_3, and that is not the proposition determined by the leading diagonal of the matrix. Another way in which

18 In other cases that Stalnaker considers, the relevant knowledge is knowledge of the referent of an indexical expression.

the theory I shall present differs from the Stalnaker-inspired theory is that I shall treat definite descriptions as Russell treats them; a sentence of the form "The *F* is *G*" will be false when there is no *F*. I shall now begin to outline that theory.

4.6. THE CONTENT OF MAKE-BELIEVE

A theory of fictional names with any plausibility must account for the variety of uses to which fictional names are put. These uses range from the author's initial act of writing or telling, through the reader's engagement with the story, to those speculations that seem to free the character from the text of origin and treat it as an autonomous object of study. These kinds of use are importantly different from one another, and in developing a theory of fictional names we must be careful to distinguish them. The result will, I hope, be a theory that combines some partial and apparently rather disparate suggestions into an explanatory whole.

There is no necessary connection between writing fiction and using fictional names. Our culture might never have hit upon the idea of "making up" fictional characters. We might have been content to write fictional stories about real people, creatures, and things generally. In that case the semantics of fictional names would not strike us as a problem. Problems about fictional names arise because authors of fiction do use these expressions in their works. It is natural, then, to begin our inquiries into the semantics of fictional names by examining their use within such fictional works. I shall call this the *fictive* use of fictional names. When Doyle wrote, as we shall assume he did, "Holmes was a pipe smoker," how are we to explain his use of the expression "Holmes"?[19]

I claimed in Chapter 1 that in writing this sentence Doyle was performing an act of fiction-making. He intended that

19 The material in this section develops a suggestion made by Alvin Plantinga (*The Nature of Necessity*, pp. 159–63) and others. See also Nicholas Wolterstorff, "Characters and their Names," *Poetics* 8 (1979): 101–27, sec. 5.

readers make believe the content of his utterance. If we are able to say what this content is, we shall know how the expression "Holmes" functions in Doyle's utterance. And we shall know what that content is when we know what a reader of Doyle's utterance will make believe as a result of reading it. Of course, a reader may be inattentive or confused, and might come to make believe just about anything as a result of his reading. The reader I have in mind here is an ideal reader: a reader whose make-believe can be regarded as appropriate to what he reads. When we know the content of this reader's make-believe, we know all that is relevant to determining the semantics of "Holmes." For there surely can be no *more* to the meaning of that term than all it can contribute to the content of the reader's make-believe. To suppose otherwise would be to suppose there is some semantically significant aspect to Doyle's use of "Holmes" that the reader (even an ideal reader) can take no account of when he reads the story. Such an aspect would affect the content of the story, but not in such a way as to affect even the most attentive reading of it, in which case fictional stories would have to be thought of as containing an essentially incommunicable element. This mystical doctrine has, I take it, no plausibility.

In what follows I'm going to use the machinery of possible worlds, so I shall assume we are considering a fiction that involves no inconsistency. Given my immediate purpose, I don't think this restriction is especially harmful. If I can show that the content of a consistent fictional story does not depend upon the assignment of a referent to "Holmes" or to any fictional name that occurs in it, it seems at least probable that the same will hold for inconsistent fictions.

To get a better sense of what is involved in reading about a fictional character, contrast the Holmes case with a case involving only a genuinely referring proper name. Suppose you and I are acquainted with Jones and you say to me, "Jones is a pipe smoker." "Jones" here functions as a directly referring expression. It functions to pick out a particular individual about whom you are telling me something. What you say is true in the actual world if Jones actually smokes a pipe, and true or false at other worlds depending on whether it's Jones himself who smokes in those worlds. "Jones," as used in this sentence, is rigid: it refers to Jones in any world where it refers to anybody. Now you may make up a story about Jones for my entertainment, it being common knowledge between us that your story is make-believe. If, in the course of your story, you say "Jones is a pipe smoker," "Jones" functions just as before as a genuine proper name. Although your utterance is fictive rather than assertative, your use of "Jones" still counts as a direct reference to Jones. "Jones" remains rigid across the transition from assertion to fiction-making.

In fiction we do sometimes use genuine proper names to pick out particular individuals and say something about them that is part of the make-believe. I remarked in Section 4.1 that this is how Tolstoy uses "Napoleon" in *War and Peace*. But "Holmes" doesn't function like that in Doyle's story. In writing his story Doyle does not invite us to pick out some particular individual and make believe that this person was involved in the events of the story. What, then, is required of the reader in order for him to understand Doyle's utterance?

Assume for a moment that the Holmes story contains only one fictional character, Holmes. What he does in the story is done in relation to real places and people, like London and Queen Victoria. From the set of possible worlds we can pick out a subset that contains all and only the *qualitative worlds* of the story. A world w is a qualitative world of the story if there is someone in w who does everything that Holmes is said in the story to do, and in which everything else that's part of the story is literal truth. That person will, for instance, be called "Holmes," live in London, have a life span that overlaps with that of Queen Victoria. Who that person is will differ from one world to another.

Suppose that, on the basis of my reading of the story, I am able to distinguish the qualitative worlds of the story from all the others. Given a complete description of a world, I can tell you whether it is one of the story's qualitative worlds. Read-

148

4.6. The content of make-believe

ing the story a bit more attentively, or having a bit more background knowledge, would certainly not enable me to pick out a proper subset of these worlds and say: "Those are the worlds in which it is really *Holmes* that does those things." When it comes to fictional stories, the limit of understanding – the theoretical ideal – is just the ability to distinguish the story's qualitative worlds.

So I can understand the story without needing to pick out a particular individual to which "Holmes" refers. Because I understand the story I must understand the expression "Holmes" as it occurs in the story. So I understand that expression without having to assign a referent to it. To understand the story I have merely to suppose that there is someone who does the things Holmes is said to do in the story. The same cannot be said for the fictional story about Jones. If all I can do is identify the qualitative worlds of that story – worlds in which *someone* does and is the things Jones is said to do and be – then I do not fully understand your use of the expression "Jones," and I consequently do not fully understand the story you are telling me. My understanding *that* story depends upon my prior understanding of the name "Jones."

It seems I can assimilate the full content of the Holmes story without assigning a reference to Holmes, just as I can assimilate the statement "Someone smokes" without asking who that someone is. And there is more than just an analogy here. Both "Holmes" and "someone" give way, on logical analysis, to the machinery of variables and quantifiers. In order to arrive at a preliminary account of fictional names let us bring back the other fictional characters of the Holmes story. When we read that Holmes, Watson, Moriarty, and the others did such and such we are to make believe that there is someone, and someone else, and . . . , and the first one was called 'Holmes' and . . . , and the nth was called so-and-so, and the first one did such and such, and so on. When we understand that, we are able to say of any possible world whether it is a qualitative world of the story. And that, as we have seen, is all there is to understanding the story. Let $F(t_1 \ldots t_n)$ be our story, where the t_is are fictional names.

4. The characters of fiction

The present proposal is that the content of the story is the content of the corresponding "Ramsey Sentence":[20]

(1) $\exists x_1 \ldots \exists x_n[F(x_1 \ldots x_n)]$,

which differs from $F(t_1 \ldots t_n)$ in that each fictional name is replaced by a variable bound by an existential quantifier.

Statement (1) says there is an n-tuple of things that satisfies the properties and relations specified in the story. If (1) represents the content of the story, the fictional names that appear in its original exposition give way to existentially quantified variables, and the content of the story is that there are n individuals that have certain properties and stand in certain relations to one another. On this interpretation the story is straightforwardly false at the actual world, true at qualitative worlds of the story and false at all the others. By fixing the truth value of the story at each world we determine the proposition expressed by the story. What is said in the story is thus meaningful, and meaningfulness is all that's required in order for us to make believe that the story is true.

This suggestion is on the right lines, but it needs to be developed further, for an important ingredient in what the reader gets from the story has been left out. When we read a story that purports to describe the activities of n individuals we do not make believe merely that there are n individuals who do these things. We make believe that there is a particular n-tuple of individuals who do these things and about whom we are learning, even when the story (explicit content plus background) does not exclude the possibility that there is another n-tuple of individuals who do the same things. Consider a not very exciting story, the text of which reads:

20 So called after Frank Ramsey. See his "Theories," in D. H. Mellor (ed.), *Foundations* (London: Routledge & Kegan Paul, 1978). Ramsey argued that if $T(t_1 \ldots t_n)$ is a scientific theory, where the t_is are theoretical terms, then the content of the theory is expressed by its Ramsey Sentence $\exists x_1 \ldots \exists x_n[T(x_1 \ldots x_n)]$. Here I simply apply Ramsey's proposal to fictional stories.

4.6. The content of make-believe

(2) Jack got up in the morning and ate breakfast.

On the theory so far advanced this really amounts to

(3) There is someone called "Jack" who got up in the morning and ate breakfast.

But (3) is inadequate as a formulation of (2), for it does not capture the evident fact that the story purports to describe the activities of a particular Jack. In many stories, of course, the claim of uniqueness can be inferred from or is explicit in the descriptions of the characters and would not need to be stated independently. It can usually be inferred from a story which says of its characters that they did things at certain narrowly circumscribed places and times. If it is said that Holmes looked out of the bedroom window of 221B Baker Street at exactly 10 a.m. on July 14, 1890, we can be sure that the story rules out there being two people called "Holmes" there at the same time; background and explicit content strongly suggest that the story is not to be understood as involving odd speculations about personal identity. But a theory of fiction ought to cover less spatiotemporally circumscribed fictional efforts like my (2), which carries no direct implication of uniqueness. And even in a fiction as sparsely described as (2), I think we take it to be part of the story that there is a particular person called "Jack" who is being described. To read (2) as a straightforward existential quantification would be to miss an important ingredient, and so (3) cannot display the logical form of (2).

About the least satisfactory response to this would be to say that the real content of (2) is not (3) but

(4) There is exactly one person called "Jack" who got up in the morning and ate breakfast.

If we had to assess the content of (2) on the assumption that it was produced in a community like ours, we would conclude, I think, that it's true in the story that many people are called "Jack" and eat breakfast. Far from regimenting the content of the text, (4) expresses something that is false in the

151

story. Unique identification of characters must be got in another way.

Now, recall from Chapter 2 that our make-believe is that the story is told to us as known fact. We make-believe that there is a teller who is responsible for the text we are reading, who has knowledge of someone called "Jack," about whom he wants to tell us. We make believe that the teller has a particular person in mind; it is *that* Jack whom the story is about. It is tempting at this point to say that the content of (2) is really

(5) There are exactly two people, the first of whom is called "Jack" and who got up and had breakfast and the second of whom tells of the activities of the first.

But this is no improvement. For the story might leave it open not only as to whether there is another person called "Jack" who does these things, but also as to whether there is another person who describes in the same way this other Jack's activities. If (2) was produced in a community where people were constantly writing brief biographical sketches of each other, relevant background might well tell us that this is true in the story. At the very least it would not be false in the story. Turning a story that says there is an n-tuple of individuals with certain properties into a story that says there is a $n + 1$-tuple of individuals, one of whom tells the story of the others, does not get us to a unique n-tuple we can identify as the characters of the story. But I think it's clear which way we should go here. It may be that (2) does not rule out the possibility that there is someone else telling a structurally identical narrative, but it does rule out the possibility that there is someone else engaged in *this very act of narration*, that is, the act of narration that produces the text I'm now reading.

I had better explain the (partly stipulative) sense I'm giving to the word "text" here. Cervantes and Pierre Menard, supposing that Menard had completed his project of writing a story word-for-word identical with Cervantes's, produced distinct texts in my sense.[21] I have before me, let us suppose,

21 See the discussion in Section 2.6.

152

4.6. The content of make-believe

a copy of a certain text; it is entitled "Don Quixote de la Mancha." Which text is it a copy of? Spelling takes us some way toward an answer. The way it's spelled tells us it is not, for instance, a copy of the text of *Northanger Abbey*. But spelling will not tell us whether it is a copy of the text of Cervantes's work or of Menard's, since their texts are spelled the same. Finding out that it is a copy of the one rather than of the other is a matter of tracing its causal history. It is either the very copy produced by Cervantes (or by Menard) or, more likely, it bears the ancestral of the copy-relation to that copy.[22] Thus the expression "the text I'm now reading" refers to the text – in the example of the previous paragraph it is Doyle's text – produced by the author whose initial act of fiction-making resulted, via the copy-relation, in the copy I have before me. We shall need this principle of textual individuation when I come to discuss a problem of Kripke's farther on.

We readers make believe that the text we are reading is the product of someone who has knowledge of certain people and their actions. He has in mind a certain *n*-tuple of individuals, and these are the characters described in *his* text – whether or not there is another *n*-tuple somewhere else doing similar things, accompanied by their own chronicler. And the teller (the fictional author) is identified as the person uniquely responsible for this text, a copy of which I'm now reading.[23] Note that it's true in the story that the fictional author is responsible for this text, but that it's not true that he is, for there is no such person as the fictional author. In fact,

---

22 *A* bears the ancestral of the copy-relation to *B* iff *A* is a copy of *B* or *A* is a copy of a copy of *B*, or . . . etc.

23 This, or something like it, was the view of G. E. Moore, who wrote that "Dickens' propositions are all of the form 'there was only one man of whom it is true both *that I'm telling you of him, and* that etc, etc.' " (See Moore's contribution to the symposium on imaginary objects, *Aristotelian Society Supplementary Volume XII* [1933]: 55–70. The quotation is from p. 69; italics in the original.) But Moore would be wrong to say, as he seems to say, that the content of the story includes an indexical self-reference by the real author – Dickens in this case. We saw in Chapter 2 that it is the fictional author who plays a role in the story, not the real author. Thus I anchor the characters to the real world via a reference to the story rather to the author.

4. The characters of fiction

Doyle is responsible for this text, but it's not true in the story that he is. This is a familiar feature of fictions. It might be true in the story that an unnamed Mafia hitman killed President Kennedy, but not true that he did; and it may be true that Oswald killed Kennedy, but not true in the story that he did.

Now the content of (2) is properly represented as

(6) There are exactly two people, the first of whom is called "Jack" and who got up and had breakfast and the second of whom tells of the activities of the first *by producing this text.*

Now I can present the standard logical form of a fictional story. Let T be the text we are reading. Previously we identified the content of T with

(1) $\exists x_1 \ldots \exists x_n [F(x_1 \ldots x_n)]$.

When we want to say there is exactly one n-tuple of things of which Φ is true we need this formulation:

$$\exists y_1 \ldots \exists y_n \forall x_1 \ldots \forall x_n [\Phi(x_1 \ldots x_n) \equiv y_1 = x_1 \,\&\, \ldots \,\&\, y_n = x_n],$$

which I abbreviate to

$$\exists^1 x_1 \ldots \exists^1 x_n [\Phi(x_1 \ldots x_n)].$$

I can now replace (1) with the more acceptable

(7) $\exists^1 x_1 \ldots \exists^1 x_{n+1}[F(x_1 \ldots x_n)$ and x_{n+1} is responsible for the text T and T sets out x_{n+1}'s knowledge of the activities of $x_1 \ldots x_n]$,

which I abbreviate to

(7') $\exists^1 x_1 \ldots \exists^1 x_{n+1}[F^{\circ}(x_1 \ldots x_{n+1})]$.

Fictional stories don't *have* to be amenable to this treatment. A philosophically self-conscious writer might make it clear that the fictional author has in mind two n-tuples of individuals, both of which fit the story he is telling us equally well; he is just not going to tell us anything that distinguishes between the two n-tuples. (Borges might have written such a story.) In that case uniqueness of instantiation would not be

4.7. *In defense of the fictional author*

part of our make-believe about the story, and we could not treat the fictional names that occur in the story in the way I suggest. But without such explicit indications to the contrary, we naturally assume the story is about a particular group of characters. (7) is the correct formulation of such a story.

I began with a question about the meaning of a particular sentence in the story: "Holmes was a pipe smoker." We see now that this was misleading. No proper part of a fictional story containing fictional names is semantically independent enough to express a proposition on its own. Only the whole story expresses a proposition, for there are quantifiers that have as their scope the whole story, picking up variables along the way. Readers have the illusion that the story is decomposable into sentential elements because it is part of their make-believe that expressions like "Holmes" really are proper names. We shall understand this better after we have investigated the way readers themselves use fictional names. This is the subject of Section 4.8.

4.7. IN DEFENSE OF THE FICTIONAL AUTHOR

The emphasis I have placed on the uniqueness of characters can help reinforce a point seen to be controversial at the end of Chapter 2: my claim that our make-believe is that the story is told as known fact. The difficulty was that certain fictions – "mindless fictions" I called them – seem to preclude their own telling; a teller is to be introduced into the fiction only at the expense of making contradictory things part of our make-believe. But I think this consequence is correct. Even stories that are explicit about the absence of a narrator require us to assume that there is one in order that we shall make sense of them. Consider the following little story in which it is explicit that there is no narrator (it owes something to a suggestion put to me by Bill Lycan):[24]

---

24 Lycan was arguing against me at the time and I don't know whether my treatment of the story will satisfy him.

155

4. The characters of fiction

(*) A lizard basked in the sun. A breeze stirred the leaves of
a flower nearby. A bird flew past. Too bad there was no
one around to record the event.

What is true in this story? That there is a lizard, a
breeze, a bird, and a flower such that . . . But the reader
of (*) will not suppose that this is *all* that's true in the
story. The content of his make-believe will not be merely
that there is at least one (or even that there is exactly one)
lizard, at least one breeze, and so on. His make-believe
will be, rather, that there is a *particular* lizard–breeze–
bird–flower quadruple that the story is about. If the text
goes on to say "The bird landed by the flower," he will
recognize that the speaker of this sentence (the fictional
author) has in mind a particular bird, the same bird he
had in mind in uttering (*). Of course, this recognition
occurs within the scope of our make-believe. We need not
assume that there is, actually, someone who has in mind
any such bird. Probably the real author of these sentences
did not have any particular bird in mind when he wrote
the story, and if he did it would not be relevant to the
story's content. Rather, it is part of the story that there is
someone who had in mind a particular bird, and consequently part of the reader's make-believe that there is
such a person when he engages imaginatively with the
story.
　There is currently a debate about whether indefinite
descriptions like "a bird" or "a man high in the inner circle" are semantically ambiguous. On the view according to
which they are semantically ambiguous the truth values of
sentences involving these expressions sometimes depend
upon what is true of some particular individual. Thus,
Donnellan claims that "We had a call from a man high in
the inner circle" is true just in case the man the speaker
had in mind in producing the sentence telephoned the
speaker. If it turned out that the man the speaker had in
mind did not call him but that he was called by some
other man high in the inner circle (perhaps without the

156

4.7. In defense of the fictional author

speaker knowing this man was high in the inner circle), then what the speaker said was false.[25]

My argument above does not depend upon assuming that Donellan's view, or any view that attributes semantic ambiguity to indefinite descriptions, is the correct one. It may be that sentences like those in (*) literally mean that *there is* a man (bird, or whatever) who has the property predicated in the sentence. That is, it may be true – and I'm inclined to think it is true – that expressions like "a bird" always function semantically as quantifiers. So I'm not claiming that the sentences in (*) are such that their being true depends upon the properties of a certain lizard–bird–flower–breeze quadruple that the speaker has in mind. I'm claiming that what is *true in the story* is that there is a particular such quadruple had in mind by the fictional author that has certain properties. We have seen already that the propositions true in a story need not correspond to propositions literally expressed by sentences of the text. If expressions like "a bird" are semantically univocal and their occurrence in sentences is always to be explained quantificationally, then, in the case we are considering, the propositions literally expressed by the sentences of (*) are indeed distinct from the propositions true in the story. And this difference would be a product of what is sometimes called the difference between semantic reference and speaker's reference.[26] When we consider semantic reference we shall say that the expression "a bird," as it occurs in (*), does not have a referential role, that it functions as a quantifier. When we consider speaker's reference we shall say that (it is make-believe that) in using the expression "a bird" the speaker meant to refer to some particular bird: the one he had in mind. But, of course, we would not be able to say this if it were not part of our make-believe that there is a speaker who

25 "Speaker Reference, Descriptions and Anaphora," in Peter Cole (ed.), *Syntax and Semantics*, vol. 9: *Pragmatics* (New York: Academic Press, 1978).

26 On which see Saul Kripke, "Speaker's Reference and Semantic Reference," in P. French, T. Uehling, and H. Wettstein (eds.), *Midwest Studies in Philosophy*, vol. 2; *Studies in the Philosophy of Language* (Minneapolis: University of Minnesota Press, 1977).

has such a bird in mind. And if we take the way of semantic ambiguity and say that we have, in (*), an example of the referential use of an indefinite description, it will once again have to be part of our make-believe that there is a speaker who has a bird in mind. For without that assumption there would be no grounds for saying that the expression functions in this way rather than as a quantifier. Either way, we cannot do without the fictional author.

Stories like (*), if we bother to think about them carefully, put a strain on the imagination. They require us to make believe that there is no one to tell the tale. And to make sense of them we must suppose the tale is told to us by someone who has knowledge of what he tells. They are stories that invite us to make believe that something is the case, and to make believe that it's not. We have seen that other genres of fiction are subject to comparable narrative tensions: certain sorts of time travel stories, for instance.

4.8. THE METAFICTIVE USE OF FICTIONAL NAMES

Fictional names are used not only by writers of fiction. They are used in other ways: first of all, in what I shall call a *metafictive* way.

While you and I are recollecting the Holmes story, I might say "Holmes was a pipe smoker." My utterance differs in important ways from Doyle's original utterance of the same sentence. In my mouth it's an assertion: something I intend to get you to believe is true, something I probably believe to be true, and which, in some sense or other, *is* true. How can it be true when uttered by me and false when uttered by Doyle? The answer was given in Chapter 2, where we decided that such statements are best understood as prefixed by an intentional operator "It is part of the story that___." This operator can transform a false proposition like *Holmes was a pipe smoker* into a true one, and generally does so whenever the proposition is part of the story. As before, we write

4.8. *The metafictive use of fictional names*

"$F_S(P)$" for "it is part of the fiction S that P" or "P is true in the fiction S."

It is, for instance, hardly controversial that "F_H(Holmes is a pipe smoker)" should come out true, where H is the Holmes story. Now what does "Holmes" mean in this sentence? It cannot, we have seen, be a proper name. If it were, understanding the sentence would involve knowing who Holmes was, and there is no such thing as knowing that. And it does not seem to function as a bound variable in the style of our previous analysis. To say that it's true in the story that Holmes is a smoker cannot amount to saying that it's true in the story that there is exactly one person called "Holmes" who smokes – the story might have it that there are two such people.

I suggest that "Holmes," as it appears within the scope of the operator **F**, functions as an abbreviated definite description. But I shall not argue that the description it abbreviates is a description readers usually have in mind when they use the expression in these contexts. No doubt readers simply take over the fictional names that occur within the story without giving the matter serious thought. They may have in mind various definite descriptions that they associate with the name "Holmes," such as "the famous detective who lived in Baker Street," "the man who solved the mystery of the Redheaded League." But which description they have in mind will vary from reader to reader, and from time to time for the same reader. My purpose is to show that there is a nonarbitrary choice of descriptions in terms of which we can make good semantic sense of what readers say. This description could then be taken as a semantic ideal; it is what a perfectly informed, retentive, and rational reader would mean by "Holmes."[27]

Recall that I represent the story's content like this:

---

27 This account of fictional names is intended to apply only to the use of such expressions as they occur within the scope of the operator **F**. A rather different account will be necessary for their occurrence within statements that report the content of the reader's make-believe, for which see Section 5.5.

4. The characters of fiction

(7') $\exists^1 x_1 \ldots \exists^1 x_{n+1} [F^{\circ}(x_1 \ldots x_{n+1})].$

We can now use the story itself to give sense to the fictional names which occur in it. If x_1 is the variable which replaced "Holmes" in our original regimentation of the story, we may define

(8) Holmes $=_{df} \imath x_1 \exists^1 x_2 \ldots \exists^1 x_{n+1} [F^{\circ}(x_1 \ldots x_{n+1})]$

(where "$\imath$" is the definite description operator, with "$\imath x F x$" being read as "the F"), which I shall abbreviate to

(8') Holmes $=_{df} \imath x F^{\#} x.$ [28]

Similar definitions can be given for all the other fictional names in the story. "Holmes" denotes, in each world, the person, if there is one, who is the first member of the unique $n+1$-tuple of things that satisfies the conditions of the story, "Watson" denotes, in each world, the person, if there is one, who is the second member, "Moriarty" the third, and so on. [29] In its metafictive use the sentence "Holmes smokes a pipe" is to be understood as

28 See Lewis, "How to Define Theoretical Terms," *Journal of Philosophy* 67 (1970): 427–46, reprinted in *Philosophical Papers*, vol. 1 (New York: Oxford University Press, 1981); "Psychophysical and Theoretical Identifications," *Australasian Journal of Philosophy* 50 (1972); 249–58; and "Truth in Fiction," esp. p. 267.

29 In a world with two qualitatively identical planets on both of which a single story is told as known fact, no one is any of the characters in the story. When uniqueness is required, indeterminacy translates into failure of reference.

This case cannot arise for fictions like the Sherlock Holmes story, which are tied to actual places like planet Earth. In a world with two qualitatively identical planets only one of them can be Earth. Saying which one it is, is not a matter of *stipulating* that one of them is Earth; it's a matter of making it clear which world you are talking about. Worlds w_1 and w_2 both contain two qualitative look-alikes of Earth. In w_1 it is planet 1 that is Earth, in w_2 it is planet 2 that is Earth. That's one of the ways in which those two worlds differ. (On this, see the remarks on pp. 15–20 of Kripke's new preface to *Naming and Necessity*.) Here one cannot afford to take counterparts of Earth as a substitute for identifying Earth across worlds. For two qualitatively identical planets may both be counterparts of Earth (see Lewis, "Counterpart Theory and Quantified Modal Logic," p. 29 of the reprint in *Philosophical Papers*, vol. 1).

The case of reference failure induced by indeterminacy *can* arise for stories that are not tied to anything we can identify in the actual world. Frank Herbert's *Dune* might be an example of such a story. (A discussion with Bill Lycan helped me to clarify this point.)

(9) $\imath x F^{\#} x$ smokes a pipe

(or, to abbreviate further, $S[\imath x F^{\#} x]$).

Now (9) is false. If I say "Holmes smoked a pipe," intending to say something true, my statement must be understood as implicitly prefixed by the operator **F**:

(10) $F_H(S[\imath x F^{\#} x])$.

This treatment of fictional names avoids a threatening circularity. A story might describe one of its characters only in terms of the character's relations to other characters. If we were to look for a description from within the story to go proxy for that character's name, we would find the name of another character occurring in that description. If the characters were all intimately connected in this way, we would be left with a set of descriptions that take in each other's washing. The method of Lewis neatly solves the problem by defining all the characters in one go.

Because fictional names in their metafictive use are abbreviated descriptions in the style of (8), metafictive statements have some odd properties. All the true ones concerning a given fiction are equivalent – they are equivalent to the proposition that expresses the whole story, bound by the **F** operator. And all the false ones are equivalent – they are equivalent to the contradictory proposition bound by the **F** operator. That's the price you pay for assuming, as I do, that fictional characters are simply carved out of the stories in which they occur, and have no kind of independent being – a point I shall have occasion to reaffirm in Section 4.11.

How much of a price are we paying here? Not much of a price, I think. In arithmetic all truths are equivalent, as are all falsehoods, yet there are great epistemic differences between arithmetical truths. Exactly how this is to be accounted for is unclear, but presumably there is some explanation, and the explanation that works for arithmetic may work for metafictive statements.

Bear in mind also that metafictive statements are not the only kinds of statements in which fictional names can occur.

4. The characters of fiction

The ideally rational and retentive reader who says, "It is true in the story that Holmes takes cocaine," is best thought of as one who is looking back over the story, recalling its structure. He is not, at the moment he is expressing this thought, absorbed in a game of make-believe while reading the story. For one who is so absorbed, I don't think that the expression "Holmes" has the sense I have ascribed to it in metafictive contexts. The absorbed reader, however great his powers of attention and memory, does not give to "Holmes" and like expressions a sense that includes all the information in the story, for it is part of his make-believe that he has received only so much information from the text so far in his reading, even if, as a matter of fact, he knows how the story will turn out. How a fictional name like "Holmes" might function for such a reader is a question I return to in Chapter 5.[30] The point to note here is that the idealized account of fictional names in their metafictive uses is not intended to apply to the use of fictional names within a make-believe, and the equivalence problem is not a problem which arises when we consider such uses.

4.9. ACCIDENTAL REFERENCE AND ABOUTNESS

We now have an answer to a problem raised by Gilbert Ryle and more recently by Saul Kripke.[31] Kripke argues that fictional names cannot be abbreviated descriptions because if they were they might turn out, accidentally, to have reference. He imagines a case where, unknown to Doyle, there is someone who does all the things ascribed to Holmes in the stories. Surely that would not be a case in which Doyle was

30 See Section 5.5.
31 See Ryle's contribution to the symposium with Moore on imaginary objects (p. 39). There Ryle took the bizarre view that in this case "we should say that while previously we had thought Pickwick Papers was only a *pretence* autobiography, we now find that, by coincidence, it is a real one" (italics in the original). See also Kripke, *Naming and Necessity*, pp. 157–8. I'm grateful to Frank Jackson for discussion of this problem. Lewis discusses the problem in his "Truth in Fiction," pp. 265–6.

writing about *that* man. But it seems that on a descriptive account he would have been. For that man (call him "Actual Holmes" or "$H_@$") would, on such an account, *be* the unique individual who fits Doyle's description. He would be Holmes.

For $H_@$ to be Holmes, everything true in Doyle's story of Holmes must be actually true of $H_@$. On my account it is true in the story that Holmes's adventures are described by someone (the fictional author) who has knowledge of Holmes's activities that he sets down in this text, the text I'm now reading (call it T_1). Is that true of $H_@$? No: T_1 is a text produced by Doyle, and it is part of the example we are considering that Doyle knew nothing of $H_@$, so T_1 cannot be said to describe his activities. $H_@$ may be written about by someone who produces a text, call it T_2, lexically identical to Doyle's – all this unknown to Doyle himself of course. And T_1 and T_2 are distinct texts (just as Cervantes's text is distinct from Pierre Menard's) because they are the products of distinct communicative acts. Being described in T_2 rather than in T_1, $H_@$ fails to satisfy the description he would need to satisfy in order to be Holmes. Tying characters to texts, along with a nice attention to the individuation of texts, enables us to solve Kripke's problem.

In the rush to solve the problem we easily overlook an important question: Is there a problem here to be solved? Suppose we adopted some theory about fictional names according to which the description "Holmes" abbreviates is a description that could possibly be satisfied by some actual world individual about whom Doyle knows nothing. Why, exactly, would this be an awkward possibility? If we admit the possibility, we don't also have to admit that Doyle would, in that situation, be writing *about $H_@$*. In *War and Peace*, Tolstoy was writing about the real Napoleon. But suppose that Tolstoy had never heard of Napoleon, that he did not believe there was anybody who did the things that Napoleon did (either the things he really did or the things he is said to do in Tolstoy's story). Would he then have been writing about Napoleon? Surely not, on account of his not having any beliefs *about* Napoleon at the time of writing his novel. For the same reasons, Doyle would not have been writing about $H_@$ in the situation Kripke imagines. Notice that a story can be about someone without its being true of that someone, as *War and Peace* is about Napoleon even though it does not describe his activities correctly. Similarly, a story can be true of someone without being about that someone. In Kripke's fantasy, Doyle's story is true of $H_@$ without being about him.

This point has nothing essentially to do with fiction. Suppose I tell a lying story, using no proper names but only definite descriptions. Suppose the story turns out to be true of someone I have never heard of. Was I talking about that person? Aboutness is a notoriously problematic relation; perhaps there is a *weak* sense in which I was talking about that person. Such a sense might be this: I used a description uniquely true of that person. In this, very weak, sense of "about" I can talk about someone I have no knowledge of and who I don't believe exists. In the extraordinary circumstances we are asked by Kripke to imagine, Doyle would be writing about $H_@$ in this sense. Given the implausible scenario, this is not an implausible addition – no more so than it would be to say, in the case of the lying story, that I was talking about the someone who fitted my description. But there is another, stronger, sense of "about" in which it is not true that I was talking about anyone when I told the pack of lies. The person who accidentally fitted the description given by my lying story is not someone *I had in mind* as being the person of whom the story is true, for I did not have anybody in mind. It would be very implausible – in fact, it would be clearly false – to say that Doyle was writing about $H_@$ in this sense of "about," and any theory with this consequence would be wrong. But this is not a consequence of a descriptive theory of fictional names. Once we distinguish senses of "about," Kripke's objection collapses.

4.10. FICTIONAL NAMES AND SINGULAR
PROPOSITIONS

Treating fictional names as complex descriptions rather than
as directly referring devices might avoid unpleasant ontological commitments, but it does not seem to do justice to all our
intuitions about fictional stories and what is true in them. For
example, it is surely true in the Holmes story that "Holmes"
is a directly referring device: that it is in fact the proper name
of a particular individual, Holmes. And it is also true in the
story that Holmes's identity is not tied to his exploits as a
detective. That is, it is true in the story that if Holmes had not
done the things described in the story he would still have
been Holmes; he would still have been identical to himself.[32]
So it seems we want

(11) "Holmes" is the proper name of **Holmes**

and

(12) **Holmes** might never have done the things described in
the stories,

to be such that truths result when they are embedded in **F.**
But in (11) and (12) "**Holmes**" cannot, it seems, be replaced
by "$\imath x F^{\#}(x)$." To so construe it would not be to capture the
propositions we want to capture: propositions expressible by
means of sentences in which "**Holmes**" itself is used rigidly
to designate an individual. (I use "**Holmes**" in order to distinguish this purportedly rigid use from the descriptive and
hence nonrigid "Holmes.") Let us call such propositions *singular*.[33] While

(11') "Holmes" is the proper name of $\imath x F^{\#}(x)$

and

32 Bill Lycan discusses modal claims about fictional characters in his "Fiction and
Essence," forthcoming.
33 On singular propositions, see David Kaplan, "How to Russell a Frege-Church,"
Journal of Philosophy 72 (1975): 716–29, esp. p. 724. See also his "Dthat," pp.
226–7.

(12') $\imath x F^{\#}(x)$ might not have been $\imath x F^{\#}(x)$

are true in the story, they don't express the singular propositions we are trying to capture. (11') is unproblematically true in the story, but it does not express what (11) is intended to express. (11') is true in a world where the $F^{\#}$ is called "Holmes," but (11) is supposed to be true in a world where the individual **Holmes** is called "Holmes." Since, by assumption, **Holmes** might not have been the $F^{\#}$, (11) and (11') do not have the same truth values in all worlds. (12') is true in the story on a reading where the first occurrence of the description has large scope, but that's not what we want to express in (12). (12') is true, when so read, in a world w when the thing that is $F^{\#}$ in w fails to be the thing that is $F^{\#}$ in some other world. But (12) is supposed to be true in w just in case the individual **Holmes** is the $F^{\#}$ in w and fails to be the $F^{\#}$ in some other world. It seems that our attempt to provide descriptive substitutes for fictional names fails to account for all that goes to make up a story.

At this point the temptation to believe in fictional people is strong. If "Holmes" rigidly designates a (fictional) person a, then we can say (11) is true in w if "Holmes" designates a in w, and (12) is true in w if a is the $F^{\#}$ in w and not the $F^{\#}$ in some other world. But for what seem to me convincing reasons I have rejected the appeal to fictional people. I'm forced to conclude that (11) and (12) do not express any propositions. Now, as Gareth Evans pointed out, if a sentence expresses no proposition on its own, any more complex sentence in which it is embedded will also express no proposition.[34] So

(13) F("Holmes" is the proper name of **Holmes**)

and

(14) F(**Holmes** might not have done the things described in the story)

express no propositions either. In that case our intuition that they are true cannot be right: so, at least, my theory tells me.

---

34 See Evans, *The Varieties of Reference*, p. 364.

4.10. Fictional names and singular propositions

A theory that clashes with intuition must provide an explanation of why intuition is wrong. I now attend to that task.

The explanation is simply that we here make a tempting but fallacious inference. It is true in *Macbeth* that Lady Macbeth had some positive number of children. So it's tempting to ask, "How many children had Lady Macbeth?" – supposing there is some positive number *n* such that it is true in *Macbeth* that Lady Macbeth had *n* children. But there is no such number, and the inference is fallacious. ω-incompleteness, as we noticed in Chapter 2, is a structural feature of fictional stories.

Now, it is similarly true in the Holmes story that "Holmes" is the proper name of someone, but there is no one of whom it is true in the stories that "Holmes" is his name. If, like those who think there is a number that is the number of Lady Macbeth's children, we. make the fallacious inference and conclude that there is such a person, it will be natural to suppose that the someone of whom it is true in the stories that his name is "Holmes" is **Holmes**. For who else could it be?

Note that at each world where the Holmes story is told as known fact there is someone whose proper name is "Holmes" (at different worlds it will generally be different persons). Similarly, there will be, at worlds where *Macbeth* is told as known fact, some particular number of children that Lady Macbeth has (at different worlds it will be different numbers).

A similar argument applies in the case of (12). It is true in the Holmes story that there is some particular person who is the $F^\#$ and might not have been the $F^\#$. We fallaciously infer that there is some particular person of whom it is true in the story that he is the $F^\#$ and might not have been. And who would that be but **Holmes**?

I said that (11) and (12) express no propositions. But

(15) "'Holmes' is the proper name of **Holmes**" expresses a true proposition

and

(16) "**Holmes** might not have done the things described in
the story" expresses a true proposition

do express propositions: false ones, as a matter of fact. And
(15) and (16) are true in the Holmes story. Following again
the inference pattern of the Lady Macbeth example, we
would then conclude that there are propositions P_1 and P_2
such that it is true in the Holmes story that (11) expresses P_1
and (12) expresses P_2. So these propositions are true in the
Holmes story. Thus, we infer that (13) and (14) are true. We
laugh at those who wonder about the number of Lady Macbeth's children. When we see how easy it is to endorse the
fallacy that underlies that wondering, we shall not laugh so
hard.

I think we now have grounds for saying that the consequences of my theory concerning the truth in fiction of singular propositions are not so very implausible.

An author can affect the kind and number of things that
are modal truths in his story, canceling the impression we
might otherwise get that statements like (12) are true in his
story, by making it explicit in the story that some kind of
superessentialism is true. In that case modal claims of the
form of (12) will not be true in the story. I'm concerned here
with the kinds of claims we are prone to make concerning
stories that have as part of their backgrounds conventional
modal assumptions.

Gareth Evans argued that what I call metafictive discourse
must be understood quite generally as involving the reader's
make-believe, and he rejects the use, made here, of the operator **F**.[35] I want to comment briefly on Evans's proposal.

Evans classed fictional names with those singular terms he
calls "Russellian" and which I have called "directly referring
devices" – terms that depend for their significance upon having a reference. If a Russellian term lacks a reference – as do
fictional names – an utterance containing it lacks sense and

35 See Evans, ibid., chap. 11. The next three references in the text are to this work.

"nothing constitutes *understanding* the utterance" (p. 71; italics in the original). And he rejected the view that metafictive discourse can be understood as prefixed by the operator **F**, appealing to the principle, mentioned already, that if "*P*" has no sense, neither does "F(*P*)" (p. 364). Instead, Evans treated metafictive discourse as a species of what he calls the "conniving" use of singular terms; the author *pretends* to refer to a particular individual by using a fictional name, and readers continue the make-believe and pretend they are referring to the same person.[36] Thus, metafictive discourse is itself pretend assertion rather than assertion.

Note that Evans treated the "in the fiction" operator **F** as if it were entirely a device of philosophers who wish to explain how it is we can make apparently serious remarks about a fiction, his claim being that the device cannot do what is required of it. But this is not the case. "It is true in the story that *P*" or, perhaps more commonly, "It is part of the story that *P*," or "In the story, *P*," are locutions people help themselves to quite naturally, and it's part of the philosopher's job to explain, if possible, the conditions under which such locutions are true. Of course, it may turn out that no sense can be made of these sorts of remarks. But a theory that does make plausible sense of them must be regarded as having an edge on a theory according to which they are nonsensical, on the grounds that it is better, other things being equal, to affirm a widely held intuition than to deny it. By refusing to treat fictional names as Russellian terms I have been able to construct a theory that does make plausible sense of remarks like "In the story, Holmes takes cocaine." To that extent the theory is preferable to Evans's own.

No doubt there are times when a reader's utterances are better construed, with Evans, as involving a pretense (or as I would prefer to say, a make-believe) rather than

---

36 "Conniving use" is Quine's expression. See *Word and Object* (Cambridge, Mass.: MIT Press, 1960), p. 50.

as implicitly prefixed by the operator **F**. Sometimes readers and movie watchers continue their make-believe after
the novel is read or the movie seen. They make-believe
they are discussing the fortunes of a particular group of
people about whom the novel or movie has informed
them. But in such cases the make-believe is essentially
superficial. At any stage it can be abandoned, as it often
is when participants become conscious of the absurdity of
their situation, and the debate continued in the fact-
stating mode. In cases like that either the operator **F** is
explicitly used or it is commonly known between the participants that the operator is intended as prefatory to all
remarks. The make-believe, so long as it continues, is
harmless, because there is always the possibility that
what is said in the course of the make-believe is capable
of being rephrased by use of the operator in a way that
makes perfect sense. If we thought, with Evans, that
remarks made in the course of the make-believe were not
so interpretable, we would be faced with a very serious
problem: the problem of how to make sense of what is
uttered. Evans himself acknowledged that what is said in
such cooperative make-believe games is serious, in the
sense that the participants' utterances are up for assessment as *"really* correct or *really* incorrect" (p. 363; italics
in the original). But I don't see how Evans's theory can
account for this serious aspect. Evans claimed that speakers in such games say something correct. But if a speaker
in such a game says something that is really correct,
there must be something really correct that he says, and
Evans's theory does not allow us to say what this correct
thing is. For Evans's theory has it that in using a fictional
name, one cannot, literally, say anything at all. By contrast, the account I have offered of metafictive discourse
enables us to describe, quite precisely, the conditions
under which someone who says P in a game of make-
believe will count as having said something correct –
namely, when $F(P)$ is true.

Evans's untimely death has left us with a somewhat

sketchy account of his proposal. It is possible I have underestimated its resources.

4.11. ROLES

There are kinds of sentences in which fictional names occur for which I have not yet provided intuitively correct truth conditions. I call these *transfictive* uses. Examples of the sorts of sentences I have in mind are

(17) Holmes's methods are quite different from those of Poirot.

(18) Holmes is more interesting than any other character in detective fiction.

(19) Holmes would have solved the Yorkshire Ripper case more quickly than the police actually did.

If we treat them at face value they come out false, because they contain nondenoting definite descriptions. Yet we cannot satisfactorily treat them as occurring within the scope of the operator **F**. Consider (17). Holmes and Poirot do not appear in the same stories, and if we take the way of treating the union of their stories as a single fiction, we shall get into trouble, for the two stories do not have a common relevant background to assist us in determining fictional truth. To create a common background we would have to resolve clashes between the backgrounds of each, and there does not seem to be a nonarbitrary way of doing this. Interfictional comparisons like the ones just mentioned must be interpreted in such a way that the respective fictions are treated as separate entities. Similarly for (18) and (19): in the story, Holmes is not a fictional character and the Yorkshire Ripper murders do not occur.[37]

Robert Howell, in reviewing the prospects for an account of fictional names along the lines I have just given, notes that

---

37 Many counterfactuals about Holmes are easier to handle than (19) because they are true in the story. Thus, it is true in the story that if Holmes had not met Watson, his activities would have been less well publicized. It is reasonable to attribute *that* belief to the implied author.

such an account cannot handle contexts like (17)–(19), and he offers this as one reason for rejecting such an account.[38] But I think the lesson to be drawn is that the account works well for fictive and metafictive contexts, badly for transfictive contexts. We need a different, but suitably related, account for transfictive contexts.

The apparent truth of these comparative statements tempts us once more to acknowledge fictional people: people whose relations to one another and to the real world would be the appropriate truth makers for such statements. Still resisting this temptation, I seek the truth makers from within a class of entities that prove themselves useful quite outside the realm of fictional discourse. I shall call these entities "roles."

Recall our definition (8′), which says that to be Holmes is to satisfy a certain definite description $\imath x F^{\#}(x)$. The question who, if anybody, is Holmes in a given world is answered by determining who, if anybody, satisfies the description in that world. So there is a (partial) function from worlds to individuals that picks out Holmes in each world where somebody is Holmes, and the value of this function for a world-argument is the individual, if there is one, who satisfies the description $\imath x F^{\#}(x)$. This function I call the *Holmes role*. I define it as follows:

(20) The Holmes Role $=_{df} f_H : \omega \rightarrow \imath x[F^{\#}_{\omega}(x)]$,

where ω is a variable ranging over worlds and '$F^{\#}_{\omega}$' denotes the extension of $F^{\#}$ in ω. Thus *being Holmes* in a world is a matter of occupying the Holmes role in that world. Roles in this technical sense correspond to intuitively more familiar entities we sometimes call "roles," but more often call "characters." We say that some characters are more interesting, or realistic, or pedestrian than others. And Peter van Inwagen points out that we sometimes say things like

38 See Howell, "Fictional Objects: How They Are and How They Aren't," *Poetics* 8 (1979): 129–77. See Section 4.2.

4.11. Roles

(21) There are characters in some nineteenth-century fictions that are presented with a greater wealth of physical detail than is any character in any eighteenth-century fiction.

It is hard to see how we could interpret (21) unless we can quantify over fictional characters. For example, it seems to follow from (21) that there are characters in nineteenth-century fiction.[39] Van Inwagen offers no account of what these characters are, but he makes it clear that commitment to characters is not a commitment to fictional people. Characters are, he says, among the "theoretical entities of literary criticism" (p. 302). And, being a theoretical entity, the character Mrs. Gamp does not *have* the property of being fat; that property is *ascribed* to that character in *Martin Chuzzlewit* (p. 305). I suggest that roles offer us a well-defined explication of van Inwagen's characters. Roles are theoretical entities, in that sense of the term which contrasts with concrete things. And the Mrs. Gamp role isn't fat; fatness is one of the defining characteristics of the role. To occupy the role in a world w one must be fat in w.

We also speak of actors playing roles, and of various interpretations of a given role. When an actor plays a role he does not literally come to occupy that role. In order to occupy the Hamlet role he would have to do and be all the things that Hamlet does and is. Rather, the actor's playing the role consists in it being make-believe that the actor does and is those things, in it being make-believe that the actor occupies the role.[40]

Fictional roles, understood in this way, belong to a larger class of entities definable in a possible worlds setting. Follow-

39 See van Inwagen's "Creatures of Fiction," *American Philosophical Quarterly* 14 (1977): 299–308, and "Fiction and Metaphysics," *Philosophy and Literature* 7 (1983): 67–77. References in the text are to "Creatures of Fiction."

40 In the context of the make-believe the audience's identification of the occupant of the role may not involve certain names and descriptions. The audience may make believe that *that* man is Hamlet, that the distinguished man speaking now is Hamlet, but not that John Gielgud is Hamlet, or that the man we saw last week in *Richard III* is Hamlet.

4. The characters of fiction

ing Pavel Tichý, I call these entities *offices*.[41] The presidency of the United States is an office: a function from worlds to individuals, which takes the value George Bush at the actual world, Jesse Jackson at some other worlds, and no value at yet others. (Strictly speaking, offices are functions from world-times to individuals, but I shall suppress the reference to time here for the sake of simplicity.) Roles are just those offices defined in terms of what is true in a story. Typically they are partial functions that take no value at the actual world. What is crucial – what makes an office a role – is that while it is not true that the function takes a value at the actual world, it is true in the story that it does.

Note that my employment of Lewis's method of definition ties roles very closely to the stories from which they are derived. For the description $\imath x F^{\#}(x)$ contains within it all the information of the Holmes story. To compute the value of the function f_H for any given world one must know what goes on in the story. Conversely, knowledge of that story is sufficient to acquaint us with that function.

I suggest that a speaker who asserts (18) is best understood as expressing a judgment about the Holmes role. He is saying that the role of Holmes is a more interesting, richer role than any other detective role in fiction. Quite how you would assess that claim is a question of aesthetics rather than of semantics, so we can afford to ignore it.

Statements (17) and (19) involve judgments about the Holmes role in a slightly different way. They are judgments about the likely consequences for an individual of *occupying* the Holmes role. To assert that Holmes's methods are quite different from Poirot's is to assert that among the defining characteristics of the Holmes role are the having of certain methods of detection, and that these are different from the methods of detection that partly define the Poirot role. And when we assert (19) we assert that among the defining characteristics of the Holmes role are the kinds of capacities that would enable their possessor to solve

41 See his "De dicto and de re," *Philosophia* 8 (1978): 1–16.

174

4.11. Roles

the case more quickly than the police actually did solve it.

As with the analysis of metafictive uses in Section 4.8, I am not concerned here to show that people uttering such statements as (17)–(19) actually have in mind the propositions I have offered by way of paraphrase. When people say things like (17)–(19) they rarely have in mind all the details of the story, and in many cases they would not be capable of retaining all the necessary detail. In making such judgments readers typically have in mind a few salient facts derived from their reading of the story. It is not my business here to analyze and legitimate all such judgments based on partial understanding. The task, as I see it, is to provide a kind of *semantic ideal,* to which a community of super readers who retain everything they read might be said to conform. If this account is an adequate representation of the semantic activities of such a community, we may be content to say merely that our own activities are to be explained, case by case, as approximations to this ideal. And this process of idealization is not, after all, terribly unrealistic. For we all accept that in making judgments like (17)–(19) we must hold ourselves responsible to the entire body of evidence that the text provides concerning the character under discussion. And that body of evidence is summarized in descriptions of the kind that occur in (8′) and (20).

I have said that roles are functions from worlds to individuals, that it is individuals who occupy roles. This may not always be so. Suppose there is a novel describing the planning of a bank robbery. But at the last moment the robbers are preempted. The last sentence of the book reads: "That night the mysterious Wapping gang robbed the bank." That's all the story tells us about the Wapping gang. We know there are several of them, it is suggested they come from Wapping, and they are said to be mysterious. Certainly we know nothing about them that could distinguish one member of the gang from any other. Thus we cannot hope to carve many distinct descriptions out of the story, one for each member of the gang (especially since we don't know how many of them there are).[42] In that case my theory says there are not several distinct characters here. There is but one character, the Wapping gang. This character is, of course, a role and a role may be occupied. But this is not a role that can be occupied by a person. It can, however, be occupied jointly by several people. Perhaps we should say that the role is to be occupied by an object that is the mereological sum of several people. Or perhaps its prospective occupants are sets (of any cardinality between, say, three and ten). Choosing, more or less arbitrarily, the first option, we could express the role as:

(22) The Wapping gang $=_{df} \imath x(x$ is the sum of several people who robbed the bank).[43]

Is this an ad hoc strategy? I think not. There are easily imaginable cases in which we would favor the treatment of a multiplicity of persons as a single character. Suppose a novel set in Revolutionary France makes frequent reference to the Mob. The Mob is described as acting in a certain way, and as having certain characteristics, for example, being furious, being easily led. Nothing is said, however, to distinguish any member of the Mob from any other. It's quite natural to regard the Mob as a single character.

Sometimes we do not merely compare characters across fictions, we *identify* them across fictions. In a sense there are many stories by Doyle about Sherlock Holmes, but I think we

42 Presumably it will be true in the story that the members of the gang are distinguished one from another in various ways. Suppose we knew that there are just two of them, that we could assume that no two people are born at the same instant, and that this is all that can be assumed as background for purposes of differentiation. We could then distinguish the members of the gang in a principled way, calling the first "Early" and the second one "Late." But if the story suggests other distinguishing properties (as it probably will), we can no longer distinguish them. Suppose we assume that one was closer to the sun in a certain direction at a certain moment. Was the closer one Early or Late? If the story does not tell us, the choice would be arbitrary. To say that Early was the closer one would be to fill out that character beyond the resources of the story. It would be to impose characters on the story, rather than to derive them from the story.
43 This is a first approximation, of course. The description will have to be integrated into the whole story in the style of (8).

may treat these stories as episodes in one big story, the whole
of which defines the Holmes character. Each separate episode contains what is merely a partial specification of the
character. But Holmes, James Bond, and other characters
have been written about (so we say) by more than one
author. Some of these stories produce consistent extensions
of the original character; it is understood in these stories that
the character did the things described in the original stories,
and did other things the new stories tell us about. In the
Flashman stories of George MacDonald Fraser, the eponymous hero (if you can call him a hero) is said to be the very
same person as the person who is described in Thomas
Hughes's *Tom Brown's Schooldays*, the latter being described
in the former as thinly disguised autobiography. *Wide Sar-
gasso Sea* by Jean Rhys purports to describe the life of Mrs.
Rochester up to her imprisonment in the attic at Thornfield
Hall. If this kind of effect is achieved without interfering with
the content of the original story, we may say that the stories
are about the same character, meaning just that the new role
is an extension of the old one. The new author is tightening
the conditions on the character; he is doing more of what the
original author did.

Sometimes, however, it seems as if different fictions contradict each other over the activities of a single character. The
contradictions can be quite startling. Homer has Helen run
off to Troy with Paris; Euripides has her spend the time in
Egypt while a look-alike languishes in Troy. Are Homer and
Euripides speaking of the same character? If "character"
means "person," the answer is no. There is no person who is
referred to in either play.[44] If "character" means "role" (and
that's what I mean by character), the answer is the same. The
defining characteristics of the two characters are different,
although they overlap – for example, both Homer–Helen and
Euripides–Helen are married to someone called "Menelaus."

44 I assume for the sake of the argument that "Helen" as used in these works is a
genuine fictional name in my sense. That is, I assume that there is no actually
existing person of whom it is true in Homer and in Euripides that "Helen" refers
to her.

One way to support the claim that both plays are about the same character would be to cut down the characters to a common core and claim that it's this core character that appears in both. I don't know how this could be done in a way that would not then legitimate a parallel strategy of cutting down, say, the James Bond character and the Holmes character to a common core and claiming that the same core character appears in the stories of Doyle and in the stories of Ian Fleming – for their characters doubtless have things in common. And what, in the end, would be gained by such a procedure, even if it could be carried out satisfactorily? Literary critics may be interested in similarities between characters, in the influence of one writer's character construction on that of another, in the relative success of one writer's characterization as compared with another's. Nothing I have said about individuating characters very finely need inhibit any of these practices. Euripides' employment of his Helen role was no doubt prompted in part by his knowledge of the Helen role employed by Homer. These roles can be compared, and judged for comparative aesthetic interest. When we study these problems a kind of shorthand develops, and we speak of "the same character." But when we speak as literary critics we don't have to clear up the semantic mess we make. When we speak as philosophers we know better.

Suppose two authors independently produce lexically identical texts. Do their stories involve the same characters? Texts that are lexically identical need not tell the same story. If Pierre Menard had succeeded in his aim of producing a text lexically identical to that of Cervantes's *Don Quixote*, but in (relative) independence from the original text, he would not have produced the same story. It's the words and sentences of the text *plus* relevant background that determine what is true in the stories, and here relevant background for the one story is different from relevant background for the other.[45]

---

45 As Borges makes clear, Freudian psychology is part of background for Menard's work, but not for Cervantes's.

4.11. Roles

What is true in the two stories will be different, and the roles the two stories define will correspondingly diverge.

Suppose background for the two stories is the same. Even then, on my account, the characters will not be the same. Pairing characters across the fictions, we shall find their properties intersect but are not coincident. Recall that a defining feature of any character is that he or she is a person about whom the (fictional) author of *this text* is writing. Of characters like Flashman it is true in the one story that he was written about by someone else, but this will not be the case for characters in the kinds of stories we are presently considering, for here the stories are independently produced and make no reference, explicit or implicit, to one another. Consider A and B, independently produced stories identical so far as spelling and background go. It will be true in A that A's protagonists are spoken of by the narrator of A, and not true in A that A's protagonists are spoken about by the narrator of B. Symmetrically for B. So the characters in A and B are pairwise distinct.[46]

One reason we are inclined to say distinct authors write about the same characters is that we confuse our own extended make-believe with the fiction itself. Thus the reader of a modern Holmes-pastiche may make believe not merely that he is reading an account of known fact, but also that Doyle's original story was a biography of the same man this is an account of. It might be part of his make-believe that the original biography was unreliable, and that the present volume corrects its errors. The reader makes believe that someone called "Holmes" was written about (unreliably) by someone called "Watson," that Watson's errors are being corrected in the volume now being read. The Holmes of the reader's make-believe, the Holmes of Doyle, and the Holmes of the later author are all different characters, with different defining characteristics. But the reader may easily conflate

---

46 Perhaps we can say instead that the circumstances of production of the text belong to relevant background for the corresponding story, and that it is therefore not possible, contrary to our original assumption, for the backgrounds of both stories to be the same.

4. The characters of fiction

them, by failing to distinguish what is make-believe in his game from what is true in each of the fictions. This unreflective consolidation can give us the impression that the stories are about the same character, and say contradictory things about him.

4.12. CONCLUSIONS

Early in this chapter I announced the nonexistence of Holmes. More precisely, fictional names as used by authors of fiction do not refer to anyone or anything. In some contexts readers use these expressions to refer to the kinds of functions I have called "roles." But roles in this sense do not act out or endure the events described in fictional stories. If these roles were occupied, there would be people who acted out or endured these events, but these roles are not occupied. That is what I mean when I say that Holmes, Alice, Flashman, and the rest of them do not exist.

There are worlds other than the actual world where the Holmes role is occupied. Someone is Holmes in a world w if he is the value of our function f_H at w. If it is possible for me to have been and done all the things Holmes is said to be and do, then there is a world in which I am and do those things and in that world I occupy the Holmes roles; I am Holmes in that world.[47] But that does not make me or the countless others about whom we could say the same thing the *subject* of the Holmes story. Doyle's use of Holmes is not a reference to me – no more than the policeman's use of "Smith's murderer" is a reference to me just because I might have murdered Smith. And my occupancy of the Holmes role in another world is not something the reader need bear in mind in order to understand or appreciate the story.

I have examined three ways in which fictional names are used. First, they occur within fictional works ("fictive" uses). Here they are to be interpreted as bound variables. Second, they occur in statements about the fiction ("metafictive"

47 Here I'm grateful to David Lewis.

180

uses). Here they are abbreviated descriptions occurring within the scope of the operator F. Third, there are statements, like our (17)–(19), that occur neither within the fiction itself nor within the scope of the operator F: statements that compare fictional characters across fiction or with real-world people or that involve quantification over fictional characters ("transfictive" uses). Such statements can be handled by introducing expressions that refer to offices or roles, and these expressions can in turn be extracted from the story's description of its characters. Each of these partial accounts of the use of fictional names is derived from the preceding one in a natural way. The whole amounts, I think, to a unified theory rather than to a patchwork of diverse suggestions. The power of the theory must be assessed in terms of its ability to explain, or to explain away, our intuitions about the truth values of statements involving fictional names. A preliminary assessment of this kind has been the aim of this chapter.

The semantics of fictional names gets more complex the farther we move away from the fiction itself. In fiction itself these expressions serve merely to introduce bound variables. When we speak about the fiction they become disguised definite descriptions: expressions that have denotation in some worlds but not in others. When we move outside the world of the fiction and say things about the character that do not correspond to what is said in the fiction, they become names of functions from worlds to individuals. In these contexts they denote superworldly, necessarily existing things.

Chapter 5

Emotion and the response to fiction

We read novels not merely to find out what is true in them, or to decide whether the author has done a decent job of plot construction, or to study the characteristics of a certain genre. We read them because we hope they will engage us, that we will be caught up in their plots, that we will be concerned – perhaps intensely concerned – for their characters, what they do and what is done to them. Like others who read *The Turn of the Screw* as a ghost story, I loathe Quint and pity Miss Jessel. And the children, at first delightful, quickly assume the aspect of a disturbing maturity. Followers of Edmund Wilson will take a different view of the story, but it will hardly be a less emotionally engaged one as they see the innocent children drawn tragically into the governess's world of delusive madness. And whether the governess opposes a real threat from the supernatural or the products of her own imagination, her courage and determination are surely admirable.

5.1. FINDING THE PROBLEM

Although we may disagree about the impact of any particular work, there is little doubt that we all, on occasion, report similar responses to fiction. But as other writers have made clear, there is something very puzzling about this. The problem is not that fiction is too trivial or irrelevant to our real concerns to be *worth* becoming emotional about. If that were the problem, it would not be especially a problem about fiction; peo-

182

5.1. Finding the problem

ple get emotional about all sorts of apparently trivial things. It is rather that, given a certain widely held conception of what emotions involve, emotional reactions to fiction seem to be *impossible*. As Colin Radford put it: "I can only be moved by someone's plight if I believe that something terrible has happened to him. If I . . . believe that he has not and is not suffering or whatever, I cannot grieve or be moved to tears."[1] Radford's point is a logical one: emotion requires belief, and the reader of fiction does not have the beliefs required for emotion. How, then, can we be horrified by ghosts we don't believe in? How can we fear for the moral and physical well-being of people we know don't exist? How can we admire a woman we know has never lived?[2]

Let us call the view that emotions are essentially belief-involving *cognitivism*. To say that I fear for the governess, while lacking the kinds of beliefs that cognitivism requires of fear, is just to say that cognitivism is false. Indeed, there is something wrong with cognitivism, but to reject it wholesale would be a mistake. The cognitive analysis of emotions contains some sereptitious legislation as well as valuable insight; the problem is to preserve the insight while getting rid of the legislation. This I propose to do. But for a while I shall play the cognitivist's game, developing a precise and not implausible (and not very original) version of the cognitivist's theory of emotions – a theory that gives belief an essential role.

What, then, of my claim to fear for the governess? My next step will be to show that, once we have this theory before us, we can develop a parallel theory of what I shall call the *quasi-*

---

1 See Radford's contribution to the symposium "How Can We Be Moved by the Fate of Anna Karenina?," *Aristotelian Society Supplementary Volumes* 49 (1975): 67–80. The quotation is from p. 68.
2 See, for example, Michael Weston's contribution to the symposium with Radford, pp. 81–93; Barrie Paskins, "On Being Moved by Anna Karenina and *Anna Karenina*," *Philosophy* 52 (1977): 344–7; Eva Schaper, "Fiction and the Suspension of Disbelief," *British Journal of Aesthetics* 18 (1978): 31–44; David Novitz, "Fiction, Imagination and Emotion," *Journal of Aesthetics and Art Criticism* 38 (1979–80): 279–88; H. O. Mounce, "Art and Real Life," *Philosophy* 55 (1980): 183–92; and William Charlton, "Feeling for the Fictitious," *British Journal of Aesthetics* 24 (1984): 206–16.

emotions – those states we get into when we encounter fiction and that we commonly describe as "pitying Anna," "fearing for the governess" and the like.[3] The quasi-emotions do not involve belief but are, in other ways, very like the emotions, which explains why I say I fear for the governess when what is true is that I quasi-fear for her. It's easy to mistake one mental state for another when the two are pretty much alike, just as it's easy to mistake a man drinking sparkling water for a man drinking champagne. Thus we solve our problem without abandoning cognitivism.

All this within the rules of the cognitivist's game. Then I shall throw out the rules and admit that the term "emotion" is too broad in its common application for us to say simply: "What I call 'pitying Anna' is *not* really an emotion." But we shall see that awkward facts about usage can be faced without rejecting the essentials of the cognitivist's solution. All we need attend to is the question of labeling.

There is a constraint worth bearing in mind here. An account of our responses to fiction (our "quasi-emotions") should draw, in a principled way, on insights into the nature of fiction itself. After all, what is characteristic of our responses to fiction is that they are responses to *fiction*, and we would expect that their being so would in some measure dictate their character. Whatever else may be said in its favor, my account will be seen to meet this constraint.

After describing some blind alleys we might be tempted to march up when thinking about fiction and the emotions, I shall try to give some structure to the issue with a sharp formulation of the problem, together with a review of the options this formulation makes available to us. I then sketch a theory of the emotions. This forms the background for a

---

3 Kendall Walton uses the term, "quasi-fear" to refer to the phenomenological aspect of fear, the feelings of bodily disturbance that go with being afraid. Similarly for quasi-pity and the phenomenological components of other emotions. I call these things "feelings" instead, reserving the "quasi" locutions for the emotionlike states that we experience when we respond to fiction and that may involve, but that are not identical to, feelings. This difference between us is merely terminological. For a substantive difference, see Section 5.6.

preliminary statement of my solution. Finally, the preliminary statement is adjusted as we distinguish between fact and stipulation.

There are ways to misunderstand the problem. One is to suppose the problem arises because Quint, Miss Jessel, the governess, and all the rest of them do not exist – to suppose that the problem is, How can we loathe, pity, or admire the nonexistent? This would be a mistake, because the problem of nonexistence is not peculiar to fictional contexts, and a solution to it, of whatever kind, will leave us with an unresolved puzzle about fiction. If I succumb to a perceptual illusion, I may fear *that man over there,* when in fact there is no man over there. But in this case I do at least believe that there is a man over there, and perhaps I also believe that he means me harm. It is the absence of exactly those kinds of beliefs in the fictional case that sets the problem of our responses to fiction apart from the kind of problem posed by perceptual illusion, historical misinformation, and other sorts of mistakes. You might resist this separation of problems if you hold, with some direct reference theorists, that no proposition is expressed by "he means me harm" in the case of a perceptual illusion and that consequently there is no more a belief in this case than there is in the case of fiction reading. But direct reference is a red herring here. For if there really is no belief in the illusion case then it is part of the illusion to which I have fallen victim that there is; I believe I have a belief even if I don't. That at least is a difference between the perceptual illusion and the case of fiction reading. And if, as argued in Chapter 4, the names of fictional characters function as disguised descriptions rather than proper names, empty or otherwise, it is not appropriate to compare sentences of fiction with sentences that purport, as in the perceptual illusion case, to express singular propositions; rather, they should be compared with sentences that involve nonrigid, descriptive terms and that are as a result semantically insensitive to what does or does not exist.

If existence isn't our problem, it seems that *belief* about existence is; isn't it the reader's failure to believe in the existence of the story's characters that creates the problem?[4] If that was so we might have reason to look kindly on those metaphysical systems which find a place for fictional entities.[5] But it is not so, and the puzzle would remain even if we could convince ourselves that fictional characters exist. There are, after all, fictional stories about real people. In *The Day of the Jackal*, de Gaulle is the intended victim of a (fictional) assassination plot. That I fear for him as the Jackal raises his rifle is just as puzzling as my fearing for a purely fictional (that is, nonexistent) character. For I do not believe de Gaulle is or ever was in the situation the novel describes (although he was in some not entirely dissimilar situations). If we focus on nonexistence, cases like this will slip through our net. So it's better to say that the beliefs lacked by the reader of fiction are beliefs concerning the *situations* of the characters.[6] The story I read involves the proposition that de Gaulle is in danger from a marksman; it is my not believing *that* proposition that makes my (apparently) fearing for de Gaulle puzzling. Of course, if and when I read a fiction and fail to believe in the existence of one of its characters, that will also generate the same sort of puzzle. But we can take it that propositions like *Sherlock Holmes exists* are just one kind of proposition about the situations of fictional characters, and so are covered by the more general formulation.

Another source of confusion is to suppose that the problem is not, How can we be moved by the fate of a fictional character? but, rather, How can we *rationally* be moved by the fate of a fictional character? Colin Radford concludes that "our being moved in certain ways by works of art . . . involves us in inconsistency and so incoherence."[7] And this from one who began, as we have already seen, with an un-

4 I am grateful to Barry Taylor for discussion of material in this paragraph.
5 See e.g. Terence Parsons, *Nonexistent Objects* (New Haven: Yale University Press, 1980).
6 In much of this chapter I use the term "reader" to refer generally to consumers of fiction in whatever media: written or oral literature, plays, films, and so on.
7 "How Can We Be Moved by the Fate of Anna Karenina?," p. 78.

compromisingly cognitive thesis: "I can only be moved by someone's plight if I believe that something terrible has happened to him. If I . . . believe that he . . . is not suffering . . . I cannot grieve or be moved to tears."[8] If there is incoherence here, it is in Radford's own position. He is like one who says that being in two places at once is an incoherent idea, so that anyone who is in two places at once is engaging in incoherent behavior. The problem is posed by an inconsistency between propositions, and we can't solve that problem by talking about incoherent behavior.

5.2. THE OPTIONS

By locating these sources of misunderstanding, we're better able to focus on the real problem. The problem is given by the existence of three plausible but mutually contradictory propositions:

(1) We have emotions concerning the situations of fictional characters.
(2) To have an emotion concerning someone's situation we must believe the propositions that describe that situation.
(3) We do not believe the propositions that describe the situations of fictional characters.

Asserting all three propositions will land us in a contradiction, resolvable by denying any one of the three. The problem is to decide which one, and further, to decide what to replace it with. For we could not be content merely to deny, say, (1); that would leave a gap in our intuitive picture of human psychological responses; a gap we should have to fill in some way.

Having listed some ways to misdescribe the problem, let me say something briefly about ways of solving it that are to be avoided. Denying (3) is one of them. Hardly anyone ever lit-

8 Ibid., p. 68. David Novitz says that his aim is "to furnish a viable account of how we can rationally be moved by the fortunes or misfortunes of fictional characters" ("Fiction, Imagination and Emotion," p. 279).

erally believes the content of a fiction when he knows it to be a fiction; if it happens at moments of forgetfulness or intense realism in the story (which I doubt), such moments are too brief to underwrite our often sustained responses to fictional events and characters. Henceforth, I shall assume the truth of (3) and consider the possibilities for rejecting either (1) or (2).

If we are to reject (1) we ought not to do so by adopting what I call the *transfer strategy*. On this view, we experience genuine emotions when we encounter fiction, but their relation to the story is causal rather than intentional; the story provokes thoughts about real people and situations, and these are the intentional objects of our emotions. Barrie Paskins, for example, claims that "our pity [for Anna] can without forcing be construed as pity for those people if any who are in the same bind as the character in the fiction."[9]

Paskins' qualification "if any" is rather problematic; what if there aren't any, or – more to the point – what if I don't believe there are any? But the basic flaw in this and similar suggestions is that they sever the *normative* connection between our responses to fiction and the fictions they are responses to. Responses to fiction are to be assessed as reasonable or unreasonable according to how well or how badly they are justified by the events of the story. And we can be persuaded that our responses to a character are inappropriate, because we have misunderstood some aspect of the story.[10] Admiring the courage and determination of the governess is reasonable, at least in part, because of what is said to happen in *The Turn of the Screw*. Admiring courageous and determined people in general is justified in quite other ways. So admiring the governess cannot *be* admiring courageous and determined people in general.

If we are to reject (2), we ought not to do so by adopting what I call the *content exclusion strategy*. On this view emotions are phenomenological states, assimilable to sensations and/or their bodily correlates. (Recall William James: "the

9 "On Being Moved by Anna Karenina and *Anna Karenina*," p. 346.
10 A point well made by Michael Weston ("How Can We Be Moved . . .?," p. 86).

feeling of these [bodily] changes as they occur is the emotion."[11] And if emotions just are feelings, having an emotion
no more requires us to have specific beliefs than having pains
does.

There are more or less plausible versions of this view, and
only the implausible versions of it will implement the content
exclusion strategy. The least plausible is an unrestricted identification of emotions with feelings along the lines of the
"water = H_2O" model beloved of early materialists. Thus we
get identities like "Fear = feeling F," "Pity = feeling G," and
so on. The observation that fear simply does not always feel
the same way might push us to substitute a disjunction of
feelings on the right-hand side, but more than likely we shall
find patterns of overlap between the different disjunctions
supposedly definitive of different mental states – and so we
shall be embarrassed to say, confronted with a feeling that
lies in more than one disjunction, what emotion its occurrence betokens. And how shall we distinguish the state of
pitying Fred from the state of pitying Jane, when they feel the
same? But distinguish them we must, when it comes to
explaining behavior. (The same objection will apply if we
move to the physiological level and try, with Ekman and his
colleagues, to distinguish the emotions in terms of differential responses in the autonomic nervous system.)[12] A more
plausible view is that to have an emotion is to be in *some* state
which occupies a certain broadly specified causal role, and
that the relevant role is occupied by a feeling (perhaps by different feelings on different occasions). On this account, the
state that realizes pity for Jane in me now might realize pity

11 William James, "What Is an Emotion?," first published in *Mind* 9 (1884): 188–205,
    and reprinted in M. Arnold (ed.), *The Nature of Emotion* (London: Penguin, 1968).
    The quotation is from p. 19 of the reprint; italics in the original. It is not clear
    whether James would say that the bodily change (he has in mind changes to the
    visceral and skeletal muscles) are themselves essential components of the emo-
    tion: whether, in other words, he would say that one is in an emotional state if
    one has the feelings of bodily disturbance without one's body actually being dis-
    turbed.
12 P. Ekman, "Autonomic Nervous System Activity Distinguishes Among Emo-
    tions," *Science* 221 (1983): 1208–10. I owe this reference to Paul Griffith.

for Fred in you now, and love for Jane in you tomorrow, because that state occupies different causal roles in different people at different times. This approach would not be available to someone who thinks of feelings as themselves functionally characterizable states, for such a person would not be able to countenance the possibility of the same feeling occupying *different* functional roles. As one skeptical of functional accounts of feeling, it is not open to me to block the move to this more sophisticated version of the emotions-are-feelings proposal. But if we make this move, we no longer have an easy route to the denial of (2); for the attempt to characterize the emotions in terms of their causes and effects will bring back what we're trying to exclude: beliefs. If fearing for a loved one is a feeling caused in a certain way, one of its causes is surely going to be beliefs about the loved one's situation, whereas my feelings for Anna Karenina are caused in some other, as yet to be examined, way. There will also be differences at the level of behavioral effects, about which I shall have more to say later. (And let no one appeal here to *typical* causal roles. Pitying Anna is not typically caused by beliefs about her situation: such an etiology would be quite pathological.) I don't want to argue that this functionalist-inspired proposal is wrong; in fact, it is rather like the proposal I shall develop concerning the emotions. My point here is that this most plausible version of the emotions-are-feelings theory turns out *not* to be a version of the content exclusion strategy. By invoking functional roles it prevents us from concentrating exclusively on feelings.

5.3. A THEORY OF EMOTION

I want now to sketch a more adequate, but not especially original, theory of the emotions. The extreme view that emotions are just subjective feelings has recently given way to the opposite view according to which emotions are purely cognitive: to have an emotion is just to judge that something is the case, or to evaluate a thing or state of affairs in some

5.3. A theory of emotion

way.[13] But this is as much a distortion as the feeling-theory. To be afraid is more than just to believe that one is in danger and to desire to avoid the danger. One can have these propositional attitudes without being in a state of fear. Neither subjective feelings nor propositional attitudes are sufficient for the presence of an emotion, although each is necessary. Nor are they jointly sufficient. To have an emotion is not just to have a certain combination of thoughts and feelings, it is to have the feelings *as a result* of having the thoughts. Pitying Jane would consist in having certain thoughts about Jane (e.g., believing that her situation is desperate, hoping that it will improve, etc.) and being caused thereby to have certain subjective feelings: the unpleasant feelings that go with pity. Such feelings are hard to describe. Perhaps they cannot be described without circularity. Perhaps all we can say is this: The feeling of pity is the feeling one has when one thinks pitying thoughts, just as we say the sensation of redness is the sensation we have when we see red things.[14]

13 See Errol Bedford, "Emotions," *Proceedings of the Aristotelian Society* 62 (1956–7): 281–304, reprinted in C. Calhoun and R. Solomon (eds.), *What Is an Emotion?*; (New York: Oxford University Press, 1984); George Pitcher, "Emotion," *Mind* 74 (1965): 326–46; Robert Solomon, *The Passions* (New York: Doubleday, 1977). For earlier work, see Thomas Reid, excerpted in D. D. Raphael (ed.), *British Moralists*, vol. 2 (Oxford: Clarendon Press, 1969), pp. 295–9. Anthony Kenny's *Action, Emotion and Will* (London: Routledge & Kegan Paul, 1963) is a recent precursor of contemporary cognitivism. Cognitive theories that emphasize the role of desire are to be found in Jenefer Robinson, "Emotion, Judgement and Desire," *Journal of Philosophy* 80 (1983): 731–40, and Joel Marks, "A Theory of Emotion," *Philosophical Studies* 42 (1982): 227–42. For a criticism of cognitivist theories, see Michael Stocker, "Psychical Feelings: Their Importance and Irreducibility," *Australasian Journal of Philosophy* 61 (1983): 5–26. The theory I propose is somewhat similar to that presented in William Lyons, *Emotion*, (New York: Cambridge University Press, 1980), and in Michael Stocker, "Emotional Thoughts," *American Philosophical Quarterly* 24 (1987): 59–69. Its closest relative is the "component analysis" of Irving Thalberg (*Perception, Emotion and Action* [Oxford: Basil Blackwell, 1977], chap. 2).

The vast amount of psychological theorizing about the emotions that has been done is not easy to assimilate to acknowledged philosophical perspectives, and the available experimental evidence is notoriously susceptible of widely differing interpretations. For a review of recent psychological work, see R. Buck, "The Psychology of Emotion," in J. E. LeDoux and W. Hirst (ed.), *Mind and Brain: Dialogues in Cognitive Neuroscience* (New York: Cambridge University Press, 1986).

14 Colors, and secondary properties generally, are themselves a disputed kind of

5. Emotion and the response to fiction

So the theory amounts to this: Our beliefs and desires, conceived of as propositional attitudes, may bear upon each other in ways that cause us to have certain kinds of feelings. Where our beliefs and desires harmonize, they tend to produce feelings we find pleasant, as with feelings of requited love, or pride in the achievements of others and of ourselves. Where our beliefs and desires are in tension, they tend to produce feelings we find unpleasant to various degrees, as with feelings of rejection, shame, and disappointment. This nexus of relationships between propositional attitudes and feelings is an emotion.

Emotions, then, have three aspects: a set of propositional attitudes, a characteristic feeling or range of feelings, and a causal relationship the one bears to the other.[15]

This simple picture would be undermined if we thought of desires themselves as feelings, or even as essentially involving feelings. For then we should have to decide whether any of the feelings we associate with an emotion are feelings constitutive of, rather than caused by, the desire that is itself constitutive of the emotion. At the very least this would complicate the straightforward account I have given of the causal structure of emotions. But although there is some tendency to think of desires as states we *feel*, we can see on reflection that this is not a very plausible view. Thus, it may happen that I have a desire I'm unaware of having, a desire I would

case in this regard. For opposing views, see Colin McGinn, *The Subjective View* (Oxford: Clarendon Press, 1983), and Christopher Peacocke, *Sense and Content* (New York: Oxford University Press, 1983). See also Stephen R. Leighton, "On Feeling Angry and Elated," *Journal of Philosophy* 85 (1988): 253–64.

15 I am not claiming that emotions are Gaul-like wholes with three parts. Here I simply specify identity conditions for emotions. Emotional episodes are type-identical when the same propositional attitude-types cause the same (or similar) feeling-types. (Perhaps I should add: cause in the same way. Here I ignore the problem of feelings deviantly caused by attitudes.) I am also not claiming that there is some specific belief–desire pair that belongs to each emotion type. Emotion-types like, say, anger or fear, are characterized by a great deal of cognitive variability. One episode of anger may involve one belief–desire pair, whereas another such episode will involve a quite different pair. No doubt there is a similar variability over a range of feelings. I claim only that two episodes will be of the same emotion-type if they involve the same beliefs, desires, and feelings.

not come to know of merely by examining my feelings, but which I might come to know of by having it pointed out to me that my behavior is hard to explain except on the assumption that I do have that desire. And although feelings come and go, I may have a desire that's with me for many years. A more useful way to think of desires is as dispositions to act in certain ways in certain circumstances.[16]

Let us sharply distinguish the theory of emotion just outlined from another theory already mentioned: that emotions are feelings that are, or typically are, caused by certain thoughts. The cognitive aspect of an emotion is a matter not of its etiology but of its very identity; the cognitive component is as essential to the emotion as is the feeling. Someone who has the feelings we associate with pity but is caused to have them in some atypical way – as the result of chemical stimulation, for instance – is not in an atypical state of pity. To be pity, the feeling must be caused by the relevant thoughts. This allows us to avoid the claim, apparently false, that each emotion involves a distinctive feeling. As I have remarked, distinct emotions can be phenomenologically very much alike as long as they involve different beliefs and desires.

On the view I propose, emotions are much closer to actions in their logical structure than they are to feelings. An action is specified in terms of beliefs and desires and behavior, where the behavior is caused by the belief and desire. An emotion differs from this in essential structure only in that feelings take the place of behavior. Emotions and actions differ in other ways, however. For example, the behavioral aspect of an action such as one's arm rising – is *made desirable* by the beliefs and desires which cause it. But the feelings we have in response to emotionally powerful thoughts, although they are caused by the thoughts, are not made desirable by them. Some feelings we have when we have an emotional experience are intrinsically desirable (i.e., they are

16 This paragraph owes much to Michael Smith, "The Humean Theory of Motivation," *Mind* 96 (1987): 36–61. See esp. sections 5 and 6.

pleasant for us) while others are intrinsically undesirable (unpleasant). But the thoughts that provoke them speak neither for nor against our having them.[17]

This theory of emotion might be objected to on the grounds that it fails to establish any connection between emotion and *behavior*. To be jealous is, among other things, to be prone to act in a certain way. But given the way I have defined emotions in terms of attitudes and feelings, the connection with behavior comes as a free bonus. For propositional attitudes and feelings are themselves to be at least partly characterized in functional terms – in terms of their connections with behavior. We can assume that the behavioral aspects of any given emotion will supervene on the behavioral aspects of its components.

Theories of the emotions like the one offered here are sometimes criticized as being false to our experience of emotions. Thus Robert Roberts claims that "Emotions are typically experienced as unified states of mind, rather than as sets of components (for example, a belief + a desire + a physiological perturbation + some behavior)."[18] Presumably Roberts will say, against my theory, that emotions are not typically experienced as a belief + a desire + a feeling, and no doubt he will be right to say this. The question is whether this is an objection to the theory. First of all, I don't see how, on anybody's account, we experience beliefs and desires at all, at least in the sense in which we experience feelings; beliefs and desires are not states with phenomenological content. Insofar as we experience our emotions at all, we experience their phenomenological components – the feelings that the beliefs and desires give rise to. And this phenomenological component is experienced, presumably, as a "unified state of mind," or of the body, since our feelings sometimes have bodily locations. But there is an extended sense of "experience," a sense in which we can be *aware of* our

17 On this, see Robert Gordon, "The Passivity of Emotions," *Philosophical Review* 95 (1986): 371–92.
18 "What an Emotion Is: A Sketch," *Philosophical Review* 97 (1988): 183–209. The quotation is from p. 184.

5.4. A solution

thoughts. And perhaps Roberts will say that I am committed to the view that when we are in emotional states, we must be aware of the thoughts that constitute them, as well as experience the feelings to which they give rise. The principle that lies behind this is the following: When we are in states with structure, our experience, in the broad sense, of those states consists in our experience of their structural components. But this principle is quite implausible. According to some, our thoughts have a quasi-sentential structure within which we can distinguish parts corresponding to the grammatical parts of a sentence. I would not think it an important objection to this view that having a thought is "typically experienced as a unified state of mind." Perhaps, when we think about it in a philosophical way, we can become aware of a quasi-sentential structure to our thoughts, even though this is not how we come to be aware of our thoughts. Something like this can be said of the emotions: We are capable, in cases where we can manage to be sufficiently analytical about our emotions, of distinguishing between the beliefs, desires, and feelings that constitute them.

Because we are rarely aware of the detailed structure of our emotions, it is plausible to suppose that there is room for error and confusion in our judgments about exactly what state we are in when we suppose ourselves to be in the grip of an emotion. Emotions turn out to be quite complex entities with identifying features that are far from transparent to introspection. It's not easy for us to say exactly what our propositional attitudes are, still harder to identify their causal ramifications. The claim that we just know that we experience pity, admiration, and the like while reading fiction cannot be sustained.

5.4. A SOLUTION

We now have a theory of the emotions. Because it's a theory that makes beliefs essential components of emotions, it represents an endorsement of (2) and, in conjunction with (3), a rejection of (1). If the theory is correct, the states we call "pitying Anna" and "fearing for the governess" – remember, "quasi-emotions" is the generic name I've given them – are not emotional states. Or so it seems. As I suggested at the beginning of the chapter, that is a conclusion I want to avoid. But let us continue our somewhat blinkered progress and consider how we should proceed on the assumption that our responses to fiction are not emotions. What I want to suggest now is that we can find an analysis of our responses to fiction with striking parallels to the analysis of emotions just presented.

In Chapter 1, I argued that a work is fiction if its author had a certain kind of intention: the intention that readers adopt the attitude of make-believe toward the propositions of the story. In Chapter 2, I noted that there are, in fact, two distinct senses of make-believe. There is the sense I have just appealed to, the sense in which someone can make believe that something or other is the case, as Emily and her friends make believe that she is a pirate captain. In this sense make-believe is a propositional attitude. It can also *be* make-believe that something or other is the case, as it is make-believe in the children's game that Emily is a pirate captain. In this sense make-believe is a propositional operator. The point I want immediately to make can be made in terms of the attitude sense. When I come to consider a view of Kendall Walton's we shall need both senses clearly before us.

To read a work of fiction is to engage in a largely internalized game of make-believe. The reader makes believe that he is reading an account of known fact, and adopts an attitude of make-believe toward the propositions of the story. He does not believe the story, he makes believe it. The difference between fiction reading and nonfiction reading is that, with the former, make-belief takes over the role that otherwise would be occupied by belief. And this suggests the following hypothesis: Our responses to fiction differ from emotions in that make-belief is substituted for belief.

What happens to someone who reads *Anna Karenina* and responds to it in a way he would describe as "pitying Anna"? The following is a first approximation that will need some

revision. Reading the novel, he plays a game of make-
believe, adopting the attitude of make-believe to the propositions of the story. He makes believe that he is reading a true
account of events, desiring certain outcomes as the story
unfolds. The interaction of his thus acquired propositional
attitudes (make-belief and desire) causes him to have feelings
of various kinds. And typically these causal processes mirror
the causal processes that would take place if his attitude was
not make-belief but straightforward belief. The subjective
feelings and bodily reactions he experiences while reading
about Anna are not unlike those he would experience on
reading about the fate of some similarly situated real person.
Putting it in functionalist terms, we may say that the functional role of make-belief is similar in this respect to that of
belief, though dissimilar in other respects. Believing someone is in danger may cause me to alert the police; making
believe he is will not.

The reader of whom we say, "He pities Anna," is thus in
a state that differs somewhat from those states I have thus far
called "emotions" in that his feelings are caused by make-
belief and desire, rather than by belief and desire. But there
is much his state has in common with an emotion: the feelings are the same (or similar), and they are caused by attitudes to propositions. Indeed, one can imagine situations in
which the very propositions are the same: compare reading
a newspaper article about an attempt on de Gaulle's life with
reading a novel that describes an exactly similar, but this time
fictional, attempt. We can illustrate this structural similarity
with a simple diagram:

Believing *P*/Desiring *Q*   Making believe *P*/Desiring *Q*

Feeling *F*   Feeling *F* (or *F**)

in which the left half represents the structure of what I have
called the emotions and the right half the parallel structure of
the quasi-emotions. The arrows represent the direction of

causation. (F^* might be qualitatively similar to but less intense than F.) In general, for any emotional state characterizable in terms of beliefs and desires of certain kinds causing feelings of a certain kind, there will be a corresponding quasi-emotion in which make-belief takes over from belief.

I've stressed the normative aspect of our quasi-emotions; the possibility of judging them reasonable or otherwise as measured against the fictions they are responses to. The same goes for the emotions: fear can be unwarranted, jealousy excessive, and we can, perhaps within limits, be argued out of our emotions. The parallel structures their analyses display suggest an account of rationality that underlies both emotions and quasi-emotions. Let us say that an emotion is *grounded* if it involves a belief that is true. Having a reasonable emotion consists in large part in having evidence that the emotion is grounded, and we argue people out of their emotions by showing them that they are not grounded. Similarly, a response to fiction is grounded if it involves a make-belief that is *true in the story* (as it is true in the story, but not, of course, true, that Anna is in a desperate situation). And we get people to change their responses by showing them that they have misinterpreted the tale in some way; by showing them that their make-believe does not correspond to what *is* true in the story. If we want to respond to the narrative, and not just to our own thoughts as provoked by a casual reading of the text, we shall want the content of our make-belief to correspond to the story as closely as may be, just as we want our beliefs to correspond to the condition of the actual world. Of course, someone who has the story right may respond to it in a way I think of both as unsatisfactory and as difficult or impossible to argue about, perhaps because the difference between us reflects a fundamental disagreement over moral value. But this shows merely that there are limits, in literature as in life, to rational debate concerning the emotions. It does not show that our response to literature is any less reason-governed than our response to life.

Thus our quasi-emotions, for all their lack of constitutive

belief, turn out to be cognitive states in a somewhat extended but real sense: they are states partly characterized by the possession of propositional content, and they are capable of being judged, within limits no doubt, as reasonable or unreasonable. In virtue of their possession of content, they are discriminable in the right ways: quasi-pity for Anna and quasi-pity for Uncle Tom will be distinguishable at the level of content, although neither involves belief.

5.5. OBJECTIONS AND REVISIONS

I want now to consider three objections to this account of the reader's response to fiction. One objection concerns the role of feeling, another the role of make-belief, and the last the role of desire. The first two will cause us little difficulty, the third will require some substantial revision of the foregoing account.

The first objection calls into question the role of feelings in the model, which I have taken to be essential to the explanation of emotions and of quasi-emotions. But there are states that we tend to categorize with the other emotions that do not, or at least do not always, involve feelings. Neither admiration nor quasi-admiration seems to have any very distinctive feelings attached to it. Even loathing might not, on occasions, feel any particular way. Perhaps if we dug a little deeper, we would be able to find feelings that go with all occurrences of emotional states; perhaps we would not. I do not especially mind what we say about this as long *as we say about quasi-emotions the same things we say about emotions*. If it is possible to identify some emotion without reference to feeling and entirely in terms of belief and desire, let us then identify the corresponding quasi-emotion entirely in terms of make-belief and desire. My claim has been that emotions and quasi-emotions differ in that make-belief takes over from belief in the latter, and that claim is consistent with there being emotions without feelings.

The second objection focuses on the functional roles that states of making believe are supposed to occupy. I have said that these states are just like beliefs in their capacity to produce feeling; how, then, do they differ from beliefs? They certainly lack the motivating potential of belief; we don't call the police during scenes of violence at the movies (as long as the violence is up there on the screen). The objection is, then, that states of making-believe are behaviorally inconsequential and so hard to explain in evolutionary terms. But I've already suggested that action-guiding potential is not absent in make-belief; it is merely different from that of belief: it gives rise to that kind of play which involves pretense, and a large body of work, theoretical and experimental, suggests that play in the immature members of human and other species assists the development of cognitive, motor, and other skills.[19] If we see play as the outward expression of make-believe, as "seriously" goal-directed action is the outcome of belief, there is little to puzzle about in our possession of this faculty. Of course, the mature reader of fiction engages in an act of make-believe that is not productive of any obvious behavior, and the act may not contribute to his cognitive enrichment in a way that confers any selective advantage. But our belief-forming capacity seems also to be oversophisticated from the point of view of natural selection. There is no problem here for make-believe that cannot also be laid at the door of other less controversial states, like belief.

Now I turn to the objection that concerns the role of desire. I have said that desire may interact with make-belief to produce the inner feelings, but not the outer behavior, that would be produced if desire interacted with belief. But what sort of a desire is it that the reader of *Anna Karenina* is supposed to have when he becomes disturbed by the prospect of Anna's suicide? What is the propositional content of the reader's desire? It seems that it must be: that Anna not throw herself under the train. It is this desire that combines with the

---

19 See, for example, "Introduction" to Jerome Bruner et al. (eds.), *Play – Its Role in Development and Evolution* (New York: Penguin Books, 1976). See also Jerome Singer et al., *The Child's World of Make-Believe* (New York: Academic Press, 1973), and *Daydreaming and Fantasies* (London: Allen & Unwin, 1976).

make-belief that Anna *does* throw herself under the train to produce certain psychical and bodily effects on the reader.

An objection to this idea is that someone could properly be said to have this desire only if he had certain beliefs that, in the case of the reader, he does not have. In that case we have traded a problem concerning emotion without belief for one concerning desire without belief. This objection seems to me on the right lines, although it has not yet been made clear why, and in what sense, one cannot have desires without beliefs. Thus, there is a sense in which I (a rabid formalist in matters mathematical) can desire to refute Gödel's theorem, even when I don't think this is even a possible thing to do. To give some direction to the discussion, I want to consider one specific argument for the conclusion that the reader cannot desire that Anna not throw herself under the train, because he does not have the right kinds of beliefs. In developing the argument I shall be able to consider, along the way, an objection to the account of fictional names of Chapter 4.

I start, then, by connecting our present discussion with what was said in Chapter 4 about fictional names. According to the doctrine there laid out, a fictional name like "Holmes" or "Anna Karenina" abbreviates a description that includes all the information given by the story. The content of Tolstoy's story is that there is a unique $n+1$-tuple, the first member of which is called "Anna" and does such and such and . . . , and the nth member of which is called "Levin" and does such and such, and the $n+1$th member of which is responsible for this story, in which he sets out his knowledge of the activities of the other n. "Anna" is then defined as the first member of that $n+1$-tuple. "Anna" denotes, in each world, the person, if there is one, who is the first member of the $n+1$-tuple of things that satisfy the conditions of the story in that world. In the style of definition (8) in Chapter 4, let the description "Anna" abbreviates be symbolized as "$\imath x A^{\#} x$." Should we now say that to desire that Anna not throw herself under the train is to desire that $\imath x A^{\#} x$ not throw herself under the train – to desire, in other words, that the following be true:

(1) $\exists x[A^{\#}x \,\&\, \forall y(A^{\#}y \to x=y) \,\&\, \sim Tx]$?

(1) is true just in case there is one and only one person who satisfies $A^{\#}$, and that person does not throw herself under a train. But one of the conditions specified in $A^{\#}$ is *throwing herself under the train*. To desire (1) would be to desire that there is a unique person who does such and such – including throwing herself under the train – who does not throw herself under the train. This does not seem to be what the reader desires. Nor is it plausible to say the reader desires not (1), but

(2) $\sim\exists x[A^{\#}x \,\&\, \forall y(A^{\#}y \to x=y) \,\&\, Tx]$,

which differs from (1) in that the negation has large scope. For (2) is equivalent to

(3) $\sim\exists x[A^{\#}x \,\&\, \forall y(A^{\#}y \to x=y)]$,

since T is just a part of $A^{\#}$. Imagine that other bad things happen to Anna in the story: suppose Anna is mugged in the street. Reading the description of the mugger's approach, the reader desires that Anna not be mugged. In the style of analysis (2), that would be to desire that

(4) $\sim\exists x[A^{\#}x \,\&\, \forall y(A^{\#}y \to x=y) \,\&\, Mx]$.

Since Anna *is* mugged in the story (we assume), M, like T, is just part of $A^{\#}$. So (4) is equivalent to (3), and hence equivalent to (2). It is hard to believe that the reader who desires that Anna not throw herself under the train and the reader who desires that Anna not be mugged have desires with logically equivalent contents. We should conclude that neither (1) nor (2) adequately represent the content of the reader's desire that Anna not throw herself under the train.

This brings us to the problem noted in Section 4.8, where I pointed out that, on my account, all true metafictional statements are logically equivalent. That account is, as I remarked in Chapter 4, an idealized account. It is an account of what such statements would mean for readers who were fully retentive of all the detail of the story: readers who reflect, in their dispassionate way, on a story they are able mentally to survey. But consider the position of a much more familiar reader: one who is caught up in the action of the story as he reads it, and who has not yet grasped, if he ever will, the full content of the story. When this reader says or thinks that he desires that Anna not throw herself under the train, "Anna" does not function as an abbreviated description of the kind specified in definition (8) of Chapter 4. "Anna" does not, for that person at that time, abbreviate "$\imath x A^{\#}x$," a definite description that includes all the information of the story. The reader is at a certain point in the narrative, and has received a certain amount of information so far; he has been told that there is a certain woman called "Anna" who has a lover called "Vronsky," and so on. He makes believe that there is a woman about whom the author knows, and that the text he, the reader, is reading sets out the author's knowledge of this woman. When the reader says he desires that Anna not jump, "Anna" may abbreviate for him a description such as "the woman called 'Anna' about whom I'm currently reading." The reader desires that the person who satisfies *that* description (which we may formalize as "$\imath x A^{*}x$") not throw herself under the train:

(5) $\exists x[A^{*}x \ \& \ \forall y(A^{*}y \rightarrow x = y) \ \& \ \sim Tx]$.

(Of course, the reader may know, from hearsay or from a previous reading, that it is true in the story that Anna throws herself under the train. But this knowledge is not yet incorporated into his make-believe; it gets incorporated later when he reads that Anna does, indeed, throw herself under the train.)

Is (5) an adequate representation of the reader's desire? The reader who desires (5) is one who desires that there is a unique person called "Anna" about whom he is reading who does not throw herself under a train. But this seems to be a desire I can have only if I desire that there is a unique person called "Anna" about whom I'm reading, and it is not plausible to suppose I have a desire of this kind whenever I read a fictional work.

The same problem arises when we consider cases of desire

outside fictional contexts. Suppose I read a newspaper report that tells me there is a man on the roof of the library, threatening to jump off. I assume, correctly, that there is just one such man. Waiting for the next report of events, I desire that the man not jump. What is the content of my desire? Is it the desire that there be a unique man on the roof who does not jump:

(6) $\exists x[Rx \ \& \ \forall y(Ry \rightarrow x = y) \ \& \sim Jx]$?

Here the same objection applies, for it is not likely that I desire that there be a unique man on the roof.

When we say an agent desires a certain outcome, we have in mind a certain range of outcomes that are viable alternatives for the agent. The outcome desired is the outcome desired more than any of the other viable alternatives. What the set of viable alternatives for an agent at a time is depends upon the agent's beliefs at that time. Because I believe the newspaper story I have read, I believe there is a man on the roof. The viable alternatives for me in this situation are all alternatives that include its being the case that there is a man on the roof, although this is not something that, in itself, I desire. Thus I desire (6) in the sense that I desire it more than any other alternative in my current set of viable alternatives. I desire (6) more than I desire that there should be a unique man on the roof who does jump, and this, we may suppose, is the only other viable alternative for me.

If this is an adequate defense of the claim that I desire (6), perhaps the same argument can be used to defend the claim that the reader desires (5). But now we face the problem that the reader does not believe there is anyone who satisfies the relevant description. He knows there is no one called "Anna" about whom he is currently reading. So we cannot characterize the relevant alternatives to (5) in terms of what the reader believes, concluding that the reader desires (5) more than any of the relevant alternatives to it. But without a class of relevant alternatives, we cannot ascribe any desire to the reader. In particular, we cannot say that the reader desires (5).

5.5. Objections and revisions

Our original worry was that a reader cannot respond emotionally to a fiction without having certain kinds of beliefs he does not in fact have. I then argued that the reader's response is a kind of state that involves not belief and desire, but make-belief and desire. Now it seems that our original worry reappears in a slightly different form: The reader cannot have the desires I ascribe to him without having beliefs he does not have.

Although the reader does not believe there is anyone called "Anna" about whom he is currently reading, he does make believe there is. This suggests we can solve the problem by saying there are, as well as states of make-belief, states of *make-desire*. We calculate desire against a background of relevant alternatives given by the agent's beliefs. We calculate make-desire against a background of relevant alternatives that are alternatives within the reader's game of make-believe. On this view, the reader does not desire that Anna not throw herself under a train, where this is understood in the sense of (5), but he does make desire this.

At first sight, this postulation of states of make-desire seems transparently ad hoc. To show that it isn't ad hoc we must find independent grounds for believing in the existence of states I have called "make-desires."

First I want to dispose of a spurious argument that might seem to provide such a ground. I have said that desires are most plausibly thought of as dispositions to act, or at least as essentially involving such dispositions. But it seems that the desire that Anna come to no harm cannot be, and cannot essentially involve, any disposition to act; there are no actions the sympathetic reader is disposed to perform when he reads that Anna is about to throw herself under the train. The reader may tremble or weep at the prospect of Anna's suicide, but these are not actions. In that case, so the argument goes, what we call "desiring that Anna come to no harm" is not really a desire. But the correct reply to this is that the dispositions associated with a given desire are complex and highly context dependent; they are dispositions to act in certain ways given other desires and beliefs. I may have a

205

desire but not be disposed to act upon it on a given occasion because I don't have the beliefs that must be combined with the desire to produce action. As we have seen, readers of fiction don't have the required beliefs. Thus it's no objection to the claim that I desire Othello not to kill Desdemona that I don't rush to the stage to save her, for I don't believe anyone on the stage is in danger.

We must look elsewhere for an argument to the conclusion that readers do not genuinely desire the outcomes they seem to desire. I begin by recalling that we are often unclear about what our desires really are. It may seem to us that we desire something, but when the opportunity for its attainment presents itself, we reject it. Admittedly, these sorts of cases are not always easy to distinguish from cases in which our desires have simply changed, but it is generally acknowledged that we may, on occasion, simply be mistaken about what we desire. Consider Fred, who tells us he would get very drunk right now if only strong drink were available to him. But it seems we know Fred better than he knows himself. We know he never does get drunk, even when he is able to do so in the most favorable conditions. We know that Fred does not want to get drunk right now. And in coming to this conclusion we don't suppose that Fred is deceiving us about his desires; we suppose that he thinks he has a desire that he does not in fact have. Fred's condition is all too common: he is a victim of his own make-believe. Fred, like most of us, carries on a double life: a life in the real world and a life in the world of his daydreams and fantasies. In some of Fred's fantasies he is a laid-back fellow who drinks to excess when the mood takes him. And Fred's fantasies sometimes have a spillover effect into the real world, especially when circumstances confine the spillover to verbal display. In his fantasies, Fred makes believe that he is a laid-back fellow, and makes desire that he should do all sorts of things that in real life he would not do, and would not desire to do. Fred's present mistake is to confuse his desires with his make-desires.

We have here, I think, the beginnings of an explanation of a puzzling phenomenon: that people sometimes act out of desires that we, as external observers, want to describe as desires that are not "in character" or not "fully theirs." Perhaps what happens is that a thought that is possessed merely as a make-desire starts to spill over into behavior of a playacting kind, but which, once it gains expression in behavior, is then interpreted by the subject as a genuine desire, and which, indeed, does become a desire as the subject tries to fit it into the structure of his own mental economy. Notice that it will be much easier to confuse our make-desires with our desires than it is to confuse our make-beliefs with our beliefs, because belief answers to an external standard in a way that desire does not. I am unlikely to confuse my make-belief that there are dragons with a belief, since its content is so obviously false.

We can discern a similar duality, though usually well under control, in our encounters with fiction. Most of us are familiar with the experience of coming, apparently, to desire outcomes in a fiction that we would not desire concerning comparable situations in real life. We find ourselves "on the side" of a fictional character who, in real life, we would shrink from as loathsome. We may also find ourselves uncharacteristically vengeful in fictional situations: a *Macbeth* in which Macduff spares Macbeth's life would, for most of us, be a very unsatisfactory play; yet we may genuinely desire that even the perpetrators of dreadful crimes be allowed to live. Our real desires, the desires upon which we would be prepared to act in appropriate circumstances, do not always seem to determine how we respond to fiction. So there is a case for saying that there are states that are like our real desires in their power to evoke feelings, but which are, nonetheless, different from our real desires; they come in tandem with our make-beliefs, not with our beliefs. In that case postulating states of make-desire ought not to be dismissed as obviously an ad hoc move.

If we say there are states of make-desire operative in fiction reading, we shall have to modify somewhat the claims I have made about the parallelism of structure between emotions and our responses to fiction. We shall have to say that a response to fiction differs from an emotion in two ways: The role of belief is taken over by make-belief, and the role of desire is taken over by make-desire. This still leaves us with a significant structural similarity.

5.6. ALTERNATIVES

There are other accounts of the response to fiction that employ the idea of make-believe. According to one of them, we do not respond emotionally to the fate of a fictional character; we make believe that we do. In *The Concept of Mind*, Gilbert Ryle said that "theatergoers and novel readers realize that they are making-believe;" "their distress and indignation are feigned."[20] But this view just seems to be wrong. However we are to describe our responses to fiction, they are not, at least not usually, feigned. One might feign a response to *Anna Karenina*, hoping to be thought a more sensitive person than one actually is, but this is not how people normally respond to the novel. In general, readers and theatergoers do not "realize," as Ryle puts it, that they are making believe, and they are very resistant (in my admittedly limited experience) to the suggestion that they are.

Kendall Walton has a more plausible proposal.[21] According to Walton, I do not really pity Anna or fear for the governess; rather it is *fictional* that I do these things. Like others who encounter fiction, I engage in a game of make-believe that creates a fiction larger than the fiction I read. It is a fiction in which I learn about the troubles of a woman whose lover abandons her, or about the struggle of a young governess against ghostly and malevolent powers, and in this fiction I am moved in appropriate ways by what I read. What is fictional in Walton's sense is different from what is really the case, but it *depends* in various ways on what is really the case. The game that the reader plays is not one in which he is free to choose what is fictional; to a significant degree, what is fic-

20 *The Concept of Mind* (London: Hutchinson, 1949), p. 92 and 107.
21 See his "Fearing Fictions" and *Mimesis as Make-Believe*, esp. sections 7.1 and 7.2.

tional is beyond his control. Thus it is fictional in his game that he is learning about the troubles of a woman called "Anna" because he is in fact reading a book in which it is part of the story that a woman called "Anna" has various problems. And it is true (really true, and not just fictional) that the reader realizes it is fictional that Anna's situation is desperate, and this realization causes him to have (to really have) certain feelings and sensations, the feelings and sensations that we normally associate with pity. It is because of this causal relationship between what the reader believes about the story and his feelings that it is fictional that the reader pities Anna; if he had had a different belief or a different set of feelings as a result of the belief, something else would be fictional about the reader: for instance, that he delights in or is merely bored by her suffering.

Generalizing Walton's analysis gives us the following picture. The reader comes to believe that P is fictional. Acquiring this belief causes him to have certain feelings Φ. It is the holding of this causal nexus that generates the make-believe truth that the reader has emotion E. And we can, in general, tell what emotion E is by asking what emotion someone would have if he were caused to feel Φ as a result of believing P (instead of believing that P is fictional). Thus, the reader of *Anna Karenina* comes to believe that it is make-believe that Anna is about to throw herself under the train, comes as a result of this to have feelings of anxiety, and this generates a fictional truth about the reader: that the reader fears for Anna.

Walton's account would need to be extended to take on board the role of desire in the causation of feelings. It is our beliefs *together with our desires* that determine how we feel. Thus, we might say that the reader's feelings are caused partly by his belief that it is fictional that Anna's situation is desperate and partly by his desire that this not be fictional.

Instead of saying that it is fictional that you pity Anna or fictional that I fear for the governess, we might, without distorting Walton's position, say that these things are make-believe. It is part of your game of make-believe that you pity

Anna, and of mine that I fear for the governess. This way of putting it has the advantage of neatly bringing out the contrast between Walton's account and my own. It is a contrast that depends upon the difference between the operator and the attitude senses of make-believe.[22] According to Walton, my feelings are caused by my belief that it is make-believe (operator) that the governess is in danger (together, we might say, with my desire that it not be make-believe that she is in danger). According to me, these feelings are caused by my make-belief (attitude) that the governess is in danger (together with my make-desire that she not be). And Walton adds something that has no counterpart in my story: that, partly because I have these feelings, it is make-believe (operator) that I fear for her.

These two accounts are not so very different. But it would be wrong to think they are equivalent, or that a choice between them would have to be arbitrary. There is at least one reason for preferring my own account. It is, let us remember, part of the story that the governess is in danger, not that it is make-believe that she is. If we adopt Walton's proposal, we shall have to say that the reader does not take any attitude toward the propositions of the story, but instead takes the attitude of belief toward propositions in which the propositions of the story are embedded. And if we do say this, it will remain a puzzle as to how our engagement with the story can generate strong feeling. We tend to distance ourselves from disturbing tales by reminding ourselves that they are "only make-believe"; if the content of the reader's thought is that it is make-believe that the governess is in danger, his feelings are likely to be inhibited. What makes me anxious is the thought that the governess is in danger: a thought I do not believe, but which I do make believe.

If we introduce considerations about desire into Walton's account, the same kind of criticism will apply. For it does not seem plausible to say that the reader desires that it not be make-believe that the governess is in danger – as if the reader

22 For which see Section 2.4.

210

wished he were reading a light comedy instead. The audience at a performance of *Othello* might be visibly moved by the prospect of Desdemona's death at Othello's hands, but they would be outraged if the management decided to substitute a happy ending; that would frustrate their desires, not satisfy them.

So I describe the matter somewhat differently. Members of the audience do desire that it be make-believe that Desdemona dies, but they also make desire that Desdemona not die, where the content *that Desdemona not die* is understood according to the suggestion of Section 5.5. And it is this state of make-desire, along with the corresponding state of make-belief, that causes members of the audience to have the unpleasant feelings they experience in the theater. Thus, I prefer to invoke make-believe as an attitude rather than as an operator in order to explain our responses to fiction.

5.7. ONE SOLUTION OR TWO?

The solution I have proposed to our problem involves a rejection of principle (1) in Section 5.2. That solution was based on the theory of emotions outlined earlier: a theory according to which emotions involve beliefs. Our responses to fiction, which involve not belief but rather make-belief, are not therefore to be classed as emotions.[23] They are states of another kind, a kind I have called "quasi-emotions."

But surely this "solution" is an altogether stipulative one. I have distinguished two kinds of states that display a certain parallelism of structure, and I have chosen to call one of them "emotional states." But what justifies this labeling rather than some other? Why not say that both kinds of states are emotions – just *different* kinds of emotions? But if we say this we can no longer say that (1) is false.

No more we can. It is time to rid ourselves of the fantasy

23 They also do not involve desires, as emotions do according to the theory. For the sake of simplicity I shall discuss the relation between emotions and quasi-emotions in terms of belief and make-belief. Nothing I want to say here would be affected by bringing desires into the picture.

that the cognitive theory of the emotions I have developed provides a philosophical analysis of the term "emotion" as understood by ordinary folk. That analysis simply will not cover much that is commonly labeled "emotion," including our responses to fiction. But this ought to cause us no alarm. Forget the labels for a moment: what we have before us are two parallel theories or, better, one big theory distinguishing two kinds of states that might not be distinguished in casual talk. The two kinds of states correspond to the two halves of the diagram on p. 197, and the theory claims that one of these kinds (left half of the diagram) is the kind of state we are in when we respond to situations believed to be actual, and that the other kind (right half of the diagram) is the kind of state we are in when we respond to situations described in fictions – situations we acknowledge to be imaginary. I have called this the distinction between "emotions" and "quasi-emotions." But as long as you agree with me that the two halves of the distinction offer a correct account of the kinds of cases they are intended to cover, you can call them what you like. If you like, we can use "emotion" to cover both. Within this terminological system we shall say that there are different kinds of emotions, these kinds being differentiated by the different kinds of propositional attitudes they involve. Thus there are different kinds of pity; the pity we feel for Anna being of a different kind from the pity we feel for real people. The first involves make-belief; the second, belief. Within this terminological system it is not (1) that comes out false but rather (2). Either way, our problem is solved.

There is yet another, and perhaps a better way, to state the solution: Dispense altogether with the unqualified – and therefore tendentious – use of "emotion," as well as with more specific unqualified emotion-terms like "fear" and "pity," and use qualifiers all the way. There are "broad emotions": anything that falls in either half of the diagram. There are "paradigm emotions": anything that falls in the left half. There are "quasi-emotions": anything that falls in the right. Thus provided for, I shall say, whenever asked whether I pity Anna Karenina, that I quasi-pity her, and so broad-pity her, but do not paradigm-pity her. Perhaps not a very elegant formulation, but it has at least the merit of being true.

5.8. EMOTIONAL CONGRUENCE

There are other questions we can ask about our responses to fiction, and we can expect that an adequate account of their structure will help us to answer them. There is, for example, a problem about the *appropriateness* of our various responses to fiction. It is appropriate, I suppose, to weep over the death of Anna Karenina, to be brought to a state of what I have called quasi-pity by her suicide. But a fictional death is not always the occasion for anguish (or quasi-anguish; I shall drop the "quasi" talk, unless the contrast between belief and make-belief is under discussion). Death and suffering as portrayed in fiction can be the occasion for boisterous humor or cynical amusement as well as for deeper and more serious responses. To weep over the death of Zipser in Tom Sharp's *Porterhouse Blue* would be an inappropriate response, even in one who thinks that death is nothing to laugh about; one who finds the story tasteless should just stop reading it. The sensitive reader is not simply one who weeps at the portrayal of suffering and rejoices at the portrayal of good fortune; he is one whose responses are *appropriate* in some as yet to be analyzed sense.

The sensitive reader is not necessarily the refined reader. Sensitivity and refinement measure different dimensions of sophistication. A sensitive but unrefined reader might be one who weeps over a Mills and Boon romance, for that's the response appropriate to the heroine's suffering. Refinement consists in not responding in this way because the work is too clichéd to be affecting. The refined and sensitive reader may laugh – but at the clichés, not at the heroine's suffering.

What we need, then, is an explanation of appropriateness. What makes it appropriate to weep over Anna Karenina and over the fate of a Mills and Boon heroine, but to laugh at the death of Zipser? I suggest that appropriateness is a matter of congruence between the reader's response and the emotion expressed in the work. *Anna Karenina* and the Mills and Boon romance are expressive of pity; *Porterhouse Blue* is expressive of boisterous humor. The sensitive reader is one who knows what emotion is expressed in the work and is therefore able to respond congruently to it; the refined reader is one who responds congruently only to works that have a certain kind of merit.

So far we have traded one problem for another. Notoriously, philosophers have found it very difficult to say what it is for a work of any kind to express an emotion. Since emotions are states of persons, we might suspect that light will be shed on this problem by taking a look once again at the "person" who has proved so valuable to us in this study: the fictional author. I have argued that what is true in the story is what it is reasonable to infer that the fictional author believes, and that the individual style of the work consists of those of its features that provide evidence concerning the personality of the fictional author. Perhaps, then, the work is expressive of an emotion just in case it provides evidence that the fictional author experienced that emotion. Bruce Vermazen has made out an excellent case for exactly this proposal: a proposal I shall adopt.[24]

Vermazen's idea seems right: when we make believe that we are being told the story of Anna Karenina by someone who knows what happened, we certainly have the impression that the teller was deeply moved by the events he describes. But the teller of *Porterhouse Blue* seems to have a quite different attitude to the death and suffering he informs us about. The way he describes these things strongly suggests that he finds them funny.

Our responses to fiction are appropriate, then, when they are congruent with the responses of the fictional author. Not, of course, congruent with real responses that anyone actually has, for the fictional author is just a character in our make-believe, and the real author may not experience the appropri-

24 See his "Expression as Expression," *Pacific Philosophical Quarterly* 67 (1986): 196–224.

ate emotion at all (as with the jaded author turning out the umpteenth romance), but congruent with the emotion we make believe is possessed by the fictional author. And here "congruent" does not mean "identical." It is make-believe that the fictional author of *Anna Karenina* feels a deep pity for Anna's situation, a pity that is a paradigm- rather than a quasi-emotion in my taxonomy. Thus, it is make-believe that the fictional author believes that Anna's situation is desperate and desires that it not be, and that these attitudes are productive in him of the feelings we associate with pity. But the reader's state is not of this kind; it is a state of "quasi-pity" in which the roles of belief and desire are taken over by make-belief and make-desire. Thus, the implied author's state and the reader's state are not the same state; they are congruent in that they differ only by the substitution of make-belief for belief and make-desire for desire. If they differ more radically – if, for example, the implied author's state is one of cynical amusement whereas the reader's state is one of (quasi-) fear for the character concerned – then the reader's response is incongruent.

5.9. PSYCHOLOGICAL KINDS

Throughout I have maintained a broadly cognitive view of both the paradigm- and the quasi-emotions; emphasizing both their propositional and their normative aspects. My theory may not encompass "moods" such as cheerfulness and free-floating anxiety, nor the fear of spiders that is unaccompanied by any belief that spiders (the ones around here, anyway) are dangerous, because these are states that are not, apparently, belief-involving. The theory was not intended to account for them, for states that do not even seem to involve belief do not generate the kind of problem with which I have been dealing. But it may be objected that, since we call these states "emotions," any adequate theory of the emotions ought to account for them as well, and my theory is to that extent inadequate. Now, we have already seen evidence that "emotion" is a term commonly used to cover states that differ

5. Emotion and the response to fiction

one from another in important structural ways (the paradigm- and quasi-emotions), and moods and phobias may simply be further examples of the heterogeneous nature of that which "emotion" is intended to cover. It is likely, then, that "emotion," as we commonly use that term, does not denote a genuine psychological *kind*.[25] In that case, future psychological theorizing may not recognize the class of what we commonly call "emotions" but will rather embody distinctions and categories that cut across our present terminology, just as the conceptual scheme of modern physics cuts across the Aristotelian distinction between the sub- and superlunary realms.

I like to think that this hypothetical psychology of the future will preserve something that is at least a recognizable descendant of my account of paradigm- and quasi-emotions. But even if that account needs substantial modification, the general form of my theory may survive. If beliefs and desires are *in some way* connected with our fears and hopes – as they must surely be – we shall be able to say that what we call fearing for the governess or hoping that Anna will find happiness are states in which the role (whatever it is) of belief and desire is taken over by make-belief and make-desire. So you may look upon the theory I have developed here as simply an *example* of the way in which the problem of our response to fiction may be tackled; a way that could be preserved within any of a variety of theoretical settings. Of course, if there literally are no such things as propositional attitudes, if we must accommodate ourselves to a radically new conceptual scheme drawn up by neuroscience, then all bets are off. But I find that an incredible hypothesis.

25 This is well argued in Paul Griffith's Ph.D. thesis *Emotion and Evolution*, Australian National University, 1988.

In conclusion

Reflecting on the theory presented in these chapters, I think we might describe it as conservative. There is very little to which I have appealed in explaining fiction that is not already required for other purposes. The author's act that is productive of fiction turns out to be a communicative act with a quite familiar structure, a structure we invoke to explain other forms of communication. Fictional truth turns out to be explainable in terms of the familiar patterns of reasoning by which we infer the beliefs of others. Fictional characters and their names turn out to be intelligible without the invocation of a realm of fictional beings. Roles are defined as functions on possible worlds, and although possible worlds are philosophically controversial, their utility for those who accept them is established in a number of areas that have nothing to do with fiction. Our response to fictional characters is explained without recourse to intentional objects of thought other than propositions, and without violation of principles of rationality. Throughout we have found no reason to abandon classical principles of logic or to postulate beings of any irreducibly fictional kinds. For these reasons the theory recommends itself.

One thing we could not have done without is the notion of make-believe, and that has remained stubbornly irreducible. But the notion is not an extravagant or unfamiliar one. Future work in philosophy and psychology may succeed in illuminating it further. I doubt if it will succeed in persuading us to discard it.

Index

Index

221

Lightning Source UK Ltd.
Milton Keynes UK
26 March 2010

151964UK00001B/182/P